Property of Steve Walker

Old Testament Survey

OLD TESTAMENT SURVEY

PAUL R. HOUSE

BROADMAN & HOLMAN PUBLISHERS
NASHVILLE, TENNESSEE

4210-15
ISBN: 0-8054-1015-5
Dewey Decimal Classification: 221
Subject Heading: Bible. OLD TESTAMENT
Library of Congress Catalog Card Number: 91-31654
Printed in the United States of America

Library of Congress Cataloging-in-Publication Data
House, Paul R. 1958-
Old Testament survey / by Paul R. House
p. cm.
ISBN 0-8054-1015-5
1. Bible. O.T.—Criticism, interpretation, etc. I. Title.
BS1171.2.H68 1992
221.6'1—dc20 91-31654
CIP

12 06 05 04 03

To the Taylor University Class of 1990
and
To the memory of John Baxter Coffey (1968-1988)

Acknowledgments

This book attempts to help beginning students understand the Old Testament. I define "beginning student" from my experiences with college freshmen who take my required Old Testament Literature course at Taylor University. Most are not yet twenty. They are intelligent and willing to learn, but they need guidance and motivation. Most of them do not know the Old Testament story, its unity, or the basic scholarly viewpoints that help interpret it. Thus, I have tried to write for students, yet I leave instructors plenty of room to develop historical, theological, and critical issues.

I appreciate Broadman Press's willingness to publish this project. Their editorial personnel offered suggestions at every stage of my writing. Everyone at Broadman was kind and generous with his or her time.

Several other people deserve my appreciation. Roy House, my father, encouraged me to write an Old Testament survey that stresses the unity of Scripture. My colleagues at Taylor University supported my efforts. Three of them—Herb Nygren, Ted Dorman, and Faye Chechowich—read and commented on parts of the manuscript. Richard Stanislaw, Academic Dean, provided financial support, and the Faculty Personnel Committee granted me a one-month leave in January 1991 to work on the book. Joanne Giger carefully typed the manuscript and told me what she thought of it. Friends like Win Corduan and Scott Hafemann kept my spirits high. My wife, Becky, and daughter, Molly, added joy to the whole process.

This book is dedicated to some special people. The Taylor University class of 1990 were my first Old Testament students in the fall of 1986. We grew up together for four years. They will do great things. John Coffey was a student and friend from that class. His death grieved many of us. I hope Roland, Joan, Joe, and Brian know John is remembered with affection.

For these and other kindnesses, I am grateful.

Paul R. House
Upland, Indiana

Contents

Chapter 19

Chapter 20

Chapter 21

Chapter 22

Old Testament Survey

Beginning the Study

Introduction

For centuries Christians and Jews alike considered the Old Testament a unified work. Jewish readers viewed the Hebrew Scriptures as a thorough account of their faith and history. Christians treated the *Old* Testament as the natural introduction to their *New* Testament. Neither group failed to acknowledge the many types of literature in the books, but both communities of faith found underlying themes and characters that bound the whole together.

Recently, though, the diversity of the Old Testament has been stressed. Children are taught that the Bible is not *a* book, but *many books.* College and seminary students tend to analyze each biblical book in isolation from other Scripture. Therefore many individuals have little sense of the wholeness of Scripture. Few people can fit specific stories into a larger biblical picture. Lacking a grasp of the overall Old Testament plot and purpose, Bible students stand baffled as they seek to understand particular passages.

This book attempts to chart some elements that unify the Old Testament. Hopefully, it can serve as a companion to Bible reading. Characters, plot, structure, and themes are highlighted so the reader will know what is happening in the Old Testament. History, theology, and criticism are not absent, but they play a secondary role. The reader is referred to other good studies of these subjects. This book will seek to help readers appreciate the unity of the Old Testament. If the student can master the introductory principles this book covers, he or she can move on to further study.

Order of the Study

Every Old Testament survey chooses a way to approach its subject. Some authors stress the content of the books. Others describe in detail the historical background of the Old Testament. Beyond these concerns, many textbooks explain the books according to when they appear in the English Bible. Still others assemble the texts in historical order. For Christians it seems logical to study the Hebrew Bible as the early church did.

The first disciples' only Scripture was the Old Testament. They believed it was inspired by God as their guide for faith and action (2 Tim. 3:16). Their Bible was divided into three specific parts: the Law, the Prophets, and the Writings. That order will be followed throughout this book. Notice how the order of the books in the Hebrew Bible differs from the English Bible:

Law	*Prophets*	*Writings*
Genesis	Joshua	Psalms
Exodus	Judges	Job
Leviticus	1 and 2 Samuel	Proverbs
Numbers	1 and 2 Kings	Ruth
Deuteronomy	Isaiah	Song of Songs
	Jeremiah	Ecclesiastes
	Ezekiel	Lamentations
	The Twelve	Esther
	(Hosea—Malachi)	Daniel
		Ezra
		Nehemiah
		1 and 2 Chronicles

Most students realize immediately that some books seem misplaced in the Hebrew Bible. After all, Ruth, Esther, Ezra, Nehemiah, and 1 and 2 Chronicles are not with the other historical works. Daniel is not among the Prophets, and Lamentations is not with Jeremiah. Some readers even doubt the Hebrew Bible's counting system. Perhaps 1 and 2 Samuel, 1 and 2 Kings, or 1 and 2 Chronicles could be one book, but how can *twelve* Minor Prophets make *one* book? The same thirty-nine books are in the Hebrew and English Bibles, so why the differences? These are vital questions if one wants to understand the early church's Bible. The answers to these questions help demonstrate the unity of the Old Testament.

Following the Hebrew order of books offers many advantages. First, the reader learns the basic events of Israel's history from creation to the fall of Jerusalem. All succeeding books therefore have a historical context to which the reader can refer. Second, the student realizes that the Prophets explain Israel's history. Third, the reader learns that the Prophets present a uniform message. Fourth, the student notes how the Writings comment on how the faithful lived given Israel's historical situation.

In other words, the Hebrew Bible's sequence shows *what* happened to Israel, *why* it happened, and *how* believers responded to both. By surveying the Old Testament in this order, the ways history, theology, and faith work together in Scripture become evident. Certainly the New Testament authors interpreted the Old Testament in this unified manner.

Literary Aspects of the Study

No piece of literature, sacred or secular, can be understood unless readers know some basic facts about the material. Characters and plot are the starting points for all literary analysis. Themes and symbols add meaning to story lines. Even knowing the differences between prose and poetry helps a reader examine literature. Certainly some knowledge of these aspects of the Old Testament will aid beginning students.

Characters

Analyzing characters means more than simply noting who appears in a story. Once characters have been identified the reader needs to know their natures. Is the character positive or negative in the story? Does the character make a significant impact on the account? What are the character's motives? What do other characters say about the individual in question? Or, does a disparity here point to character weakness or plot irony? Further, do the character's actions and words agree? Asking these and other questions about Old Testament figures will guide the reader's perception of the significance of each individual character. Normally, the characters who impact the plot the most are the most significant in the story.

Plot

Plot involves what happens in a story and why it happens. Good plots are formed by the ideas, dreams, and conflicts of its characters and are logically ordered. A mere tracing of events does not explain a plot. Rather, motives and explanations determine plot. The fact that Israel leaves Egypt (Ex. 1) tells a story, but to know that God *causes* Israel to be freed uncovers a plot.

Generally, plots may be comic or tragic. Tragic stories begin very hopefully but eventually end sadly. Israel's failure to enter the promised land (Num. 13—19) is a tragic account. Comic plots are not necessarily funny or satirical. When literary scholars say a plot is "comic," they mean the story has a pleasant, or happy, ending. All may seem negative in the middle of the story, but any problems are resolved by the plot's end. David's rise to Israel's throne despite

Saul's hatred represents a comic plot. Realizing whether a plot is comic or tragic is vital to understanding Old Testament stories.

Themes

Locating themes in literature helps the reader understand the purpose behind characters and plots. Why certain accounts appear in Scripture can often be explained by a book's theme. For example, the major theme of Judges is, "In those days there was no king in Israel; all the people did what was right in their own eyes" (Judg. 21:25, NRSV). Therefore, the author includes many occurrences that may shock or repulse the reader.

Many students fear the word *theology.* Though the study of theology can become quite complicated, at its beginning level theology identifies and studies great Bible themes. When readers begin to locate major themes in the Old Testament, they are doing very basic theology. For example, to see that Isaiah stresses salvation is a first step towards defining salvation in the Old Testament.

Symbols

Simply put, *symbols* are images, words, or phrases that represent something beyond themselves. Symbols point to deeper meaning or reality. The temple represents God's presence among Israel. Ezekiel uses his vision of dry bones (Ezek. 37:1-14) to illustrate Israel's renewal. In the Prophets, Hosea's wife Gomer is unfaithful to her husband. Hosea then claims that Israel is just as unfaithful to God. So symbols make themes come alive. They challenge readers to envision and think about a message instead of just absorbing it.

Prose

Most of the Old Testament is written in a nonpoetic style. This statement is particularly true of the Law and Former Prophets. Prose is action oriented. It describes events and the importance of those events. Rarely will prose convey abstract meaning or reveal in great detail the inner feelings of a character. Books that have a fixed starting and stopping place, like Samuel and Kings, are best served by prose, since they tell specific actions and events.

Prose proceeds logically. Whether a text describes the life of an individual, tribe, or nation, prose has a beginning, middle, and end. The author may comment on why events happen but always bases those comments on the story itself. Each story has unique elements that make it creative and artistic.

Poetry

Each major section (Law, Prophets, or Writings) of the Old Testament contains poetry. The Prophets and the Writings use poetry the most. Old Testament poets write sermons, songs, complaints, and predictions. Quite obviously, then, ancient poetry is flexible.

Hebrew poetry differs from English verse. Rhyme seldom appears in Hebrew poetry, and stanzas are not immediately apparent. Its rhythm does not always follow a set pattern, which separates it from traditional Greek, Roman, Italian, and English poetry. Old Testament poetry has its own pattern, however, and uses imagery, word play, and other poetic devices.

Old Testament poetry is shaped by thought and sense patterns. Rather than two lines rhyming, Hebrew poetry matches the ideas of consecutive lines. Two lines may say basically the same or almost opposite things. Several lines often work together to present a message. At least three types of poetry appear in the Old Testament. The first type of poetry is called synonymous poetry; the second, antithetical poetry; and the third, synthetic poetry.[1]

In synonymous poetry two lines say practically the same things, as in Psalm 3:1:

> O Lord, how many are my foes!
> How many rise up against me!

Together the two lines drive home the writer's desperate situation. Proverbs 19:4 illustrates antithetical poetry with lines that state opposite ideas:

> Wealth brings many friends,
> but a poor man's friend deserts him.

Even though the phrases are different, they both show the relative importance of wealth. Since synthetic poetry normally uses many lines, an example will not be quoted. Passages like Zephaniah 1:14-16, Joel 1:1-20, and Psalm 139:1-6 illustrate that type of poetry. A succession of lines, images, and themes shape the poems here.

Like all other nations' poetry, Hebrew verse is reflective in nature. Presentation of specific events gives way to statements about the poet's feelings about life. For instance, 2 Kings 24—25 describes the fall of Jerusalem, while Psalm 137 tells how the poet responds to that catastrophe. So poetry revolves around the thoughts of the author.

Poetry will be discussed later in the book, so it is not necessary to master all its aspects now. Still, poetry appears as early as Genesis, so some understanding of its principles will help the beginning reader. An appreciation of both prose and poetry will grow as the perceptive student sees both in the Old Testament.

Historical Aspects of the Study

Though this book focuses on literary content, it will not totally neglect historical matters. After all, much of the Old Testament's plot grows out of major historical events. Events like the exodus, the entering of the promised land, and the destruction of Jerusalem help shape whole series of books. Therefore, some explanation of dates and persons will be offered. When these historical references appear, however, every effort is made to fit them into the overall Old Testament story.

Conclusion

No survey can cover every important aspect of the Old Testament. The greatness of the subject makes that attempt impossible. Hopefully this study can provide a basic grasp of the Old Testament that will lead the reader to further analysis and greater insight. Most importantly, if learning the basics of the Old Testament helps the reader to *enjoy* the text, a lifelong love for the Bible may result.

Questions for Reflection

1. How might reading it in the new sequence affect your understanding of the Old Testament?
2. How does focusing on the Old Testament's literary aspects change your attitude about its contents?
3. What are your basic assumptions about studying the Old Testament?

Note

1. These categories were first recognized by Robert Lowth in *Lectures on the Sacred Poetry of the Hebrews* (1753; Andover: Codman Press, 1829).

Part I
The Pentateuch

Introduction

Practically every important Old Testament idea is introduced somewhere in the first five books of the Bible. These books are called the Pentateuch after the Greek *penta* (five) and *teuchos* (tool, vessel, book). They contain God's law (*torah* in Hebrew). To most modern readers the word *law* means "rules, regulations, and restrictions." Certainly the Pentateuch has such material, but *torah* also means "instruction." These books attempt to teach the reader how to live.

Two types of laws are found in the Pentateuch. The first is the command, such as occurs in the Ten Commandments (Ex. 20:1-17). A second category of law is the case law (Ex. 21:1-11). Case laws tell the people what punishment fits specific crimes. Apparently, case laws are built on the commands. Most of these laws appear in Exodus, Leviticus, Numbers, and Deuteronomy.

Before the reader ever reaches Exodus 20, however, the Pentateuch offers a different kind of "instruction." The text teaches how the world came into existence, how sin began, how the Jewish nation was born, how Israel went to Egypt, and how Moses led Israel to freedom (Gen. 1—Ex. 19). Through these chapters one meets the forefathers (patriarchs) and first mothers (matriarchs) of Israel. God is revealed as Creator, Covenant-maker, Sustainer, and Deliverer. The Pentateuch definitely instructs its learners in a variety of ways.

Who wrote the Pentateuch? Biblical scholars have debated this question for over one hundred years.[1] Many believe Moses authored all but a few verses of the books, while others say the material was written by many people over a long period of time. More and more, though, scholars on both sides of this issue simply deal with the text as it is. Certainly, the beginning reader must start at that point. Correct decisions on difficult issues cannot be made until the text itself has been mastered.

When studying the Pentateuch, one should read the books as parts of a larger whole. David Clines has shown that the books can basically be divided into four major movements.[2] These movements explain the Pentateuch's plot. In Genesis 12:1-9 God promises Abraham, the father of Israel, a son, a homeland, and a special relationship with Himself. Thus Clines says that the Pentateuch unfolds as follows:

Genesis 1—11: The Need for Abraham
Genesis 12—50: The Giving of a Son
Exodus—Leviticus: The Giving of the Law, or Covenant
Numbers—Deuteronomy: The Giving of the Land.[3]

Together these books report history from the beginning of the earth to the time just prior to the Jews entering their homeland.

Various characters and themes unify this plot. Adam, the first man, and Noah, who preserved the human race, are the major figures in Genesis 1—11. Abraham and his descendants Isaac, Jacob, and Joseph then appear to illustrate how Israel began. These men also serve as symbols that God always keeps His promises. Moses dominates the rest of the story. He both explains God's special relationship to Israel by giving them the law (or covenant) and by taking them to the border of the promised land. Perhaps the Old Testament has no more significant character.

As the student examines the Pentateuch's characters and plot, certain themes will emerge. The Law, the land, the election of Israel, the love of God, and the problem of sin are just a few of these topics. These themes work with the plot and characters to make the Pentateuch a unified and fascinating piece of inspired literature.

Notes

1. Julius Wellhausen popularized the idea that Moses did not write the Pentateuch, which disagreed with the traditional view. Compare *Prolegomena to the History of Israel* (1878; Gloucester, Mass.: Peter Smith, 1983). For a conservative response to Wellhausen and his followers consult R. K. Harrison, *Introduction to the Old Testament* (Grand Rapids: Wm. B. Eerdmans, 1969), 495-541.

2. David J. A. Clines, *The Theme of the Pentateuch* (Sheffield: JSOT Press, 1986).

3. Clines, 29.

1
Genesis: *The Need and Promise of Salvation*

Introduction

Genesis introduces us to Scripture on a grand scale, letting us become spectators in the creation of the world. Quickly, the story moves from the universe to individual people in our kind of world. This reveals what we are to expect the rest of the way. The Bible does not focus on philosophical truths. The Bible focuses on people and their needs in relationship to the world and to God.

The Bible's universal scope and interest become apparent in the first chapters. Genesis 1—11 sets the stage for all that is to follow. Human beings appear here at their finest and at their worst. God's plan and humanity's prideful rebellion interact to show the universal need for further divine action if the human plight is to be solved.

The scene opens in a chaotic darkness. The divine voice penetrates the darkness to form a world, a universe, with all the parts we know today. Each part pleases the Creator. Two human beings are the most pleasing of all. Then a perfect garden becomes the focus. Here God creates and places Adam, His highest creation. Creation is not complete. Adam needs a partner before life is complete. Investigation of all created beings fails to discover such a partner, so God makes one from a part of Adam. The idyllic situation does not last long. Temptation and sin quickly mar the picture. Man and woman have to leave the garden behind, never again to be accessible for humanity. Life in the world we know as the real world begins. In such a world sin, pride, and trouble escalate until the entire universe is corrupted. God destroys the universe to start over again with Noah, a man of faith, but also a man who quickly falls to temptation. Again human corruption reaches universal proportions. Human pride tries to lift itself to meet the Creator on His own ground. The Creator easily but sadly scatters humanity over the face of the earth, separating the peoples by making communication difficult if not impossible.

Major Events in Old Testament History*	
Lives of Abraham, Isaac, Jacob, Joseph	2000-1700 B.C.
Egyptian Period	1700-1290 B.C.
The Exodus	1450/1290 B.C.
Wilderness Wandering	1290-1250 B.C.
Period of the Judges	1250-1050 B.C.
The United Kingdom	1050-930 B.C.
The Divided Kingdom	930-722 B.C.
Fall of Northern Israel	722 B.C.
The Kingdom of Judah	722-587 B.C.
The Fall of Jerusalem	587 B.C.
The Exile	587-538 B.C.
Return to Israel	538-535 B.C.
Careers of Ezra and Nehemiah	450 B.C.

* All dates approximate

Thus Genesis 1—11 prepares us to understand the world we live in. It forces us to see our temptation, our pride, our fall. It leaves us to wonder how God will work in this kind of world to bring hope and salvation to His creation and its population. It shows us the issues we must deal with to understand our universe and to cope with life in that universe. The remainder of the Bible will work out Genesis 1—11's introduction to the problems of the nature of creation, humanity, sin, pride, temptation, judgment, hope, and salvation. As in these opening chapters, the rest of the Bible's story will feature God as the Director, no matter who appears to occupy center stage at any one moment.

Genesis 1—11: The Need for Abraham

Plot: The creation of a good world that becomes ruined by sin
Major Characters: Adam, Eve, Cain, Abel, and Noah
Major Events: The creation of the world, the origin of sin, the great flood, God's promises to Noah, and the building of the Tower of Babel

Genesis 1—2: The Creation of the World

Genesis opens with the claim that God existed before the earth. At whatever date the universe was formed, God made it. The text uses three words to describe how God shaped the world. First, it says He "created" (*bara*). No other individual in the Old Testament is said to "create." Therefore, what was accomplished only God could do. No one else can create. Second, the writer declared that God spoke (*'amar*) things into existence. God is so powerful that His mere words make events happen. Finally, several verses claim that God "made" (*'asah*) portions of the world. This word is quite common in the Old Testament. Apparently the text wants the reader to know God was actively involved in the creation process. He does not just speak from a distance. He actually touches the world in a personal way.

Two accounts of creation appear in Genesis 1—2. Genesis 1:1—2:3 focuses on the world as a whole, while 2:4-25 stresses the creation of the human race. These twin versions do not contradict one another. Rather, the first telling lays a general foundation for a discussion of the human race. Certainly, God's relationship to human beings is the Bible's main idea.

Genesis 1:1—2:3 describes creation as a systematic process. God speaks into existence or makes a thing. Then, usually, He names the new part of creation. Next, He pronounces it "good." Finally, the story reports "there was evening, and there was morning" and numbers the day. Sometimes, the order of these elements differs, but they are still present. Notice that at this point the creation is flawless. No sin or imperfection has crept into what God created.

As each new day unfolds, creation becomes more complete. First, the Lord lights a dark world. Next He separates water from water so the sky can appear. Then, land emerges, and vegetation grows on that land. As a dividing time for things to grow, seasons are formed. Further, God puts sea creatures and land animals in their proper places. Finally, God forms human beings to rule over all creation. So, days one to four explain the beginning of the world itself, while days five to six deal with the start of the creatures that inhabit the world.

Human beings receive a special place in God's world. Unlike the sea and land animals, men and women are made in God's image (1:26-27). Whatever else "God's image" may mean, people are told to  rule the earth, much like God rules all things (1:28-30). Humans are responsible for caring for creation. Having placed those most like Himself in charge of what He made, God says everything on earth is "very good." No fault mars any part of God's work.

On the seventh day God rested from His efforts (2:2-3). The Hebrew word for "rest" is *shabat*, from which the word *sabbath* comes. This word meant "to cease," so it came to mean "to rest." God was not tired. Rather, His work was done. Because God stopped on the seventh day, it is a special time of "ceasing." People do get tired. This seventh day is, therefore, a much-needed renewal period. Being the only time people did not work, the seventh day became the day of worship. Again, it is vital to note that at this point the world is complete, good, and satisfactory to God.

Genesis 2:4-25 gives more details about day six of creation. Since the Bible is about God's relationship to people, it is logical that specific accounts of how humans were created follow the general story in 1:1—2:3. The Lord makes a man out of dust (2:4-7). Once more, God is actively involved in creation. Nothing has happened by chance.

The Hebrew word for *man* here is *adam,* from which comes the name Adam. Adam is placed in a special home, the garden of Eden, to work and care for the land (2:15). Only one rule binds the man. He may not eat from a tree that teaches the knowledge of good and evil. God withheld nothing else from the first human (2:16-17). As he rules the garden, the man fulfills God's earlier command (1:28).

Despite his good home and important labor, Adam needs a helper, or mate (2:18). God sees the other animals have mates, but Adam lives alone. Therefore, the Lord fashions a woman from the man's side (2:21). Immediately, Adam understands the link between himself and the new creature (2:23). This close relationship causes men and women to leave their families and be "one flesh." As the first couple were of the same flesh, so all couples should be totally committed to one another (2:24).

It is extremely important to understand Genesis 2:25. Because the people are morally flawless, they are both naked and yet feel no shame (2:25). This parallels God's attitude that all creation "was very good" (1:31). All is well in Eden.

Genesis 3:1—6:4: The Fall into Sin

Very swiftly the plot changes in chapter 3. All creation is spoiled. The man and woman cease to be good. Even the earth suffers. What causes this drastic shift?

Genesis 3:1 introduces a negative character, a serpent, who tempts the woman to break God's single command (compare 2:16-17). He asks her what God's rule is (3:1), denies God's goodness (3:4-5), and promises that the tree's fruit will make her wise (3:5). With doubts about God planted in her mind, she looks at the fruit, desires it, and eats (3:6). Then she gives the fruit to her husband (3:6). Both break God's law. Sin enters the human race.

Their sin has direct consequences. They do know more, as the serpent promised, but what they learn bothers them. Now they feel shame over their nakedness (3:7). The ease they felt in 2:25 is totally broken. Ashamed of themselves, they fear God. They flee from His presence (3:8-10). Sin has separated them from the Lord. Further, they make excuses for their disobedience, each blaming someone else for the catastrophe (3:11-13).

God punishes the three characters for their actions. The serpent must crawl in dirt and will be cursed above all animals. More importantly, God says an offspring of the woman will crush the serpent's head (3:15). This promise has been called the *protoevangelion,* or first offer of good news. Hope still exists for the human race. The serpent will not always prevail.

Adam and his mate received penalities that still affect human experience. The woman will bear children in pain. She will desire her husband, but also know the frustration of having him rule over her (3:16). The man must grow his food by hard labor. Frustration will accompany his labor, since the ground will yield thorns alongside crops (3:17-19). No longer will the land support humans without a struggle.

Thus punishment is evident in three areas: spiritual, physical, and emotional. People no longer have a free intimacy with God or with one another. Even the serpent is stung by a spiritual threat (3:15). Their actions have changed the earth itself into a demanding taskmaster. Physical labor will not always be rewarded. The "good" creation has been completely changed. A good creature has been ruined. Whereas Genesis 1—2 ends with blessings, Genesis 3 ends with Adam and his wife (whom he names Eve in 3:20) driven from the garden of Eden.

Despite this grim turn of events, however, some hope remains. God has promised to bruise the serpent. He also still cares for human beings (3:21-24). So two great Old Testament themes emerge in Genesis 1—3: (1) the human race is sinful; (2) sin spoils a good creation. The careful reader knows something more. God can overcome sin. How will God do so?

No defeat of sin occurs in Genesis 4:1—6:4. Instead, the world goes from bad to worse. Cain, Adam's son, kills his brother Abel (4:1-15). In pride Lamech acts cruelly (4:23-24). The earth even becomes polluted by children of angels and human women (6:1-4). Only Enoch walks with God (5:21-24). Obviously, the world has grown totally lawless. Some cleansing action must be taken, and only God can take it.

Genesis 6:5—11:9: The Punishing Flood

Just how wicked the human race has become is made clear in 6:5: "Every inclination of the thoughts of his heart was only evil all the time." God decided to destroy the earth by a flood. Only a righteous man named Noah, great-grandson of Enoch, and his family will escape the great punishment by making a boxlike boat (6:8-22). When the day of judgment comes, rain begins to fall and continues to do so for forty days and nights. Everything on earth drowns in the deluge. The world has been temporarily purged of evil.

When Noah leaves the safety of his ship, he makes a sacrifice to God (8:20). God accepts this offering, and promises never again to destroy the earth by water (8:21-22). Two more great themes appear at this point. First, punishment will always follow sin. Second, God always desires to save and forgive rather than condemn. Genesis 8 marks an upturn in the story. Noah acts justly towards God, the Lord blesses the human race again, and sin has been punished. If this trend continues, perhaps a return to the garden of Eden is possible.

Scholars have long noted that many countries outside Israel also have flood stories. Egypt, Babylon, Greece—indeed most countries surrounded by water—have a tale of a flood that kills all but one person. Probably the most famous of these stories is the Babylonian flood account. In this story the gods become angry with humans and want to kill them. One god warns a man called Utnapishtim to build a cube-shaped boat and escape a coming flood. The hero does so and even takes animals on his ship. Once rescued, Utnapishtim offers sacrifices to the gods. Obviously, some of these items resemble some material in Genesis.

Many differences between the two texts exist as well. The length of the flood, the reason for the flood, the nature of God, the number of animals put on the boat, and the dimensions of the boat are examples of these differences. Some scholars believe Genesis copied the Babylonian story, but the variations in the accounts make that conclusion unlikely. Probably, both stories refer back to the original flood. The Genesis story is the superior telling of the event, since its view of God and the human race is so much more advanced than its Babylonian counterpart.

Any hope that the promises in Genesis 8 will lead to the elimination of sin is dashed in Genesis 9:1—11:9. Noah himself becomes drunk and lies uncovered in his tent (9:21). While in this condition, Noah's son Ham defiles his father (9:22). Though Noah's other two sons, Shem and Japheth, cover their father, the damage has been done. Not even Noah and his family fully serve God. All of civilization sins as well. In 11:1-9, "the whole world" seeks to build "a tower that reaches to the heavens" (11:4). Why? So they can "make a name" for themselves. Here humans use technology to exalt themselves. To stop this project, God confuses their language, so communication becomes impossible. Subsequently, they scatter throughout the earth. Once more the creation proves other than "good."

After the tower story the reader is left wondering how humanity can be salvaged. Sin has permeated the account since Genesis 3:6. If left unchecked, sin will overrun creation and force God to punish it again. Adam and Noah have failed to provide consistent spiritual leadership. Some other individual is needed if God's threat to the serpent (3:15) is to come true.

Genesis 11:10—50:26: God's Answer to Sin

Plot: God combats sin by choosing Abraham and his family to serve Him. God promises many things to this family, but events often place the fulfillment of the promises in jeopardy.

Major Characters: Abraham (Sarah), Isaac (Rebekah), Jacob (Rachel and Leah), and Joseph

Major Events: The call of Abraham, the potential sacrificing of Isaac, Jacob's deception of his father and brother, Jacob's visions of God, and Joseph's saving of the family

---

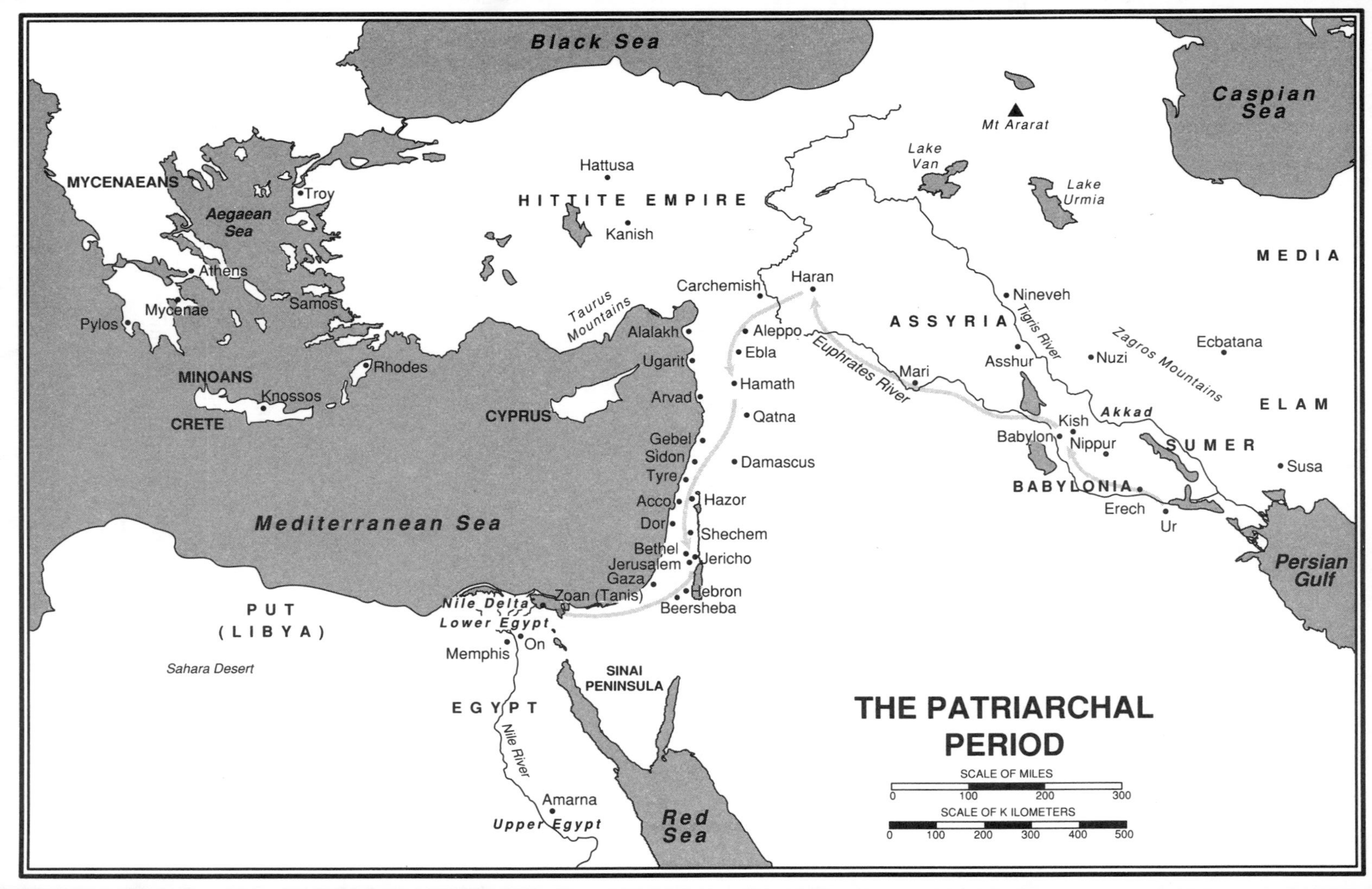
THE PATRIARCHAL PERIOD
SCALE OF MILES
0 100 200 300
SCALE OF K ILOMETERS
0 100 200 300 400 500
Black Sea
Caspian Sea
Mt Ararat
Lake Van
Lake Urmia
MEDIA
ELAM
SUMER
Susa
Persian Gulf
Ecbatana
Zagros Mountains
Nuzi
Akkad
Nineveh
Tigris River
ASSYRIA
Asshur
Kish
Babylon
Nippur
BABYLONIA
Erech
Ur
Mari
Euphrates River
Haran
Carchemish
HITTITE EMPIRE
Hattusa
Kanish
Taurus Mountains
Aleppo
Ebla
Hamath
Qatna
Damascus
Alalakh
Ugarit
Arvad
Gebel
Sidon
Tyre
Acco
Dor
Hazor
Shechem
Bethel
Jerusalem
Jericho
Gaza
Hebron
Beersheba
Zoan (Tanis)
Nile Delta
Lower Egypt
On
Memphis
EGYPT
Nile River
Amarna
Upper Egypt
SINAI PENINSULA
Red Sea
PUT (LIBYA)
Sahara Desert
Mediterranean Sea
CYPRUS
MYCENAEANS
Troy
Aegaean Sea
Athens
Samos
Mycenae
Pylos
Rhodes
MINOANS
Knossos
CRETE

Genesis 11:10—12:9: The Call of Abraham

Scripture teaches that God is never unprepared. He has a plan to meet every problem. In the midst of continual sin and chaos, the author quietly introduces the person who will lead the human race in a positive direction: Abram. Terah has three sons: Abram, Nahor, and Haran. Abram's wife is Sarai, who the text notes has borne no children. Thus Abram has no heir. His family originally comes from Ur, a highly developed city. The clan moves from Ur to Haran, where they dwell for some time (11:31).

It is important to learn some basic aspects of Abram's historical background. Scholars debate the exact date of Abram's life, but virtually all experts believe he lived between 2100 and 1700 B.C. Much has been learned about this time period through the science of archaeology. R. K. Harrison defines archaeology as the attempt "to evaluate the significance of the material remains of past human activity."[1] Archaeologists discover and evaluate ancient civilizations. They uncover such items as pottery, tools, and written records, all of which help explain what living in ancient times was like.

Probably the most instructive archaeological discovery related to Abram's time was made in 1925. At a place called Nuzu in Iraq, some twenty thousand clay tablets were found that explain many of the customs of Abram's day.[2] Marriage, adoption, and transfer of land are just a few of the practices covered in these "Nuzi tablets." From these tablets we also learn that Abram, Isaac, and Jacob were common names.

As was already mentioned, Abram's home (Ur) was a significant city. Ur produced large amounts of literature, as the Nuzi tablets demonstrate. It was a center of business and trade. Most of Ur's citizens worshiped a sun god, and Joshua 24:2 indicates that Abram's family may have as well.

Archaeologists and historians have also determined that from 2100 to 1700 B.C. many groups of people migrated from place to place. So Abram's constant moving was not unusual. There were few wars, which allowed great population shifts.

What can be learned from this brief analysis of Abram's historical background? First, one can know that Abram was not a primitive man. He came from a highly developed culture. Second, the Nuzi texts offer insight into the Bible's historical situation. Customs that sound odd today were popular in ancient times. Third, Abram's struggles are better understood. Traveling as a stranger throughout the Middle East presented several problems. Finally, readers can compare Abram's situation to their own and apply the Bible to everyday life. The Bible speaks to contemporary life, but it does so from an ancient vantage point.

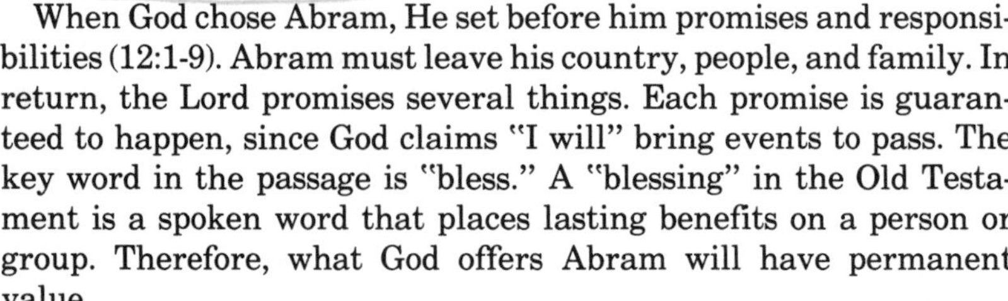

When God chose Abram, He set before him promises and responsibilities (12:1-9). Abram must leave his country, people, and family. In return, the Lord promises several things. Each promise is guaranteed to happen, since God claims "I will" bring events to pass. The key word in the passage is "bless." A "blessing" in the Old Testament is a spoken word that places lasting benefits on a person or group. Therefore, what God offers Abram will have permanent value.

God's promises focus on an heir, land, and a relationship with Abram. The first blessing is that Abram will begin a great nation, which will make his name great. Clearly, he must have children for this offer to be realized. Implied in God's command to go to a new land (12:1) is the idea that Abram's family will gain a homeland. When the Lord states that He will bless those who bless Abram and curse those who curse him, a special relationship has surfaced. God will protect Abram. Abram's family will be God's way of fighting sin. Through them, all nations can enjoy the Lord's blessing. Further, Genesis 12:7 notes that God appears again to Abram and confirms His promise of land. The Canaanites are in the land, but the land will belong to Abram's "offspring."

Genesis 12:10—25:11: Abraham's Struggle for Faith

Though Abram receives fabulous promises in Genesis 12:1-9, he is in no way perfect. His first struggle for faith occurs as he enters the land of promise. Incredibly, famine pervades the land of promise (12:10-20). Abram and Sarai, therefore, go to Egypt. To save himself, Abram poses as Sarai's brother. They are discovered, but the Lord protects them. Rather than trust God, Abram has attempted to help himself. He is not yet a man of faith.

Abram's greatest struggle of faith, however, comes as he waits for a son. He proves himself just in dealing with his nephew Lot (Gen. 13—14), but no heir arrives. When God next appears to him and repeats His promises (15:1), Abram complains about this problem (15:2-3). Once more, the Lord reassures Abram of the future (15:4-5), and Abram believes. Here he demonstrates great faith.

Many years pass. In Genesis 12 Abram is seventy-five years old. Genesis 16:16 observes he is eighty-six. Abram and Sarai have begun to doubt they can have children. So they make use of a common practice. Sarai's handmaid, named Hagar, acts as a surrogate mother for her mistress (16:1-2). Hagar bears a son named Ishmael, who becomes the father of the Arab peoples. God loves and protects this child. Still, Abram and Sarai fail the test of faith. They do not fully trust God to give them a child. Is Abram a man of faith?

Thirteen more years transpire (17:1). By now the author has introduced great tension into the plot. Is *God* faithful or not? Can or should Abram cling to the original promises? Once more God appears to Abram (17:1). This time He will "confirm" his covenant, or agreement, with Abram (17:2). To show this confirmation, the Lord changes Abram's name ("exalted father") to Abraham ("father of many"). This name change means God has increased His blessing. Abraham will have many descendants, an everlasting covenant, and the land of Canaan as a home (17:7-8).

This episode closes with two important aspects. First, God tells Abraham that Sarai's name will be changed to Sarah ("princess"). Though very aged, she will have a son. Because Abraham laughs, the new child's name will be Isaac, which means "laughter." Ishmael will not serve as the main heir. God blesses him (17:20), but Isaac is the long-awaited heir who will continue Abraham's relationship with God (17:21). To show his faith, Abraham obediently circumcises himself, Ishmael, and his male servants (17:27). Thus circumcision became the initiation rite of Jewish males into the Lord's covenant.

Isaac's laughter-filled birth provides a temporary relief in the plot's tension. Finally, the long-awaited son arrives (21:1-7). Chapters 18—19 prepare the reader for this important event by repeating the promise of a son to Abraham and Sarah (18:1-15) and eliminating Lot as an heir of faith (18:16—19:38). Hagar and Ishmael are sent away after the birth to emphasize Isaac's unique position (21:8-21). The first part of God's pledge to Abraham now seems secure.

Abraham has gotten a son, but is he now totally a man of faith? The author leaves some doubt about this issue in chapter 20 shortly before Isaac's conception, where Abraham and Sarah repeat their deception of 12:10-20. Does Abraham trust the Lord yet? If not, he can hardly answer the sin problems raised in Genesis 1—11.

All questions about Abraham's faithfulness are removed in Genesis 22. Without warning, God commands Abraham to sacrifice Isaac (22:2). Once ordered, Abraham does not hesitate. He takes Isaac, two servants, and wood for the sacrificial fire and goes to "the place God had told him about" (22:3, NIV). Carefully, slowly, the writer tells the story. Abraham sees the place (22:4). He dismisses the servants, even telling them he and Isaac will return (22:5). Even as he carries the firewood, young Isaac inquires why they have no animal to kill (22:6-7). Abraham answers that God "will provide the lamb for the burnt offering" (22:8). Is this a statement of faith, or is it merely calculated to soothe Isaac? The text does not say.

Finally, Abraham builds an altar, ties his son to it, and prepares to kill Isaac. At the last second—indeed, when his hand is in the air—

God stops Abraham (22:10-11). The Lord declares, "Now I know that you fear God, because you have not withheld from me your son, your only son" (22:12, NIV). Quite clearly, Abraham has become a person of faith. The ultimate test has been passed. Now *the reader* knows he is faithful. Surely this type of commitment can lead to the defeat of sin. God does provide a lamb for the sacrifice (22:13), so Abraham's earlier statement is vindicated.

Most of the remaining years of Abraham's life are consumed with final matters. Sarah dies, so Abraham buys a burial site in modern-day Hebron (23:1-20). The bargaining ritual recounted in chapter 23 is reflected in the Nuzi texts. Genesis's longest chapter (chap. 24) is devoted to finding Isaac a wife. Once Rebekah is secured for Isaac, Abraham can die in peace (25:7-11).

It is impossible to measure the significance of Abraham. He begins the Jewish race. He receives the eternal promises of God. Through him three major religions—Judaism, Christianity, and Islam—trace their roots. Most of all, for the story at least, he reverses the situation found in Genesis 1—11. As the man of faith, he can help defeat the serpent. As a possessor of land, perhaps, he can ease the curses placed on the human race. As a blesser of all nations, the Tower-of-Babel curse may be reversed. In short, all that God intends to do for the human race can be found in the life of Abraham.

Genesis 25:12—26:35: Isaac: An Interlude in the Plot

New readers of Genesis may be surprised at the minor role Isaac plays in the story. After all, the text waits twenty-five years to unveil him! He is the promised son from whom God will make a great nation. Still, he "merely" provides a bridge between Abraham and Jacob. Isaac is very passive. A wife is chosen for him. He repeats Abraham's trick of calling his wife his sister when in danger (26:1-11), refuses to fight when his wells are taken (26:12-32), and is tricked by his wife and youngest son (27:1-40).

Despite this passive nature, Isaac trusts God and receives the same covenant promises as Abraham. God comes to Isaac twice in Genesis 26. In the first appearance the Lord commands Isaac to stay in Canaan because the land will be given to him and his descendants (v. 3). Both visions promise Isaac many offspring (vv. 4,24), and the first claims "all nations on earth" will be blessed through him (v. 4). Each time God makes these pledges for Abraham's sake (vv. 5,24). The promises continue.

Therefore, Isaac may not be as important as his father, but he is hardly insignificant. God furthers the work begun in Abraham through him. An heir has been given, and that heir trusts God. Canaan does not yet belong to Abraham's descendants, but if God can keep one promise, surely He can keep the rest.

Since God provides an heir for Abraham, it is not surprising that Isaac has sons as well. Like Sarah, Rebekah is barren at first (25:21). When Isaac prays, though, she becomes pregnant with twins (25:22). Even before birth, the babies "jostle" one another, which puzzles Rebekah (25:22). Upon asking God about the situation, she is told two nations are in her womb, that one is the stronger and that the older will serve the younger (25:23). These odd events warn the reader of conflict to come. They also indicate that when they are born the children will be unique characters indeed.

Two stories are told about Rebekah's offspring in 25:24-34. First, the text reveals that the first baby boy was red and hairy. So the oldest son is called both Esau, which may mean "hairy," and Edom, which means "red." The second son seems competitive, so much so that he is born grabbing his brother's heel. Thus, he is named Jacob, which means "heel grabber" and which came to mean "deceiver." Already, one can sense the tension between "Red" and "Deceiver."

The second story examines the first of two major conflicts between Jacob and Esau. These brothers have different personalities and interests. Esau loves the outdoors while Jacob stays at home. Unfortunately, Isaac favors Esau, and Rebekah favors Jacob (25:27-28). One day, Jacob, the home person, is cooking stew. Esau comes home hungry and asks for some of the "red stuff" Jacob is cooking. So the red man wants red food. Jacob, ever the competitive one, asks for Esau's birthright—that is, his future leadership of the clan—in exchange for the stew. Oddly, Esau makes the bargain. Perhaps it is selfish of Jacob to suggest the trade, but the text says, "Esau despised his birthright" (25:34). For temporary gratification Esau forfeits his future.

Genesis: 27—36: Jacob: The Reluctant Heir of Faith

Which of these two sons will bear the faith of Abraham and Isaac? The older son cares little for the vital things in life. The younger son will only help his brother if he gains something in return. Obviously, the tension of the heir continues. With Isaac the tension lay in his birth, while with Jacob and Esau the tension rests in their worthiness.

Jacob outmaneuvers Esau again in chapter 27. Isaac has grown old, and his eyesight has failed (27:1). He does not know how long he will live, so he desires to prepare to die. Chief among his concluding tasks is the passing of the covenant to his oldest son. Isaac sends Esau to hunt game and cook food before the blessing. Rebekah hears the plan, however, dresses Jacob like Esau, and sends the younger son to be blessed. Confused, Isaac blesses Jacob (27:27-29). The promises God made to Abraham and Isaac are transferred to Jacob. Thus, he gains not only Esau's birthright but his special promises as well.

Of course, Esau resents this turn of events. His only comfort comes from planning to kill Jacob (27:41). Jacob's only recourse is to flee. Rebekah sends him to her brother Laban in Haran, which sounds like a merciful idea at the time (27:43). Ironically, Jacob cannot use the advantages his trickery has gained him.

On the way to Haran, Jacob has a vision of heaven (28:10-22). During this dream God offers him the promises of Abraham and Isaac. Land, offspring, and relationship are again at the heart of the covenant (28:13-15). Rather than accept God's offer unreservedly, though, Jacob vows to follow the Lord *if* he can return "safely" to Canaan (28:20-22). Therefore, Jacob will have his own struggle for faith. In him, then, the search for an heir and the struggle to believe are revived. Still, he is the person God chooses to further the reversal of Genesis 1—11.

Haran does not prove to be a safe place for Jacob. He does find his uncle Laban, but he soon learns Laban is as treacherous as he himself. Many troubles plague the heel grabber. He falls in love with Laban's daughter Rachel and works seven years for her. On his wedding night Rachel's older, and less attractive (29:17), sister, Leah, is exchanged for Rachel (29:23). The text humorously notes, "When morning came, there was Leah!" Jacob, outraged, asks, "Why have you deceived me?" The trickster has been tricked, and he must work seven more years for Rachel. Obviously, life with Laban is difficult.

After his marriage Jacob begins to father heirs of his own. Even this process causes strife. Leah is not Jacob's favorite, but she bears sons. Jacob loves Rachel the most, but she is barren. Rachel, therefore, repeats the custom of giving the handmaid as a surrogate. Leah does the same when she stops having children. Finally, Rachel has a son named Joseph. In all, eleven sons and a daughter are mentioned in the text (29:31—30:24). Certainly, Jacob does not share Abraham's need for a son. Throughout this time period Rachel and Leah vie for Jacob's affections (note 30:14-16). This competition did not lead to domestic peace, and it had long-lasting consequences.

Along with his domestic problems, Jacob has difficulty with Laban, for whom he works. The two men squabble over their flocks, and God directs Jacob to flee Laban and head back to Canaan (31:3-21). Jacob has Laban's daughters, flocks (honestly gotten), and grandchildren. When they flee, Rachel steals Laban's household gods, which conveyed inheritance rights, so Laban chases them. This time it is Laban who asks, "Why did you run off secretly and deceive me?" (31:27) Their battle to deceive one another has ended. They agree never to bother the other again (31:38-55).

At this point in the story Jacob stands between equal dangers. He cannot go back to Haran and live with Laban, but his last memory of Esau was unpleasant. His relationship with God has advanced in that he obeys God's command to flee, but the Lord has given no guarantees about the future (compare 31:3). Will Esau kill him? Once more the promised heir is in jeopardy.

Jacob travels homeward and prepares to meet Esau by sending ahead gifts of goats, sheep, camels, cattle, and donkeys (32:14-15). Since he expects trouble, he divides the family into two groups, with the children of the handmaids first, Leah and her sons second, and Rachel and Joseph last (32:7-8; 33:1-2). Though Jacob knows God has sent him home, he does not yet fully trust the Lord. He has yet to demonstrate the faith of Abraham and Isaac.

God comes to Jacob in this time of extreme crisis. Jacob sends his family ahead and spends the night alone. During the night a "man" wrestles with Jacob. This wrestler is powerful, for he "touches" Jacob's hip and dislocates it (32:25). As day approaches, the "man" asks to be released. Jacob, in dire need of help, asks for a blessing (32:26). In response, the "man" changes Jacob's name to Israel (he "struggles with God"). Like Abraham's name change, this event signals God's blessing. Jacob has struggled with God and men and has won (32:28). Another way to translate the verse is that as Jacob draws his strength from God he will overcome.[3]

Whatever else this story means, it indicates that God will keep His promise to protect Jacob (28:14-15). He can meet Esau and survive. The episode also changes Jacob. As Israel he will be a man of faith. He leaves the wrestling match changed, for he has wrestled with the Lord. Having seen God face-to-face (32:30), he cannot be the same.

Throughout the rest of his life Jacob/Israel acts in faith. When he encounters Esau, all is well (33:1-4). Esau forgives his brother. Both men have prospered (33:9). Upon his return home Jacob puts all foreign gods out of his house and keeps his promise to serve the Lord (28:20-22; 35:1-15). Thus he fulfills his role as the bearer of the covenant of Abraham and Isaac. Having struggled with men and wrestled with God, he now lives in peace. One more son, Benjamin, is born to him, but in the birthing process Rachel dies (35:16-19). His father Isaac dies as well (35:27-29). Despite these natural pains, Jacob's life seems more tranquil than before.

Though Jacob lives on, it is appropriate to summarize his character and place in the plot now. Quite obviously, Jacob is not a perfect man. He can lie and deceive. He even tries to bargain with God. More importantly, however, he is a man who changes. Jacob grows into a man of faith. He also helps fulfill God's promise to Abraham of many heirs. Indeed, Jacob's twelve sons become the heads of the nation Israel's twelve tribes. The heir promise is nearly fulfilled, though not yet totally secure. The land and covenant promises await completion. Finally, Jacob's life proves that God's purposes are worked out through all types of people. If God can work through Jacob, then He can also use many other imperfect people.

Genesis 37—50: Joseph: The Completion of the Heir Promise

After Jacob's move towards faith the reader may think all tension about an heir has been resolved. After all, Isaac and Jacob were mere individuals, but Jacob has twelve sons! Genesis 37—50 shows, though, that the whole nation, or family, can be placed in jeopardy. Unless the Lord protects Israel, the whole group can disappear.

Just as Isaac's heir of faith was not the oldest son, so Jacob's most significant son is a younger one. Joseph is the son of Rachel, Jacob's favorite wife. Therefore, he is Jacob's favorite son and receives a special coat from his father (37:3). This gift causes Joseph's brothers to hate him (37:4).

Like Abraham, Isaac, and Jacob, he has dreams. Joseph dreams that his father, his brothers, and eventually the whole world will bow down to him (37:5-9). The text does not clearly state that Joseph's telling of the dreams reveals undue pride, but it does say his brothers hate him even more when they hear the dreams (37:11). Jacob, though, keeps the dreams in mind.

In 37:1-11 the author prepares the reader for the major plot elements of Genesis 37—50. First, the hatred of Joseph's brothers will explode shortly. Second, Joseph will have great power. Third, he will be God's present link to the old promises. Thus alerted, the reader should not be surprised at what follows.

Because they hate Joseph, the ten brothers seize him, cast him into a pit, and eventually sell him into slavery (37:12-35). To cover their act, they dip the special coat in blood and act as if Joseph has been killed (37:31-33). Of course, Jacob is devastated (37:34-35). His favorite has disappeared. Meanwhile, Joseph is sold to an Egyptian (37:36).

These events throw the plot into turmoil again. The chosen son has been persecuted, and the remaining heirs are hardly men of faith. Under the circumstances, God's promise of an heir is endangered. Unless something dramatic happens, the whole plan to reverse Genesis 1—11 cannot succeed.

Joseph's situation gets worse in Genesis 39. Sold to an Egyptian named Potiphar, he does good work and is given authority over his master's household. God blesses Potiphar because of Joseph (39:1-6). Unfortunately, Potiphar's wife lusts after Joseph. When he refuses her advances, she has him jailed on false charges (39:7-20). At this point in this story it hardly pays to be faithful.

Almost incredibly, jail proves the best place for Joseph. While there, God blesses him, and he "rules" the jail as he ruled Potiphar's household (39:21-23). Two other inmates have dreams. Neither man can interpret them, but Joseph can. He predicts that Pharaoh's chief cupbearer will be restored to his former position, while the Pharaoh's baker will be executed (40:9-22). Both these interpretations are correct. Though Joseph asks the cupbearer to help free him, the man forgets him (40:23). What is important here is that the man of faith can interpret dreams through God's power (40:8).

Dreams enter the story again in chapter 41. This time they help release Joseph from prison. Pharaoh, the king of Egypt, first dreams of seven healthy cows that are eaten by ugly, gaunt cows (41:1-4). His second dream is that seven good heads of grain are swallowed by seven blighted heads of grain (41:5-7). When no one can interpret these dreams, the cupbearer finally remembers Joseph. Brought from prison, Joseph claims seven very productive years will come, followed by seven extremely lean years (41:25-32). Next, Joseph advises the king to place a suitable person in charge of storing up food during the good years (41:33-36). Because of his wisdom, Joseph receives the task. He is now second in command in Egypt (41:37-40). During the good years Joseph "stored up huge quantities of grain" (41:49, NIV). The famine years come too, and the whole world needs grain (42:57). Many nations buy grain from Egypt.

Certainly, Joseph has saved the day for Egypt, but what about Israel? Back in Canaan, famine also reigns. Jacob hears Egypt has grain, so he sends his ten oldest sons to buy food. Benjamin stays home. Unknown to the brothers, when they reach Egypt, they will have to buy grain from Joseph. When they meet, he knows them; but they do not recognize him. Obviously, they do not expect Joseph to be a high-ranking Egyptian official.

Now comes Joseph's greatest test of faith. He could take revenge on them, or he could sell them grain and not tell them who he is and that more famine will come. Either way the promises to Abraham fail to come true.

Joseph decides to test his brothers to see if they have changed. First, he accuses them of being spies (42:14). Next, he demands they bring their youngest brother (Benjamin) to him to prove they are not spies (42:20). Then, he keeps a brother (Simeon) as a hostage until they return (42:24). Jacob only agrees to send Benjamin when they again run out of food (43:1-15). Joseph has a cup placed in Benjamin's sack to make him look like a thief (44:1-17). Why? To see if they will protect Benjamin. All is lost if they treat him as they did Joseph. Because they offer to take Benjamin's place in prison to spare their father further grief (44:25-34), Joseph knows they have changed.

Finally, Joseph reveals himself to his brothers (45:1-3). He demonstrates a great deal of emotion, not only because of their presence, but because he now understands why he has suffered so greatly. Joseph declares: "But God sent me ahead of you to preserve for you a remnant on earth and to save your lives by a great deliverance. So then, it was not you who sent me here, but God" (Gen. 45:7-8, NIV). God has kept all twelve heirs alive by allowing one to go to Egypt, suffer, and be exalted. Joseph has passed his test of faith. His certification as a man of faith saves the whole clan.

Genesis concludes with the traveling of Jacob and his clan to Egypt, the death of Jacob, and the death of Joseph. All twelve tribes now reside outside Canaan, the land of promise. Certainly, the promise to Abraham of many descendants has begun to be fulfilled, but the promises about land and covenant seem remote. Still faithful, Joseph directs his brothers to bury him in Canaan when they go to the promised land (50:25). So the book ends with a reminder to the reader that God will honor *all* the promises made in Genesis 12:1-9. Thus the problem of sin described in Genesis 1—11 can be solved.

All of Israel is saved because Joseph is a person of faith. His decision to pardon his brothers means Jacob's clan will survive. His belief that God has used him to help others marks him as the true heir of Abraham's relationship with God.

Conclusion

Genesis offers the reader a comprehensive introduction to the Bible. Sin emerges as the major problem the human race has to overcome, and God acts through people to defeat sin. He also offers promises that serve as an outline for the first five Old Testament books. The mystery of Abraham's heir has been solved, and the numerous descendants have begun to appear, but His other promises are yet to reach fulfillment.[4]

Questions for Reflection

1. How does being made in God's image affect your relationship to God? How does it affect your image of yourself?
2. Do the curses placed on Adam and Eve apply to today? If so, how?

3. How do God's promises to Abraham impact the rest of the Bible?
4. What does God's choice of Jacob say about God's character? 
5. Describe Joseph's personality. Is he too good to be true? Were his brothers at least partially justified in their treatment of Joseph?

Notes

1. R. K. Harrison, *Introduction to the Old Testament* (Grand Rapids: Wm. B. Eerdmans, 1969), 85.

2. Compare Bernhard W. Anderson, *Understanding the Old Testament,* 3d ed. (Englewood Cliffs, N.J.: Prentice-Hall, 1975), 30-31.

3. The Greek Old Testament, the Septuagint, can be translated this way. I am indebted to one of my students, Mr. James Bunce, for this insight.

4. For further study see Eugene F. Roop, *Genesis,* Believers Church Bible Commentary (Scottdate, Penn.: Herald Press, 1987); Victor Hamilton, *The Book of Genesis Chapters 1—17,* The New International Commentary on the Old Testament (Grand Rapids: Wm. B. Eerdmans, 1990); Walter Brueggemann, *Genesis,* Interpretation (Atlanta: John Knox, 1982); Gerhard von Rad, *Genesis,* The Old Testament Library (Philadelphia: Westminster, 1961); Gordon J. Wenham, *Genesis 1—15,* vol. 1 in *Word Biblical Commentary* (Waco, Tex.: Word Books, 1987).

2
Exodus—Leviticus: *God Gives the Covenant*

Plot: God keeps the promise to have a special relationship with Abraham's heirs by making a covenant with them. God chooses Moses to lead Israel out of Egypt, then uses him to reveal and explain the covenant to them. At the end of this section Israel should be ready to conquer the promised land.
Major Characters: Moses, Egypt's Pharaoh, Aaron, and the Lord
Major Events: Israel's enslavement in Egypt, Moses' call, Israel's deliverance, God's giving of the covenant, Israel's rebellion against God, and the Lord's explanation of correct worship

Introduction

Exodus begins with Israel living securely in Egypt. They are guests of the Pharaoh, who protects them because of Joseph's service to Egypt. Yet by book's end Israel resides outside of Egypt. They have escaped slavery in Egypt and have moved towards the land God promised Abraham. Moses has become their leader. What events cause their situation to change so drastically? At what point in history do these events happen?

As we have already seen, Abraham, Isaac, Jacob, and Joseph lived about 2100 to 1700 B.C. During this era Egypt was strong politically, economically, and militarily.[1] In the years 1700 to 1550, though, Egypt was dominated by a foreign people called the Hyksos.[2] The defeat of this invader began a period of Egyptian power that lasted from 1550 to 1200 B.C.[3] Egypt dominated its region during these years. Virtually all historians place the events of Exodus—Deuteronomy in this era.

The last possible date for Israel's departure, or exodus, from Egypt is about 1230 B.C. An Egyptian monument discovered in 1895 states that Pharaoh Merneptah defeated Israel's army in Canaan near that time.[4] Obviously, if Israel lost a skirmish in the promised land in 1230 B.C., then they must have left Egypt by then!

The earliest possible date for the exodus is more difficult to determine. First Kings 6:1 says Solomon built the temple 480 years after Israel left Egypt. Since Solomon completed construction about 960 B.C., adding 480 years to this date makes 1440 B.C. the approximate year of Israel's deliverance. Also, some scholars believe that archaeological evidence indicates Pithom and Rameses, cities Jewish slaves built (Ex. 1:8-11), were finished before 1440 B.C. They also think this date best explains the timing of Israel's conquest of the promised land.[5] So perhaps Israel left Egypt about 1440 B.C. and entered Canaan about 1400 B.C. This theory has Israel in their homeland long before Merneptah defeats them.

Other authorities note that the 480 years mentioned in 1 Kings 6:1 may be a symbolic or approximate number. Too, they think Pithom and Rameses were not completed until about 1300 B.C. Further, Moab and Edom, nations mentioned in Exodus—Deuteronomy, apparently were not countries until 1300 B.C., according to these scholars. These opinions, plus their conviction that archaeological data implies that Canaan was invaded about 1250 B.C., lead to a 1290 B.C. date for the Exodus.[6]

It is impossible at the present time to say with total certainty which date is correct. So it is proper to conclude that the exodus occurs in 1440 or 1290 B.C. Either date falls within the 1550-1200 B.C. period in Egypt. Thus, God delivers Israel when Egypt is strong. Both options demonstrate God's great power and love for Israel.

Much of Leviticus seems odd to modern readers. Animals are killed, then burned. Grain is burned. Rules covering subjects as diverse as skin infections and bestiality appear. Festivals are mentioned, and priestly rules abound. To a casual reader Leviticus is complicated, confusing, and uninteresting. If we remember what has happened in Exodus, however, the book makes more sense.

Exodus unfolds the basics of the covenant. It also demonstrates that Israel does not always keep the covenant, and it introduces where the Jews worship. Yet Exodus does not explain in any detail what the people should do if they sin again. Nor does it identify who will lead worship, or how the nation can avoid sin altogether. These issues are addressed in Leviticus, with the matter of how sins are forgiven handled first.

Exodus 1—4: Israel's Enslavement and Moses' Call

After Jacob and Joseph die, Abraham's heirs multiply in Egypt. Indeed, they become so numerous that seemingly "the land was filled with them" (Ex. 1:7). Their growth makes Egypt nervous, however, so Pharaoh (their leader) decides to enslave the Jews (1:8-11). Israel is forced to build "Pithom and Rameses as store cities for Pharaoh" (1:11, NIV). They still increase in number, despite their horrible situation (1:12-14). Therefore, Pharaoh attempts to kill all Jewish male babies, but God defeats this plan as well (1:15-21). Abraham *will* have the descendants he was promised.

Mere survival in Egypt does not fulfill the promise of land. Israel must leave Egypt and return to Canaan. To do this, they will need someone to lead this great number of people. Exodus 2 introduces this person.

Moses is miraculously saved from death while still a baby. Frustrated with the continuing increase in the Jewish population, Pharaoh commands that all Israelite male babies be drowned (1:22). Moses' parents hide their son as long as they can, but eventually give up hope. His mother takes a basket, daubs it with tar, puts Moses in this crude boat, and leaves him in the Nile river (2:1-4). Miriam, his sister, stands "at a distance to see what would happen to him" (2:4, NIV).

At this point an apparently disastrous event happens. Pharaoh's own daughter discovers the basket (2:5-6). Readers should expect her to kill the baby. Instead, she feels sorry for Moses and decides to adopt him! Miriam, a quick-thinking girl, offers her mother as a nurse for Moses (2:7-9). When he grows up, Moses lives with his adoptive mother (2:10). This unusual beginning marks Moses for greatness.

By the time he is an adult, Moses appreciates his heritage. When he sees an Egyptian beating a Jew, he kills the aggressor (2:11-12). Later, he tries to admonish two Jews for fighting one another, but they reject his authority and broadcast his earlier murder (2:14). Afraid for his life, Moses flees to the desert area called Midian (2:15-17). There he marries, has children, and works for his father-in-law (2:18-22). Meanwhile, after many years, the Pharaoh who seeks Moses' life dies; yet Israel remains enslaved (2:23). They cry out to God, and He answers them (2:24). Because of the covenant with Abraham, the Lord decides to act on Israel's behalf (2:24-25).

Despite his past mistakes, God decides to use Moses to deliver the slaves. While tending sheep in the desert, Moses notices a bush on fire that does not burn up (3:1-2). When he turns to observe this strange phenomenon, God speaks to him, saying that the place is "holy ground" (3:5), that is, a place where God appears. The Lord informs Moses that Israel's slavery has lasted long enough. Moses must demand that Pharaoh release the Jews (3:6-10).

This command seems ridiculous to Moses. He protests and offers reasons why he should not confront Pharaoh. First, he reminds God that he is a nobody. How can he "bring the Israelites out of Egypt?" (3:11). God promises to be with him at all times and even pledges to bring the people to the very place where they are talking (3:12). Second, Moses does not know God's name. Who should he say has sent him? God says, "I am [or will be] what [or who] I am [or will be]," and then identifies Himself as the God of the covenant. "I am" has been with Abraham, Isaac, and Jacob (3:14-15). Thus, the God who never dies sends him. Based on this identification, the Lord tells Moses to assemble Israel's elders and tell them they will soon be delivered (3:16-17). To reassure Moses, the Lord promises to force Pharaoh to release them. He also guarantees that Egypt will even give Israel money to leave (3:18-22).

Still, Moses remains unwilling. He offers a third excuse, "What if they do not believe me?" (4:1, NIV). God gives him three miracles to perform: turning a stick into a snake, making his skin leprous, and changing water into blood (4:1-9). Next, Moses says he is a poor speaker (4:10). The Lord says Moses will be told what to say (4:11-12). Finally, Moses simply asks God to send someone else (4:13). At this plea the Lord explodes. God promises that Aaron, Moses' brother, will help him speak and angrily sends Moses to his task (4:14-17).

Eventually, a reluctant Moses leaves his job and takes up his commission (4:18-26). Just as God had said, Aaron comes to help Moses (4:27-28). Together they deliver God's message to Israel's elders and perform their miraculous signs (4:29-30). Perhaps out of desperation, the elders believe (4:31). They agree to follow God's plan. One very real problem remains, though. The Lord warns Moses that Pharaoh will only release Israel after a long struggle, one in which God will harden the Egyptian leader's heart before he releases the Jews (4:21).

Now Israel has a leader, however uncertain and untested. They have God's promise to set them free. Still, they lack the means to effect their freedom. God has already said Pharaoh will be stubborn. How will they gain their freedom? How will Abraham's heirs receive their covenant and secure their land?

Exodus 5—19: Israel's Exodus

Armed with their people's support, Moses and Aaron meet Pharaoh. They confront him with the news that Yahweh, their God, commands him to "Let my people go, so that they may celebrate a festival to me in the desert" (5:1). Pharaoh's response sets the stage for chapters 5—15. He asks, "Who is Yahweh that I should obey his command to let Israel go?" Further, he has never heard of the Lord. Pharaoh declares, "I do not know Yahweh, and I most certainly will not let Israel go" (5:2). This thinly veiled challenge gives Yahweh the chance to introduce Himself to Pharaoh. It also allows the Lord to demonstrate His power and His love for Israel.

Very soon, Pharaoh will know Yahweh's name. For now, he is free to oppress the Jews even more. Like his predecessors, Pharaoh decides that Israel will be less of a problem if they are forced to work harder (compare 1:8-14). Then they will have no time to dream of three-day festivals for Yahweh (5:3-4). He orders that the slaves be forced to gather their own ingredients for the bricks they make each day (5:6-9). Despite this added burden, they are to continue to produce as many bricks as ever (5:10-14). Of course, the people complain, but the Egyptians blame the change on Moses (5:15-18). The Jews then turn against him (5:19-21), and he protests to God (5:22-23).

Though things have not gone well so far, God is hardly discouraged. Yahweh instructs Moses to tell the people they will be set free (6:1-8). God remembers that they need a covenant and land, but the people refuse to listen to Moses "because of their discouragement and cruel bondage" (6:9, NIV). Likewise, Moses repeats his earlier fears. The people do not listen to him (6:12), and he is not a good speaker (6:30). At this low point, Yahweh reminds Moses that Aaron will help him, that God will perform miraculous signs, and that Israel will leave Egypt (7:1-4). In short, Egypt will come to know that Yahweh is Lord (7:5). Clearly, God has accepted Pharaoh's challenge (see 5:2).

Since Pharaoh has refused to release Israel, Moses must persuade him further. God has him work the first of the three miracles he learned in the desert. Moses throws his staff down in Pharaoh's presence, and it becomes a snake. Horrors! Pharaoh's sorcerers can do the same "trick." Moses' snake eats all theirs, but Pharaoh remains unimpressed. His "heart becomes hard . . . just as the Lord had said" (7:13). He has not yet learned God's identity.

Now God sends a series of ten plagues against Pharaoh and his people. These calamities will show Pharaoh slowly and painfully that the Lord must be obeyed. Both Israel and Egypt will learn "to know" God, an idea that appears seven times in the plague stories.[7]

Each plague reveals a little more of God's authority, and each one also pushes Pharaoh closer to freeing Israel. Sadly, only death on a large scale will finally convince him to release them.

At first, Pharaoh's magicians can duplicate Moses' signs. He turns the Nile's waters into blood, which kills fish and makes it impossible to drink (7:14-21). The magicians also turn water into blood (7:22); thus, despite the hardship his decision creates for his people, Pharaoh refuses to let Israel leave (7:23-24). A week later the Lord causes frogs to cover the land (8:5-6), but the sorcerers do the same (8:7). Pharaoh asks Moses to end the plague, however, and Moses agrees to remove them at a set time to teach Pharaoh "there is not one like the Lord" (8:10). In return for removing the frogs, Pharaoh promises Moses that Israel may celebrate a three-day festival. Then he changes his mind. Next, God sends huge swarms of gnats. This time the magicians *cannot* repeat the signs. They tell Pharaoh this plague is from God, but he refuses to listen (8:16-19).

The afflictions intensify. Flies fill the land, except where the Jews live (8:20-24). Thus Yahweh shows that the disasters are not quirks of nature. Rather, the Lord distinguishes between Israel and their oppressors. Again, Pharaoh agrees to let the people take a holiday to sacrifice to Yahweh, only to break his promise when the plague ends (8:28-32). Next, Egypt's cattle are killed (9:1-7). Pharaoh remains stubborn after this disaster, when Egypt is subsequently afflicted with boils (9:8-12) and when hail destroys Egypt's crops (9:13-35).

Sensing that he is losing his battle with God, Pharaoh begins to bargain with Moses when he hears that locusts will eat what the hail did not ruin. First, Pharaoh says that only Israel's *men* may celebrate the festival (10:10-11). Moses rejects this compromise, so the locusts eat "all that was left after the hail—everything growing in the fields and the fruit on the trees" (10:15, NIV). Second, after darkness covers Egypt—again except for where Israel lives—Pharaoh states that all the Jews can leave but that they must not take their animals (10:21-24). Since Israel wants to offer sacrifices to Yahweh, Moses again refuses to agree (10:25-26). Totally frustrated, Pharaoh warns Moses that he will be executed if he ever approaches Pharaoh again (10:27-28). Apparently, Pharaoh still believes he can dismiss Moses and his God.

Every compromise has failed. Pharaoh remains unyielding while God's power has become evident and Moses has become famous (11:3). One more awful plague will free Israel. Every firstborn male will die, causing Egypt to *demand* that Israel leave (11:4-10; compare 4:21-23). In one horrible night the Lord will demonstrate His authority over Pharaoh and his gods (12:12).

Israel's children will be spared death because their parents will sacrifice a lamb and put some of its blood on the front of their homes (12:1-7). Because of this blood, God will "pass over," or spare Israel (12:13). To remember this deliverance, the nation is commanded to celebrate a Passover ceremony every year as a "permanent statue" (12:14). During this annual observance they will eat unleavened bread to remember their hurried departure from Egypt (12:15-19) and bitter herbs to recall their bitter bondage (12:8). Since the Passover begins Israel's national life, its celebration begins each new year (12:2). It also allows parents to share their faith with their children (12:24-28). This great holy day will permanently remind Israel of God's love for them.

Just as God had threatened, Egypt's firstborn sons and cattle die (12:29-30). Of course, this event causes the nation great grief. Pharaoh finally orders the Jews to leave Egypt. Indeed, the Egyptians are so afraid of Israel that they give them silver, gold, and clothing to take with them (12:31-36). Over 600,000 Jews leave along with several people of other nationalities (12:28-37). After over four centuries away from Canaan (12:40-41) the Jews head towards the promised land. Abraham's heirs finally seem on their way to gaining a homeland and making a covenant with God.

Despite his obvious defeat, Pharaoh makes one more attempt to keep his slaves. God leads Israel "around by the desert road toward the Red Sea" (13:18) so that the people will not have to fight any battles so soon after their deliverance (13:17). Pharaoh chases them with six hundred chariots (14:7). With the people trapped between the Egyptians and the sea, Moses stretches his hands over the waters (14:21). God then parts the seas, has the people cross over on dry land, and holds back the chariots (14:19-22). Finally, God allows the Egyptians to pursue Israel, only to drown them in the resurgent waters (14:23-28). Israel is at last totally free from bondage, and they celebrate their salvation in song (15:1-21).

Three great themes emerge from chapters 5—15. First, Pharaoh and Egypt learn God's identity. Yahweh rules over nature and human beings. No person or god can overpower the Lord. Second, Israel also discovers God's greatness. Since Yahweh acts on their behalf, they should love and appreciate God. Third, the Lord redeems Israel. This idea dominates the rest of the Old Testament. The exodus event is a symbol and proof of Yahweh's kindness to the Jews in the rest of the Torah, but it is especially prominent in the Prophets and Writings. Indeed, their deliverance is the foundation for all their major beliefs about God.

Once on "the desert road," Moses must figure out how to feed his nation. Within a few days of the exodus, the people complain of hunger. They even say they wish they were back in Egypt (16:3)! So the

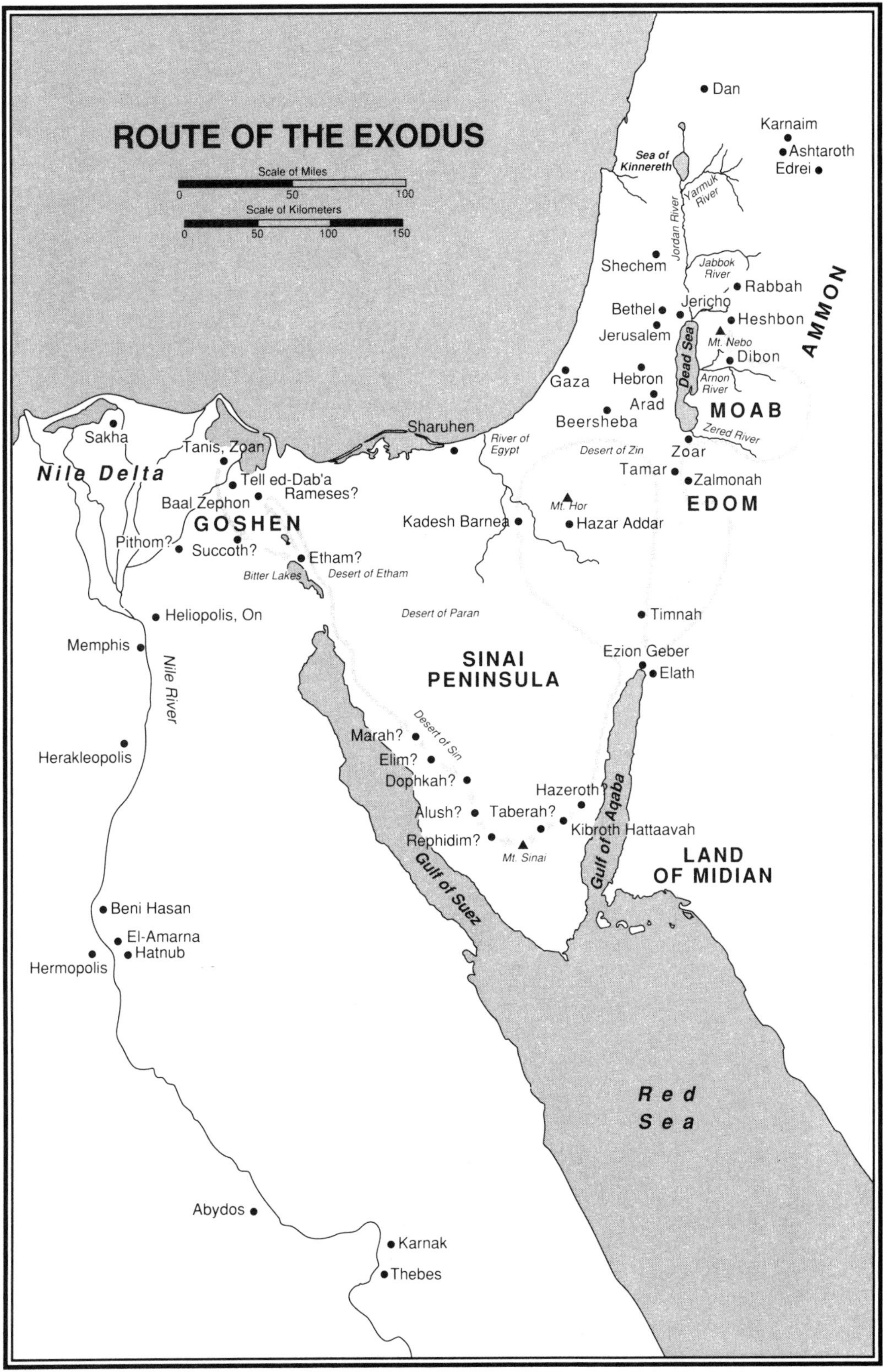
ROUTE OF THE EXODUS
Scale of Miles
0
50
100
Scale of Kilometers
0
50
100
150
Dan
Karnaim
Ashtaroth
Edrei
Sea of Kinnereth
Yarmuk River
Jordan River
Shechem
Jabbok River
Rabbah
AMMON
Bethel
Jericho
Heshbon
Jerusalem
Mt. Nebo
Dead Sea
Dibon
Gaza
Hebron
Arnon River
Arad
MOAB
Beersheba
Zered River
Sakha
Tanis, Zoan
Sharuhen
River of Egypt
Desert of Zin
Zoar
Nile Delta
Tamar
Zalmonah
Tell ed-Dab'a
Rameses?
Baal Zephon
Mt. Hor
EDOM
GOSHEN
Kadesh Barnea
Hazar Addar
Pithom?
Succoth?
Etham?
Bitter Lakes
Desert of Etham
Heliopolis, On
Desert of Paran
Timnah
Memphis
Nile River
Ezion Geber
Elath
SINAI PENINSULA
Desert of Sin
Marah?
Herakleopolis
Elim?
Dophkah?
Hazeroth
Alush?
Taberah?
Kibroth Hattaavah
Rephidim?
Mt. Sinai
Gulf of Aqaba
LAND OF MIDIAN
Gulf of Suez
Beni Hasan
El-Amarna
Hatnub
Hermopolis
Red Sea
Abydos
Karnak
Thebes

Lord provides daily food for them. Each morning "thin flakes like frost" cover the ground (16:14, NIV). This substance can be made into various types of bread and cakes. When the people see it for the first time, they ask, "*Man who*?"—which is Hebrew for "What is it?" Therefore, they call it "manna" (16:31). Though not particularly exciting food, it feeds them every day until they reach Canaan (16:35). Eventually, the people also complain of thirst, and God has Moses get water from a rock (17:1-7). Again, Yahweh meets all of their basic needs.

After three months' journey Israel arrives at Mount Sinai, near where Moses received his first vision of God (19:2). God now prepares the people to receive their covenant, an event that will fulfill God's second major promise to Abraham. Yahweh promises to make Israel a "holy," or special, nation with priestly duties representing God to all other nations (19:6). Of all the world's nations, they will be God's "treasured possession" (19:5). As they wait under the mountain, the people see lightning and a cloud and hear thunder (19:16). God is about to reveal the terms of their relationship to Him. Only Moses speaks to the Lord, lest the people defile the holy place in some way (19:23).

Israel stands at a crossroads in their history. They have fled Egypt with no place to go except where God leads. Deep in the desert, they wait for new instructions from a new Master. How they respond to what God says will dictate the next part of the story. What will Yahweh say? Will Israel agree to keep the terms God outlines? How will the second promise to Abraham be fulfilled?

Exodus 20—24: The Heart of the Covenant

It is important to define what the Bible means when it says God made a covenant with Israel. Moshe Weinfeld says that *covenant* (*berith* in Hebrew) first meant "bond" or "fetter."[8] Those making covenants accepted mutual obligations and were bound to the agreement. Thus, *covenant* came to mean "commitment," "friendship," and "binding oath."[9] Covenants were long-term, binding relationships that could not be easily severed.[10] Nations, individuals, families, and religious groups made covenants in the ancient world.

Ceremonies helped seal covenants. When two parties had agreed, a covenant meal was eaten, or an oath was recited. As covenants became more formal, a book containing the covenant's promises were written and put in a secure place.[11] Solemn moments like these heightened the seriousness of covenant making. Covenants were not entered into casually, as the ratification ceremony indicated.

Covenant breaking was a great offense. When it occurred, nations went to war, and clans feuded. Individuals sought restitution from their unfaithful partners. To mark the unfortunate occasion, the covenant's basic requirements, often written on stones, were smashed. New stones were cut only if a new covenant was made.[12] Most covenant documents included warnings for those who dared to break their solemn promises.

So what was a covenant during Moses' day? To Israel and their neighbors it was an absolutely binding relationship. Makers of covenants were to be totally loyal to one another, since their lives were linked through this agreement. Mutual benefits were expected, and covenant breakers were punished.

All of Israel's neighbors made covenants. Yet one unique feature separated Israel from other nations. Only Israel made this absolute commitment to its God.[13] No other group gave itself so totally to a deity, and no other group believed their god loved or promised as much as Yahweh. Therefore, Exodus 20—24 describes a unique and crucial moment in Israel's history. What they agree to now will affect the nation for the rest of the Old Testament.

Exodus 20—24 presents the simplest part of the covenant. Instructions on the worship center, sacrifices, priestly duties, and other more-complicated aspects of the covenant come later. For now, the Lord delivers ten foundational commands, then explains how these standards apply to daily life through a series of case studies.[14] Once the people receive this information from Moses, they will have to decide whether to accept or reject Yahweh's requirements.

The Ten Commandments can be divided into two broad categories. Each of the first four statements govern Israel's relationship to God, while the last six focus on interpersonal issues. Both emphases are vital to the new nation's survival. The basis of the covenant also has two parts: the identity of the Lord and God's past action on the Jews' behalf (20:2). Because Yahweh is the God of Abraham, Isaac, and Jacob, He has ended their slavery. So God's faithfulness and love undergird the standards the covenant professes.

To have a proper relationship with God, Israel must abide by four logical principles. First, because the Lord delivered them, they must have no god but Yahweh (20:3). Too, the Old Testament teaches that there is only one living God, so worshiping anyone or anything else is foolish. This first command dictates the essence of Israel's commitment to Yahweh. Second, God prohibits images of gods (20:4-6). No part of creation can be used as a picture of the Lord. God is not a form or figure that people can fashion and manipulate. Third, Yahweh's name must be honored (20:7). No misuse of God's name, whether through cursing or falsely claimed authority, can be tolerated, or Israel will lose respect for the Lord. Fourth, a special day is set aside for worship and rest. This *Sabbath,* or "day of ceasing labor," allows Israel to renew its covenant commitments free from daily concerns. Obviously, each new command leads to the next.

If the Jews obey God, then they can treat one another with respect. The final six commands help achieve this goal. First, parents deserve "glory" or "honor" from their children (20:12). Just as respect for Yahweh is the heart of Israel's religion, so respect for the family unit is the foundation of their society. Second, murder is prohibited (20:13). The taking of an innocent life may be the ultimate injustice against another person, as the Cain and Abel story (Gen. 4) demonstrates. Third, adultery must be avoided (20:14). Not only does it destroy the family, and thus society, it is also stealing, which is the subject of the fourth human-related command (20:15). Clearly, the taking of property or spouse leaves the wronged party without what is rightly theirs. Fifth, giving false witness against neighbors is denounced (20:16). Lying tarnishes reputations and corrupts judicial systems. Finally, coveting, the desire to have someone else's spouse, servants, or possessions, is outlawed (20:17). This last order is a summary command since coveting leads to idolatry, lying, stealing, and adultery.

Further explanations of how the Ten Commandments apply to religious and community life appear in Exodus 20:22—23:19. These case laws seem to be listed almost at random, but they all get their moral force from the Ten Commandments, and they all stress fairness to Yahweh and other people. The standard for all punishment for sin is "an eye for an eye," which simply means that punishment should match the crime. Excessive sentences cannot be prescribed for minor crimes. Again, fairness is the goal of the covenant.

Various topics are covered in this section. Idols are prohibited again, and altars built for Yahweh are to be simple and dignified (20:22-26). Hebrew servants are to be treated well. Because of the simple agricultural economy of the time, some Jews became indentured servants for six years (21:2). At the end of that time they were to go free (21:2-4). Neither male nor female servant may be abused (21:5-11). When personal injuries are inflicted in the community, restitution must be paid. Crimes such as murder, kidnapping, or criminal neglect that causes death require the death penalty as restitution (21:12-17,29). Lesser injuries incur "only" financial settlements (21:18-36). These rules apply to pains inflicted on slaves and free persons alike (21:20-21,26-27).

Stolen or abused property also requires restitution. What is stolen must be returned, and the thief must pay damages (22:1-3). Anyone who borrows an animal and does not care for it properly has to cover the owner's loss (22:14-15). Again, these judgments aim at fairness.

The restitution does not exceed the expense of the crime.

Social concerns also receive treatment. Men may not use women sexually without punishment. To do so results in either marriage or payment of damages to the irate father (22:16-17). Witchcraft, idolatry, and bestiality are not allowed (22:18-20). Because Israel was once weak and oppressed (22:21), they are to take particularly good care of the helpless. Widows, orphans, and the poor are to be treated with great compassion (22:22-27). How can these ideals be upheld? By truth telling and equity in the courts (23:1-3); by showing kindness for neighbors and having respect for their property (23:4-5); and by eliminating favoritism and oppression (23:6-9).

Only a few religious obligations are mentioned, but they are extremely important. Sabbath rest should be observed by the people, and must extend to their land, animals, households, and servants as well (23:10-13). Rest and renewal will thus restore the covenant community on a regular basis. Further, annual religious festivals are to be observed so that Israel can reflect on its relationship to God and one another (23:14-19). Finally, Yahweh promises to do great things for the people if they will agree to obey these standards. God promises to conquer their enemies and give His people a satisfying life if they ratify the covenant. Their victories will be "little by little," but they will also be inevitable (23:20-33).

Now the people must decide. Will they accept God's offer? The principles of fairness to God and fairness to each other are quite simple. Without hesitation, Israel agrees. They say as a body, "Everything the Lord has said we will do" (24:3, NIV). Moses writes down the commands and case laws to create a permanent record of this covenant agreement (24:4). Israel will obey God. Yahweh will bless Israel. Sacrifices seal the agreement (24:5-7). God then calls Moses up Mount Sinai to receive tablets containing the ten basic laws, and presumably, to get instruction on further parts of the covenant (24:12). He leaves Israel's elders in charge of the people (24:13-14) and stays "on the mountain forty days and forty nights" (24:18, NIV). After hundreds of years of delay the Lord has begun to fulfill the second part of the promises to Abraham. Israel has a special relationship—a special agreement—with the Lord. Israel is a covenant people. Still no land.

Exodus 25—31: Instructions for the Tabernacle and Priesthood

Now that the people of Israel have accepted their covenant obligations, they need a place to worship their covenant partner. Therefore, Yahweh tells Moses how to build a portable sanctuary that they can take with them wherever they go. This tabernacle is quite simple in design. It houses an ark (or box) that will hold the stone tablets that contain the Ten Commandments (25:10-22). It also shelters a table (25:23-30), lampstand (25:31-40), ceremonial altar (27:1-8), incense altar (30:1-10), and a basin for washing the priest's hands and feet (30:17-21). Each of these items is necessary to facilitate prayer and sacrifice in the worship center.

The tabernacle has three distinct areas: the courtyard, the holy place, and the holy of holies. The courtyard is the open space between the curtains that separate the place of worship from the rest of the camp and the tent that holds the holy place and holy of holies. Animal sacrifices are offered in the courtyard. Inside the holy place, the lampstand, table, and incense altar are used for prayer. The holy of holies is a room within the holy place where the ark of the covenant is kept.

Priests will help the people offer their sacrifices and care for the tabernacle and its furnishing (28:1). They will be set apart for this work in special services (Ex. 29). Aaron and his descendants are to serve as priests throughout Israel's history and will wear special garments made for them (28:6-43).

Yahweh instructs Moses to commission two men, Bezalel and Oholiab, to build the tabernacle and all its utensils (31:1-11). God gave these craftsmen special abilities, skills, and knowledge for this task (31:3-6). When he has gotten all the plans for the worship center, its priests, and its builders, Moses is ready to go back to the people. God gives him two tablets that symbolize Israel's covenant with Yahweh (31:18). Israel now has some basic standards, a prospective place to worship, and a priesthood to lead them. What could possibly alter the positive direction their future seems to be taking?

Exodus 32—34: Covenant Breaking and Covenant Renewal

As Exodus 24:18 notes, Moses leaves the people under Aaron's leadership for forty days. In fact, his absence lasts so long that the people fear he has died or left them (32:1). Therefore, they encourage Aaron to "make us gods who will go before us" (32:1, NIV). Without arguing, Aaron, who Moses has been told will be the people's main priestly leader, makes an idol for them. He collects gold from the group and fashions "an idol cast in the shape of a calf" (32:4, NIV). Forgetting all Yahweh has done, they declare, "These are your gods, O Israel, that brought you out of Egypt" (32:4). Clearly, they have broken the most basic of the covenant's ten foundational commands. They have both made an idol and worshiped it (compare Ex. 20:3-6).

Aaron compounds these sins by declaring a festival (supposedly to Yahweh!) that quickly turns into an orgy complete with gluttony, drunkenness, and immorality (32:5-6). By acting this way, they break their covenant commitments to one another. The great covenant has not even lasted six weeks!

Meanwhile, on Mount Sinai Moses has no idea what the people have done. God tells him to return to camp "because your people . . . have become corrupt" (32:7, NIV). Indeed, Yahweh is angry enough to consider destroying Israel and making a new nation from Moses' family (32:9-10). Perhaps God is simply testing Moses' commitment to leadership. If so, Moses passes. He asks God to spare the people, and God relents (32:11-14). Once Moses sees Israel's party, however, his anger "burns." He breaks the covenant stones on which the Ten Commandments are written (32:15-19). Besides demonstrating his anger, this action symbolizes the broken covenant. Upon seeing the golden idol, Moses gets angrier. He burns the idol, throws its powder into the people's water, and makes them drink the mixture (32:20).

Moses acts decisively to end the drunken festival. First, he confronts Aaron, who claims he merely put the gold in the fire, "and out came this calf!" (32:24, NIV). He prefaces this almost-humorous excuse by blaming the people for pressuring him (32:22). Second, Moses has the Levites kill those who are still sinning. Sadly, about three thousand persons die (32:25-29). Third, he informs Israel of their sin, then promises to ask Yahweh to forgive them and to renew the shattered covenant (32:30). Fourth, Moses requests that God kill him and forgive the people (32:31-32). His strategy works—to a point. The Lord forgives Israel but refuses to lead them into Canaan (32:33—33:6), so the covenant relationship remains broken.

Mostly because of Moses' continued prayers for the people (compare 33:7-23), Yahweh decides to give Israel a second chance. God orders Moses to cut new covenant stones (34:1-3), and he gratefully does so (34:4-9). Yahweh now pledges to give Israel a homeland if they will reject idolatry, keep the laws already given—especially the Sabbath observance, and celebrate the prescribed festivals (34:10-26). Since the covenant has been restored, Moses' status as God's representative is magnified (34:27-35). His leadership has saved the nation from the deserved consequences of its own sinfulness.

Exodus 35—40: Building the Tabernacle

Israel makes the most of its second chance. They obey God. They provide the materials, funds, and workmen for the tabernacle (35:4—36:7). In fact, they give so generously that Yahweh restrains them from giving too much (36:5-7)! Bezalel and Oholiab make all the parts of the tabernacle and priestly garments chapters 25—31 describe (chaps. 36—39). Finally, the tabernacle is completed, and the people walk behind it and the ark of the covenant, where the new covenant stones are stored (40:34-38). God is so pleased that "the glory of the Lord" fills the worship center (40:34-35).

Clearly God's love and Moses' leadership have given Israel new life. Israel now has the opportunity to receive the rest of the covenant. They have standards, and they have a place to worship their God. What they do not have is a way to deal appropriately with their sins. What if they act like they did in chapter 32 again? Is having Moses pray for them the only way their sins can be covered?

Leviticus 1—7: A System for Forgiving Sins

Five types of sacrifices are to be offered. Each one has its own specific purpose and unique form of presentation. Three types deal with sins that have been committed, while two allow worshipers to express joy and gratitude to God. Allowances are made for the poorer members of the covenant community. Their sacrifices do not cost as much as those wealthier Jews offer.

Burnt, sin, and *guilt* offerings cover the people's sins. More specifically, a *burnt offering* is to be given for general unintentional sins (1:3-17). Poor worshipers bring two birds (1:14-17) while those who can afford to do so offer a male from their herd or flock of sheep or goats (1:10-13). As its name indicates, this sacrifice is totally destroyed by fire. It is an offering that is given freely to Yahweh. *Sin offerings* are brought "when anyone sins unintentionally and does what is forbidden in any of the Lord's commands" (4:1, NIV). It too consists of a male from the herd or flock, or two birds, but only its fatty portion is burned. The priests may eat the rest (6:24-30). *Guilt offerings* cover unintentional sins that harm a neighbor. When this situation occurs, the worshiper must make restitution first, then bring the same animals as in the sin offering (5:14—6:7).

Grain and *peace offerings* express gratitude to God. Part of a *grain* (or cereal) *offering* is burned; the priests may eat the rest (2:1-3). *Peace offerings* are male or female animals that are treated like sin offerings (3:1-16). These sacrifices are offered in hopes that God will continue to bless the people.

A set ritual is observed every time an animal is brought to the tabernacle. First, it is presented for inspection at the entrance of the worship area (1:3; 4:4; 5:18). Second, the worshiper places a hand on the animal's head (1:4; 4:4), which means the person claims responsibility for its death. Third, the worshiper kills the sacrifice (1:5; 4:4). This act also forces the individual to see the consequences of sin.

Fourth, the priests sprinkle some of the animal's blood on the altar, and the appropriate portion is destroyed.

Several theological truths emerge from Leviticus 1—7. First, God forgives sin (Lev. 4:35; 5:18 among others). The people's obedience to God's directions restores the covenant relationship. Second, these offerings are specific and personal. Excuse making and blaming others for individual transgressions are eliminated. Third, this system demonstrates God's fairness. Rich and poor alike stand equal before God, and both can afford the sacrifices Yahweh requires. Fourth, all these elements point to God's mercy. Regardless of the sin, a loving, covenant Lord stands ready to forgive it.

Leviticus 8—10: Priests for Covenant Worship

Priests are mentioned many times in Exodus 20—Leviticus 7. Aaron serves as the first high (or chief) priest (Ex. 29:1-9). Because of his position, he receives clothing to wear that highlights his prominence (Ex. 39:1-31). Due to the golden calf incident, however, the priests have not yet begun their ministry. Without them the sacrifices and other aspects of worship cannot occur. So it is logical that the Lord instructs Moses to ordain the priests and help them begin their work.

Aaron, his sons, and the whole tribe of Levi are to be Israel's high priest, priests, and priestly assistants. To ordain, or set apart, the priests, Moses carries out several symbolic acts. After gathering the people to witness the ceremony (8:1-4), he first washes Aaron and his sons, then gives them their special clothes (8:5-9). Next, he anoints the prospective priests and the utensils of the tabernacle with oil (8:10-13). Then Moses makes sacrifices for the priests' sins and presents a ram as a special ordination offering (8:14-29). Finally, even the ministers' garments are consecrated (8:30). The whole ordination ceremony lasts seven days (8:31-36).

Without delay Aaron and his sons start completing their tasks. They offer sacrifices and lead worship (9:1-22), and Yahweh approves of what they do (9:23-24). After this positive start, tragedy strikes. Nadab and Abihu, Aaron's sons, offer "unauthorized fire before the Lord, contrary to his command" (10:1, NIV). Because of this error, fire comes from the Lord and kills them (10:2). Moses tells Aaron that this event proves the seriousness of God's rules about priestly conduct (10:3). None of God's commands is trivial or open to human innovation. Those who lead the covenant nation's worship must have total respect for Yahweh and the covenant itself.

Leviticus 11—15: Causes for Sacrifices

With a priesthood, sacrificial system, and worship center in place, the important question rises: When and why do we use them? Put another way, besides idolatry like that practiced in Exodus 32:1-6, what could the people do that requires offering a sacrifice? Leviticus 1—7 speaks of sin, guilt, and restitution, but what specific acts and circumstances cause *Yahweh* to ask for restitution? What makes a person "unclean," or in need of a fresh start with God and the covenant community?

A variety of things can make an individual "unclean." For example, eating "unclean" food makes one unclean and thus obligated to offer sacrifices (chap. 11). Exactly why the animals listed in Leviticus 11 are unclean is not clear to us, but the people do not seem to protest the Lord's decision. Whatever the reasoning behind the prohibitions, obedience to these laws marks Israel as an unusual nation, totally committed to their God. Childbirth (12:1-8), skin diseases (13:1-45), mildew (13:47-59), and bodily discharges (15:1-33) make people and places unclean. Most of these rules protect the people from health risks. When the risk is removed, an individual may offer an appropriate sacrifice and resume an active life in the community (for example, Lev. 14). No one is declared "unclean" for life unless the unfortunate condition persists.

Modern readers often have difficulty understanding why diseased people, such as lepers (13:45-46), are ostracized from the group. We must remember that ancient peoples had few medicines. Epidemics could kill whole cities. Thus, their safest means of avoiding outbreaks of disease was to isolate infected persons.

Leviticus 16: The Comprehensive Sacrifice

One nagging question remains about the sacrificial system. Israel possesses the basic standards of their covenant. They have a place to worship and priests to lead that worship. Their sins are forgiven by a set of sacrifices, and they know what specific circumstances make them "unclean." What if they fail to offer sacrifices when they sin? Is there any way for them to renew their relationship with God?

Once a year, Aaron must offer sacrifices to cleanse the priests, the tabernacle, and the people (16:14-33). Then God will forgive whatever sins have been committed during the previous year (16:21-22). This ceremony occurs in four stages. First, as worshipers stand outside the tabernacle, Aaron offers a "sin offering to make atonement for himself and his household" (16:6, NIV). Second, he slaughters a goat as a sin offering for the people (16:15). Third, he uses some of the blood from the bull and goat to cleanse ceremonially the worship area (16:18-19). Fourth, he places his hands on a live goat's head and confesses the people's sins. This transfers the sins to the goat. Then he has the animal taken far into the desert (16:20-22). Israel must observe this ritual every year so they can be "clean from all . . . sins" (16:30, NIV). Regardless of the nature of their sins, God forgives the people (16:29-34).

This Day of Atonement has tremendous symbolic significance. Its comprehensive nature reveals Yahweh's power and love. Further, the priest's rare entry into the holy of holies emphasizes Israel's own commitment to the covenant. Finally, the drama of the goat going to the wilderness provides an accurate picture of how God forgives sins. Once covered, the Lord acts as if all transgressions no longer exist.

Leviticus 17—26: Becoming a Holy People

God is not content to allow Israel to simply avoid sin. Now the people learn how they can move towards moral excellence. Long called "the holiness code," these chapters insist that Israel must be holy because their God is holy (see 19:2; 20:26).[15] By "holy" the author means that the Jews are "special," "unique," and "set apart" for God's purposes (compare Ex. 19:6). They are to demonstrate these qualities by the ways they respond to God and how they treat one another.

As in chapters 11—16, the laws in the holiness code cover very practical matters. Though the topics discussed in chapters 17—26 are quite diverse, each subject deals with religious, private, or community life. Religious observances and how they set Israel apart from other nations are described in chapter 18:21-26. Personal holiness, especially as it relates to sexual purity, is the subject of chapters 18—20. Chapter 19, the heart of the whole law, stresses love for neighbors, and chapter 26 closes the section by reminding Israel of the benefits of obeying the covenant.

Worship remains the focus of the law. Thus, Yahweh explains again that all sacrifices must be brought to the tabernacle (17:1-4). Otherwise, the people may be tempted to make offerings to idols (17:7). Priests must set a strong moral example for the people so worship can maintain credibility. They are to have high standards for marriage (21:7-15), total respect for their work (22:1-16), and a comprehensive knowledge of the sacrificial system (22:17-33). The people must faithfully observe the special feasts Yahweh has instituted (chaps. 23—25). Israel's celebration of the festivals sets them apart as a grateful nation committed to Yahweh.

Sexual relationships have long been a universal concern. Generally, people want to know who they may marry, and they also are interested in what constitutes "normal" human sexuality. Leviticus 18—20 addresses these issues through a series of prohibitions. First, Israel may not marry "close relatives" (18:6). Incestuous relationships such as father-child, mother-child, brother-sister, and nephew-aunt, among others are thereby eliminated (18:7-18). Second, adultery and sexual acts performed in pagan cultic worship must be avoided (18:19-21). Third, homosexuality and bestiality are denounced as "detestable" and "perversion" (18:22-23). Anyone who ignores these warnings will be punished (chap. 20). God sets these standards so that Israel will be different from the nations they will conquer in Canaan (18:1-5,24-28). Again, holiness is the goal.

All these rules are meant to help Israel love their neighbor as much as they love themselves (19:18). To show this love the people should care for their poor (19:9-10), practice honesty (19:11-13), promote justice (19:13-18), and encourage purity of worship (19:26-30). If they will obey the whole covenant, then God will bless every aspect of their lives (26:1-12). Disobedience, though, will bring certain discipline, then punishment, and death if they do not repent (26:14-46). Clearly, God desires to love them and see them love one another (26:40-45). Judgment is a last resort.

Leviticus 27: Devotion to Yahweh

The covenant concludes with commands about what belongs to God. This emphasis is appropriate, since the covenant as a whole stresses that the people are devoting themselves to the Lord. As God's special nation, the Jews are to give Yahweh a tenth of their wealth (27:30-33). If they volunteer to give more, because of a vow or out of joy, they must keep their pledge (27:1-29). Their land and property come from God, so such gifts are not unreasonable.

Conclusion

When Exodus and Leviticus end, Israel possesses a comprehensive statement of what God expects from them. They know the basics of this covenant, as well as its finer points. They have a place to worship, leaders to guide worship, and sacrifices that will cover their sins. Beyond these vital ingredients, they now possess a national identity: they are Yahweh's holy people. This relationship entitles them to a new homeland. Given all these factors, Leviticus 27 marks a high point in Scripture. Abraham has heirs, and those heirs have a covenant. Can land be far behind?[16]

Questions for Reflection

1. Why do you think God allowed Israel to remain enslaved for so long? 
2. Does God favor the oppressed of the world? If so, how?
3. Using Leviticus as a guide, define holiness. What are some ways we can demonstrate holiness today?
4. What value do the long descriptions of tabernacle building and ritual requirements in Exodus and Leviticus have for modern believers?

Notes

1. John Bright, *A History of Israel*, 2d ed. (Philadelphia: Westminster Press, 1972), 51.

2. Bright, 60-62.

3. Bright, 106-13.

4. R. K. Harrison, *Introduction to the Old Testament* (Grand Rapids: Wm. B. Eerdmans, 1969), 322-23. The monument lists several victories, including the fact that "Israel is laid waste, his seed is not." Compare James B. Pritchard, ed., *Ancient Near Eastern Texts Relating to the Old Testament*, 2d ed. (Princeton: Princeton University Press, 1955), 378.

5. Read John J. Bimson, *Redating the Exodus and Conquest*, 2d ed., JSOT Supplement Series 5 (Sheffield: Almond Press, 1981); and Gleason L. Archer, Jr., *A Survey of Old Testament Introduction*, rev. ed. (Chicago: Moody Press, 1979), 223-34 for representatives of this opinion.

6. Compare Harrison, 174-77, and Bright, 121-22.

7. Compare Victor P. Hamilton, *Handbook on the Pentateuch* (Grand Rapids: Baker, 1982), 163-66.

8. Moshe Weinfeld, "*berith,*" *Theological Dictionary of the Old Testament,* 12 vols., ed. G. Johannes Botterweck and Helmer Ringgren, and trans. John T. Willis, Geoffrey W. Bromiley, and David E. Green (Grand Rapids: Wm. B. Eerdmans, 1974 -), 2:255. See also D. J. McCarthy, *Old Testament Covenant* (Richmond, Va.: John Knox, 1972).

9. Weinfeld, 256-59.

10. Weinfeld, 261.

11. Weinfeld, 266-67.

12. Weinfeld, 265.

13. Weinfeld, 278-79.

14. Brevard Childs, *Introduction to the Old Testament as Scripture* (Philadelphia: Fortress, 1980), 174.

15. Martin Noth, *Leviticus: A Commentary,* trans. J. E. Anderson (Philadelphia: Westminster, 1965), 128.

16. For further study see R. Alan Cole, *Exodus,* vol. 2 in *Tyndale Old Testament Commentaries* (Downers Grove, Ill.: Inter-Varsity, 1973); Roy L. Honeycutt, "Exodus" in *The Broadman Bible Commentary,* vol. 1, rev. ed. (Nash-

ville: Broadman Press, 1973), 289-456; Brevard Childs, *Exodus,* Old Testament Library (Philadelphia: Westminster, 1974); Terence E. Fretheim, *Exodus,* Interpretation (Louisville: John Knox, 1991); John I. Durham, *Exodus,* vol. 3 in *Word Biblical Commentary* (Waco, Tex.: Word Books, 1987); Robert L. Cate, *Exodus,* vol. 2 in *Layman's Bible Book Commentary* (Nashville: Broadman Press, 1979); G. J. Wenham, *The Book of Leviticus,* The New International Commentary on the Old Testament (Grand Rapids: Wm. B. Eerdmans, 1979); Jacob Milgrom, *Leviticus 1—16,* vol. 3 in *The Anchor Bible* (New York: Doubleday, 1991); R. E. Clements, "Leviticus" in *The Broadman Bible Commentary,* vol. 2 (Nashville: Broadman Press, 1970).

3
Numbers—Deuteronomy: *The Struggle for Land*

Plot: Israel comes to the edge of Canaan, then refuses to fight for the land. Because they reject God's promise, Yahweh sentences them to forty years in the desert. When a new generation matures, the Lord promises them the land. When Deuteronomy ends, the nation is poised on the edge of Canaan, ready to conquer again.

Major Characters: Moses, Yahweh, Aaron, Joshua, Caleb, and Korah

Major Events: The first Passover, Israel's preparation to leave Sinai and enter Canaan, the people's refusal to enter the land and subsequent exile, the death of the first generation, Moses' instructions to the new generation, and Moses' death

---

Introduction

Numbers and Deuteronomy might appear unnecessary to the plot. Exodus and Leviticus have prepared Israel to enter the land. All they need are marching orders. As so often happens, God sees things differently. Israel must learn how to live as covenant people in the wilderness with God before they are ready to receive the promise of the land and the security of life in it. Thus God has the people numbered, the camp set up and purified, and then issues the orders to move out. Immediately, Israel finds a better way to do things. They want a different leadership style and team. Despite this, God leads them to the border of the land and lets them send spies to see the land and set up strategy to conquer it. The spies, however, return in fear, frustration, and faithlessness. This leads to forty years of divine discipline. Only the next generation will enter the promised land. Meanwhile, the old generation wanders and murmurs through the wilderness and then into the countries bordering the promised land.

God shows His power against their enemies, allows two and a half tribes to opt for land east of the Jordan outside the land of promise, and prepares the people for life in the land. Aaron and Miriam die. Finally, in Deuteronomy, Moses reminds the people of God's love, God's actions, and God's expectations for the people in the land. He leads the people to renew the covenant with God and then installs Joshua as his successor. Finally, Moses goes up the mountain to view the promised land and die. Numbers and Deuteronomy thus mark recessive elements in the plot, delaying the action for a whole generation and forcing Israel to see and accept God's conditions for life as His people in His promised land.

Numbers 1—10: Departure from Sinai

This section is one of the most hopeful texts in the Old Testament. A very eventful year (1:1) has passed. Israel has left Egypt, accepted a covenant, and rested near Mount Sinai. Now they prepare to leave Sinai and go conquer Canaan. They take a census (Num. 1—2), organize their priests (Num. 3—4), purify their camp (Num. 5), and dedicate certain people and offerings (Num. 6—7). These objectives completed, they ordain the priests and Levites (Num. 8), celebrate their first Passover after leaving Egypt (Num. 9), and leave Mount Sinai (Num. 10). Each activity indicates that Israel is ready to enter their new homeland.

If everything goes as planned, the people's next stop should be in Canaan; but even the book's Hebrew title warns that something will go wrong. Instead of "Numbers," a title taken from the the Latin *arithmoi*, the Hebrew title is "in the wilderness" (*bemidbar*). Why will Israel be "in the wilderness" at the end of the book? What could possibly go wrong?

Numbers 11—20: Losing the Land

Without question, Numbers 11—20 describes some of the most tragic events in the Bible. From the heights of marching to the promised land the people fall to the depths of dying in the desert. Even Moses loses the privilege of entering Canaan. This whole segment chronicles one disaster and missed opportunity after another.

Hints of problems appear in chapters 11—12. Despite what God has done on their behalf, the people complain about their living conditions (11:1-3). Certainly, life in the desert was not pleasant, but they have been promised that this situation is temporary. They will soon be in Canaan. Next, they demand meat instead of manna. God gives them quail, yet also sends a plague because of their complaining (11:4-35). Finally, Aaron and Miriam oppose Moses because he marries an Ethiopian woman (12:1-2). God defends Moses by striking Miriam with leprosy, then heals her when Moses prays for her (12:3-16). Moses remains Yahweh's chosen ruler, but these petty disputes are ominous. All is not well in Israel.

Israel now travels within striking distance of the promised land. To help them know their opponents' strengths and weaknesses, Yahweh has Moses send leaders to spy on the Canaanites (13:1-16). Moses instructs them to assess the land, its cities, and its people (13:17-20). This information will help Moses know where to invade. The spies carry out their mission. In the process they discover that the land is extremely fruitful (13:21-25).

Their task complete, the spies make their report. First, they admit that the land "does flow with milk and honey" (13:27, NIV). Life there would be preferable to living in the desert. Second, they state that the inhabitants of Canaan are numerous and powerful, and the cities are heavily fortified (13:28). Third, they note that several people groups would have to be eliminated before the Jews could conquer the land (13:29). Thus, though Caleb and Joshua are in favor of invasion, the majority of the spies counsel against attack. They even spread lies to advance their opinion, claiming that the land eats people and that *all* the Canaanites are giants (13:30-33). God's promise of a homeland and Israel's commitment to the covenant are both in jeopardy.

Responses now come from the people, their leaders, and the Lord. Bitterly disappointed, the people cry and wish for death (14:1-2). They now believe their wives and children will be killed by the Canaanites (14:3), which makes them want to choose new leaders and return to Egypt (14:4). Moses, Aaron, Joshua, and Caleb try again to convince the people to move forward. According to them only rebellion can stop their ultimate victory (14:5-9). Because of these pleadings, the nation decides to stone Moses and Aaron (14:10).

At this crucial moment *the Lord* responds. Angered at Israel's unbelief, Yahweh proposes to begin a new nation from Moses' descendants (14:10-12). As in Exodus 32:11-14 Moses declines this honor and instead prays for the people (14:13-19). God relents, but only partially. With stunning decisiveness the Lord denies anyone over twenty years old the right to enter the promised land. Only Joshua and Caleb, the two faithful spies, will live in Canaan (14:20-30). Then Yahweh sentences the older generation to eventual death in the desert and kills the ten lying spies (14:27-38). The children they thought would die in Canaan will inherit it—just as God promised Abraham (14:31). It will just not be *this* generation who possesses the land.

Too late, the people realize their mistake. They offer to go and fight, but Moses tells them they have lost their chance. God will not be with them, so they will be routed (14:39-43). They go anyway, and Moses' prediction comes true (14:44-45). Yahweh's sentence will be served. The whole heir, covenant, and land (Gen. 12:1-9) process has been suspended for forty years.

More woes follow. After some further instructions on sacrifices (chap. 15), a group rebels against Moses. Led by Korah, this faction apparently resents the notion that only Moses can represent Israel before God. They argue that all the people are holy and that God will hear anyone (16:1-3). To defend himself, Moses suggests that Aaron and the rebels offer fire before God (16:5-11). Whomever the Lord accepts will be declared Yahweh's representative. Not only does God not affirm Korah, the ground opens and devours him and his family (16:31-33). Fire consumes the other leaders of the faction (16:34-35). Moses remains the leader, but the text hints that he is losing patience with the nation (see 16:15).

After more laws pertaining to the priests (chaps. 17—18) and purity (chap. 19), still another, perhaps greater, tragedy occurs. Once again, Israel is thirsty. Once again, they complain (20:1-2). As usual, they wish they were dead, or at least back in Egypt (20:3-5). Perhaps by now, Moses also wishes they were dead. Yahweh tells Moses and Aaron to get water by speaking to a rock (20:6-9). Instead of speaking to the rock, though, Moses strikes the rock (20:11). Worse still, he takes credit for the miracle instead of honoring God (20:10). Because of this prideful insubordination, neither Moses nor Aaron will enter the promised land. Like the rebellious nation they lead, they will die in the desert. Indeed, Aaron dies fairly soon (20:22-29).

To sympathetic readers, Moses' punishment seems much too harsh. After delivering, leading, and interceding he will not take the new generation into Canaan. As with earlier stories, such as that of Nadab and Abihu (Lev. 10:1-23), this episode emphasizes God's holiness and authority. No one, not even Moses, can claim the Lord's glory. To do so constitutes blasphemy, or taking God's name in vain. Still, one wishes Moses could be pardoned, even with this understanding. That he continues to lead Israel and serve God after this development demonstrates Moses' character and commitment to the Lord.

Numbers 21—36: A New People for the Land

Slowly, painfully, the old generation begins to die. Yahweh remains faithful to them, for Israel continues to have food, clothing, and guidance; they even win some battles (21:1-3, 21-35). Yet they also complain and die for their insolence (21:4-9). They worship other gods and participate in immorality as they did in the golden calf story (compare Ex. 32:1-6 and Num. 25:1-9). Given their instability, is Yahweh through with Israel? Is there any hope for their future?

The Balaam stories (Num. 22—24) are unusual, to say the least. A pagan prophet hears from the Lord. His donkey also speaks to him. Though he has been hired to place a curse on Israel, he cannot do so. What does this strange account mean? Though no one has the final word on this text's interpretation, one idea is evident: Yahweh still plans to fulfill the promises made to Abraham. Balaam says Israel will be numerous (23:7-10), God will be with them, blessing their friends and cursing their enemies (24:3-9), and God will help them conquer the land (24:15-19). Nothing can thwart Yahweh's purpose.

Eventually, the old generation dies (Num. 26). God begins to reaffirm various laws (27:1-11). Just as important, Yahweh also instructs Moses to prepare Joshua to be the nation's new leader and Eleazar to be their new priest (27:12-23). These men will now supervise offerings, festivals, and vows (Num. 28—30).

Yahweh gives the new generation a taste of victory by allowing them to defeat the Midianites, who had earlier enticed Israel into idolatry (Num. 31; compare 25:16-18). After this battle, representatives of the tribes of Gad and Reuben ask Moses to allow their families to settle east of the Jordan River instead of in the promised land. Moses agrees, but only after making them promise to help conquer Canaan (chap. 32). That the nation speaks of invasion and conquest at all reveals that the new generation intends to obey God and possess the land.

Finally, this tragic book concludes. Moses recounts the sad history of Israel's travels in the desert and warns the people to follow the Lord (Num. 33). There follows a discussion of what part of Canaan each tribe will possess and the naming of new leaders (Num. 34). Moses explains how the Levites are to be treated (Num. 35) and rules that women may inherit land (Num. 36). Clearly the book's last few chapters point to a more hopeful future. Israel can expect to approach Canaan again. In fact, they have journeyed within close range of the land already. Horrible things have happened, but a new era is dawning.

Deuteronomy 1—4: The Land and the Past

When Numbers ends, a new generation has emerged. Raised in the desert, this group seems determined to avoid their parents' fate. Likewise, Moses is determined to guide them towards success in Canaan. He gives them advice on a number of issues, including how to wage war, establish their worship, choose future leaders, and deal with false prophets. To convey this information he presents a revised covenant. He then asks the new generation to embrace it as their own.

Several scholars have noted that Deuteronomy is composed as a covenant (or treaty) between God and Israel. The covenant takes its structure from the most common treaty format of Moses' day and consists of six parts.[1] After an introduction that names the parties making the agreement, the treaty describes the history of these parties' relationship. Next, general and specific regulations for keeping the covenant appear. Finally, blessings and curses for keeping or breaking the treaty are noted, followed by a list of witnesses to the agreement. Thus, Peter Craigie suggests that Deuteronomy can be divided as follows:

1. Preamble (1:1-5).
2. Historical Prologue (1:6—4:49).
3. General Stipulations (chaps. 5—11).
4. Specific Stipulations (chaps. 12—26).
5. Blessings and Curses (chaps. 27—28).
6. Witnesses (see 30:19; 31:19; 32:1-43).[2]

Seen this way, Deuteronomy summarizes Israel's past and helps shape their future.

Other writers, especially E. W. Nicholson,[3] question this division of the book. They also debate whether this treaty form was most prominent in Moses' lifetime or a later period. Despite these needed cautions, it is legitimate to discuss Deuteronomy as a treaty between Yahweh and Israel. As the book unfolds, what God expects and the people's willingness to obey become evident.

Moses first reminds the nation of their history (Deut. 1—4). Even though this generation did not participate in the events of Exodus 1—Numbers 20, Moses says "you" chose spies, rebelled against God, and so on (see 1:9,14). He links them to their parents' mistakes to encourage them to keep Yahweh's commands in the future. Because they refused to invade Canaan (1:19-46), the Lord made them live in the desert forty years (2:1-25). Later, they won some victories that prepared them to conquer the promised land (2:26—3:11). Moses concludes this historical section of the treaty by reminding the people that obedience is the key to their future (Deut. 4). Just as a weaker nation must obey its stronger covenant partner, so Israel must abide by Yahweh's standards if they are to inherit the land.

Deuteronomy 5—11: Basic Rules for Possessing the Land

Having completed his brief summary of their past, Moses reviews the basics of the Sinai covenant. He also establishes the bases of their national life. Three ideas receive special treatment. First, Moses tells the people to keep the Ten Commandments and the other foundational covenant laws (Deut. 5). Their future in the land depends on this faithfulness (5:33). Second, they must love God above all else, an effort that involves their hearts, minds, and strength (6:4-9). This love motivates their obedience to Yahweh and eliminates idolatry (Deut. 8). Third, God has chosen them to be a special people. Because of the promises to Abraham, the Lord continues to bless this sometimes stubborn and rebellious group (9:1-6). If Israel remembers and responds correctly to these truths, their love for God will lead to a long stay in Canaan (Deut. 11).

The new generation must understand and implement the covenant's basic stipulations before it can hope to obey more detailed instructions. Once grasped, however, the basic requirements unlock new opportunities for blessing. Will Israel respond to this new divine initiative?

Deuteronomy 12—26: Specific Rules for Possessing the Land

Many of the standards explained in chapters 12—26 are familiar to readers. After all, they appeared earlier in the Pentateuch. For instance, Israel must not worship other gods (Deut. 13). They should avoid unclean foods (Deut. 14), cancel the debts of the poor (Deut. 15), and observe their national religious festivals (Deut. 16). Judges are to be just (16:18-20; 17:8-13), priests are to be provided for (18:1-8), and property rights and marital bonds are to be upheld (Deut. 22). These laws are new *to this generation,* though, so they deserve particular emphasis.

Because they will soon enter a new land, the people also receive some new instructions. When they enter Canaan, they must worship Yahweh in one central place (12:4-7). Of course, they may pray and praise God wherever they live and work, but God will choose a permanent location for their major festivals (12:8-29). This emphasis on a particular worship center helps guard against the tendency to bow down to idols at various local shrines (12:1-4,29-32).

Other rules apply directly to life in the new land. A few of their cities are set aside as places of refuge for innocent parties who are threatened by persons seeking unjust revenge (Deut. 19). Again, mercy motivates the covenant. When they fight wars, they must totally destroy their enemies (Deut. 20). Yet, if they take a woman captive, they may not abuse her sexually. They must marry her and give her all privileges of a wife (21:10-14). To show their gratitude for their new home, they are to give tithes and offerings from what the land yields (Deut. 26). Such gifts will support needy and defenseless persons (26:12-15).

Two sets of laws about life in Canaan are particularly vital for understanding the rest of the Old Testament. Moses senses that Israel will eventually want a king, so he sets rules for the rulers (17:14-20). Israelite kings must come from the people and live simply (17:15-17). They should "follow carefully all the words of this law and these decrees" (17:18-20, NIV). Moses also knows that prophets will always exist. They will preach various doctrines and come from many countries (see Balaam). So he says, a prophet must preach worship of Yahweh alone (18:17-20). Further, true prophets speak the truth. If their predictions come true (and if they preach Yahweh), they are sent from God. If not, they are liars. These laws about rulers and preachers save Israel from political and spiritual ruin.

Various rules complete the specific requirements of the covenant. These include statements on divorce (24:1-4), the poor (24:17-18), caring for widows (25:5-10), and a number of other issues. These laws combine God's mercy and justice, and they deserve Israel's active allegiance.

On the one hand, this revised covenant has gotten complicated. Rules for many situations now exist. Yet, on the other hand, it has remained quite simple. The Ten Commandments still undergird the law. That fact has not changed. Truth, fidelity, and commitment to Yahweh still define God's standards. In this way the law remains understandable to all. Few Israelites can fail to grasp what the covenant requires.

Deuteronomy 27—28: Incentives to Keep the Covenant

As in Leviticus 26, Moses realizes that Israel needs reasons to keep the law. Mere promise of land did not ensure faithfulness in Numbers 13—14. Therefore, Moses chooses a picturesque and creative way to encourage them to renew the covenant. He tells them of a place called Shechem in the new land. This city has special significance because Abraham was first promised a homeland there (Gen. 12:6). Nearby, two adjacent mountains illustrate Israel's choice of accepting or rejecting the covenant.

On one side of a valley stands Ebal, a rocky, barren mass. On the other side is Gerizim, a mountain that has trees and vegetation. Ebal represents what will happen to Israel if they reject Yahweh's standards. Gerizim symbolizes the richness of their lives if they will honor the Lord (27:1-13). The people may choose either barrenness or fruitfulness, cursing or blessing. Their future in the land depends on this decision.

If Israel chooses Gerizim (blessing), they will be blessed in their homes, on their jobs, and in the world beyond Canaan (28:1-6). All their enemies will tremble before them (28:7). They will truly exist as a unique and special people of Yahweh (28:8-14). If, however, Israel refuses the covenant, they will suffer reverses in all walks of life (28:15-19). Plagues will hinder them (28:20-24). Enemies will scatter them (28:25-29). Eventually, they will be driven into exile, where they will long for home (28:63-68). Indeed, their lives will be barren as Ebal. Surely this generation has already experienced such existence in the desert. Which mountain will they choose?

Deuteronomy 29—33: Accepting the Covenant

Without dissent the nation accepts this updated covenant (29:1). They agree with Moses' version of their history (Deut. 29) and choose life instead of death, Gerizim instead of Ebal (30:19-20). This final phase of his career virtually completed, Moses establishes his longtime aide and military commander Joshua as his successor (31:1-8). He also makes a copy of the law and places it in the ark (31:9-13) as a witness of Israel's pledge to follow Yahweh. Though he knows the people will not always serve God, Moses blesses all twelve tribes (Deut. 32—33) and hopes for the best.

Perhaps the clearest summary of the covenant's importance for Israel's future appears in 32:46-47. Moses says:

> Take to heart all the words I have declared to you today, so that you may command your children to obey carefully all the words of this law. They are not idle words to you. They are your life. By them you will live long in the land you are crossing the Jordan to possess.

Their future is guaranteed as long as they take their covenant responsibilities seriously. Indeed, their life in and possession of Canaan depend on it. All else is secondary to following God.

The great covenant ends in chapter 33. Israel, the vassal, has agreed to serve their Lord. Therefore, they are promised great blessing. No other ancient nation had this understanding of their god. Israel believed their God alone ruled all history and thereby chose them as a special people. Israel alone believed God calls people to a relationship based on mutual love and respect. If Israel will practice covenant faithfulness, they can soon inherit the promised land.

Deuteronomy 34: The Death of Moses

After addressing the people and encouraging Joshua, Moses climbs Mount Nebo, views Canaan from a distance, and dies (34:1-5). No person, not even Abraham, impacts Old Testament faith like Moses (34:10-12). As miracle worker, deliverer, lawgiver, and prophet, Moses is the most diverse and talented leader in the Hebrew Bible. Without him Israel could not have survived as a nation. With him they develop from a slave people to a conquering army. Though not flawless, his blend of boldness and humility make him a model servant of Yahweh.

Conclusion

At the end of the Pentateuch Israel is poised outside Canaan, ready to possess their new home. God's plan to overcome human sin by choosing a holy nation has advanced. Promises made to Abraham in Genesis 12:1-9 are either fulfilled or near completion. He no longer lacks heir or covenant, and land will not be missing much longer. Israel has overcome their initial rejection of Canaan. A new, courageous, generation is in place. As in Numbers 1—10, the text has reached a high point. Will Israel finally be faithful to their always-faithful Lord?[4]

Questions for Reflection

1. How does Israel's decision not to attack Canaan alter their future? Do we make similar life-changing decisions?
2. Was God's punishment of Moses too harsh? Why or why not?
3. How does the covenant demonstrate God's kindness?
4. Was the covenant difficult to understand? Was it hard to keep?
5. What role did love play in Israel's covenant relationship with God?

Notes

1. Compare Meredith G. Kline, *Treaty of the Great King* (Grand Rapids: Wm. B. Eerdmans, 1963).

2. Peter Craigie, *Commentary on the Book of Deuteronomy* (Grand Rapids: Wm. B. Eerdmans, 1976), 24.

3. E. W. Nicholson, *God and His People: Covenant and Theology in the Old Testament* (Oxford: Clarendon Press, 1986). More recently Weinfeld, *Deuteronomy 1—11,* vol. 5 in *The Anchor Bible* (New York: Doubleday, 1991), 6-7, has argued that Deuteronomy is not a covenant between two parties but a loyalty oath the king imposed on vassals. Weinfeld sees connections in Deuteronomy to both the old Hittite tradition from about 1400 B.C. and the Assyrian tradition about 675 B.C.

4. See also Patrick D. Miller, *Deuteronomy,* Interpretation (Louisville: John Knox, 1990); A. D. H. Mayes, *Deuteronomy,* The New Century Bible Commentary (Grand Rapids: Wm. B. Eerdmans, 1979); Roy L. Honeycutt, *Leviticus, Numbers, Deuteronomy*, vol. 3 in *Layman's Bible Book Commentary* (Broadman Press, 1979); Duane L. Christensen, *Deuteronomy 1—11,* vol. 6A in *Word Biblical Commentary* (Dallas: Word Books, 1991); R. K. Harrison, *Numbers,* The Wycliffe Exegetical Commentary (Chicago: Moody Press, 1990); Philip J. Budd, *Numbers,* vol. 5 in *Word Biblical Commentary* (Waco, Tex.: Word Books, 1984).

Part II
The Former Prophets

Introduction

Deuteronomy leaves readers in suspense. Israel camps just outside the promised land, poised to complete God's promises to Abraham. Moses has said they will succeed, but he is dead. Israel was at a similar pivotal position in Numbers and failed to conquer. Will the people waste a second chance to claim their homeland? God has promised to fight for them. Will this second generation of Israelites believe Yahweh, or be as rebellious as their parents?

Frankly, Israel's chances for success are not strong. Canaan has several fortified cities with large populations, and Israel has limited combat experience. Even if they manage to win the war, Israel has no system of government. How will they organize to secure and manage the land? Can they hold on to what they capture?

Joshua—Kings address these and other related issues. These books tell what happened in history, and explain why it happened. They report events and state the theological factors involved in Israel's history. They feature human heroes and villains, yet always point to the Lord of history. For example, 1 Kings 1—11 discusses Solomon's wealth and political savvy, but it also emphasizes his weakening relationship to the Lord and its consequences. Thus, the books present a "sacred history" of Israel, a history accurate and insightful at the same time. They take both the human and divine elements of history seriously.

How does the author achieve this balance? A writer must have criteria to judge events and characters. Without question, the biblical writers judged Israel's leaders and people by the covenant in Deuteronomy. In fact, Deuteronomy's influence is so evident in Joshua—Kings that Martin Noth calls these books a "deuteronomistic history."[1] The kings are measured by the standards sketched in Deuteronomy 17:14-20. The people are blessed or punished according to the principles outlined in Deuteronomy 27—28. Israel cannot keep their land if they break their promises to God.

Thus we read to see how Israel will measure up and how God will react. We begin by asking how the second generation will capture the land. Will they finally complete God's promises to Abraham? If so, how will they divide and cultivate their inheritance?

Note

1. Martin Noth, *The Deuteronomistic History* (1957; reprint, Sheffield: Sheffield Academic Press, 1981). For more recent assessment see M. O'Brien, *The Deuteronomic History Hypothesis: A Reassessment* (Göttingen: Vandenhoeck and Ruprecht, 1989); B. Peckham, *The Composition of the Deuteronomistic History* (Atlanta: Scholars Press, 1985); Terence E. Fretheim, *Deuteronomic History,* Interpreting Biblical Texts (Nashville: Abingdon Press, 1983).

4
Joshua: *God Gives the Land*

Plot: Joshua leads Israel's conquest of Canaan. Israel divides the land and chooses to live as a covenant community within their inherited country.
Major Characters: Joshua, Rahab, Achan, Caleb, Eleazar, and Phinehas
Major Events: The conquest of Jericho, Ai, Gibeon, and certain northern and southern cities; the division of the land; and the covenant renewal ceremony at Shechem

Introduction

Joshua is an exciting and positive book. Israel finally conquers the land God promised to Abraham. Why does the nation accomplish this task now? Because the new generation is determined to obey the Lord. They refuse to stay in the desert and do whatever their leaders and Yahweh demand. They do not repeat their parents' mistakes.

Joshua unfolds in three parts. First, chapters 1—12 describe how Israel conquers most of the promised land. Details about significant battles appear, including theological reasons for Israel's success or failure. Second, chapters 13—22 state how the nation's twelve tribes divide the land. Each tribe has its own territory, much as the United States has fifty separate states. Third, the book concludes with a covenant renewal ceremony in chapters 23—24. A now-retired Joshua encourages the people to obey God's laws and, thereby, keep the land. Each section focuses on Yahweh's faithfulness in offering Canaan to Israel and on Israel's challenge to respond in faithfulness.

Joshua 1—12: The Promised Land Conquered

Israel needs a capable leader if they are to conquer the land. God has chosen Joshua for this task (Deut. 31:1-8). Joshua has served as

Moses' assistant for years (Ex. 32:17) and, as a spy, favored attacking Canaan (Num. 14:6-10). No one else has his experience and potential for leadership. Still, he has never led the people. He has yet to prove he can replace Moses.

Because of his awesome responsibility, Joshua needs encouragement from Yahweh before Israel enters the land (1:1-9). God promises to never "leave or forsake" him (1:5). Yahweh also pledges to give the promised land to the people (1:3-4) and make Joshua great like Moses (1:5). In return, Joshua must lead the people, keep the covenant, read the law of Moses as Deuteronomy 17:18-20 commanded, and depend on God's presence (1:6-9). Three times Yahweh tells him to be "strong and courageous" (1:6,7,9), which may speak to his natural fears. After this reassurance Joshua is ready to lead. He tells the nation to prepare to cross the Jordan River and enter the land (1:10-15). The people comply but only after adding their own plea that Joshua "be strong and courageous!" (1:16-18).

Joshua decides to attack Jericho first (2:1). Since Jericho is located in the middle of the region, Joshua apparently intends to cut Canaan into two parts. Then Israel can move north and south from their central power base. So he sends two spies to view that city (2:1). The men enter Jericho and go to "the house of a prostitute named Rahab" (2:1, NIV). Undoubtedly, they exercise caution, yet the king learns of their presence (2:2-3). When the king's messengers come to arrest the spies, Rahab says that they have left town; but she has actually hidden them in her home (2:4-6). Her lie works, for the king's men leave town to pursue the spies (2:7).

Once alone with the two Israelites, Rahab confesses that she believes God will give Jericho to Israel (2:8-11). She, therefore, asks the spies to spare her and her family's lives when they destroy the town (2:12-13). They agree, and she helps them escape (2:14-16). In effect, Rahab joins Israel. She will become part of the people of God because of her faith and actions. Meanwhile, the spies tell Joshua that Jericho is theirs (2:24).

With great purpose, the people break camp and cross the Jordan. Priests carry the ark in front of the people, symbolizing Yahweh's leadership of Israel. God even causes the river to stop flowing while they cross. As soon as they complete the crossing, the waters return to their place (Josh. 3—4). Clearly, this event signals a new exodus of sorts. Just as their parents went through the parted Red Sea to the wilderness (Ex. 14), so now they leave the desert by crossing the Jordan to their new home. In Canaan the daily manna ceases, since they can now eat the fruit of the land (5:10-12). God has met, and will continue to meet, their physical needs.

Jericho falls in spectacular fashion. For six days Israel's army

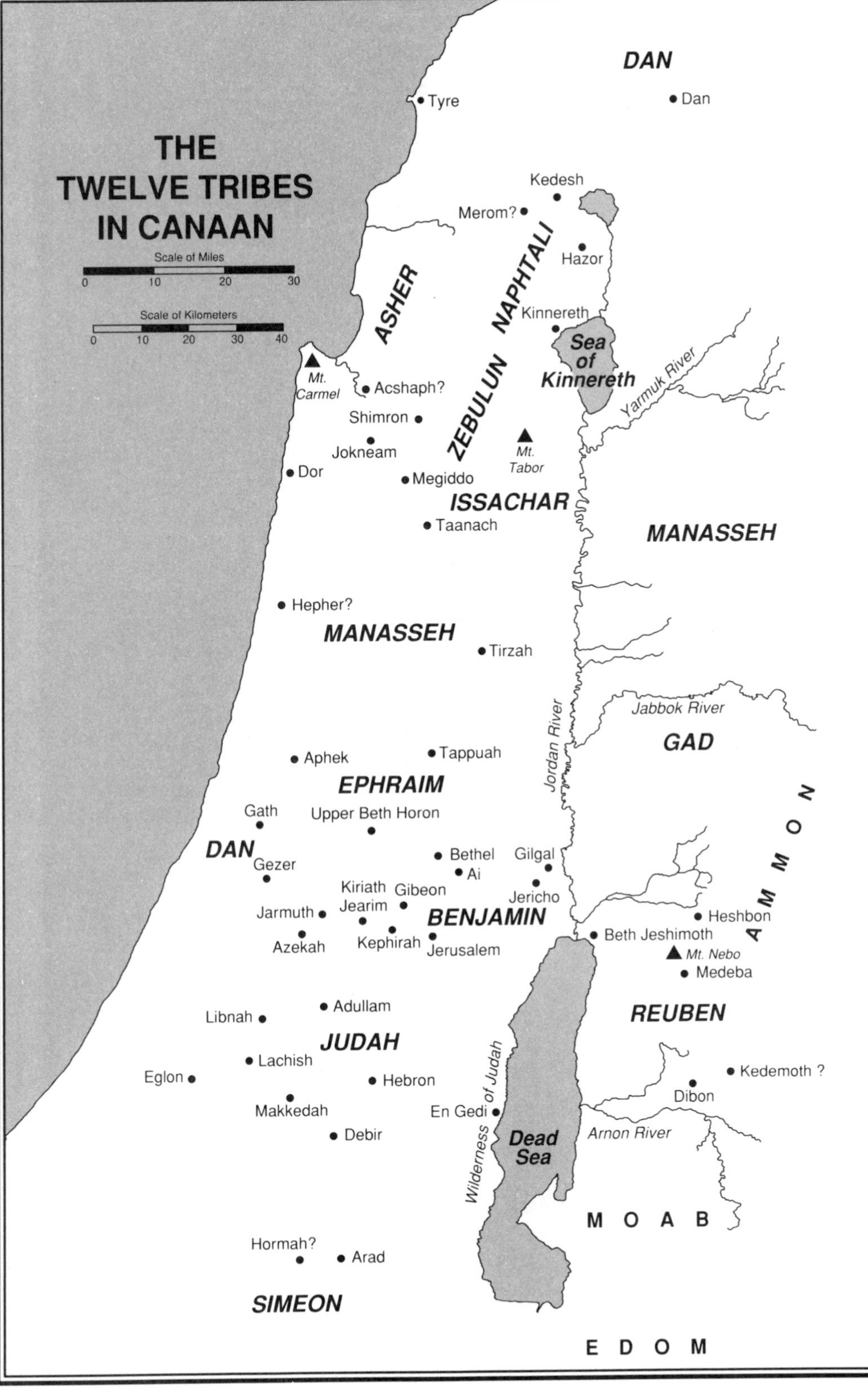
THE TWELVE TRIBES IN CANAAN
Scale of Miles
0 10 20 30
Scale of Kilometers
0 10 20 30 40
DAN
Tyre
Dan
Kedesh
Merom?
Hazor
ASHER
NAPHTALI
Kinnereth
Sea of Kinnereth
Yarmuk River
Mt. Carmel
Acshaph?
Shimron
ZEBULUN
Mt. Tabor
Jokneam
Dor
Megiddo
ISSACHAR
Taanach
MANASSEH
Hepher?
MANASSEH
Tirzah
Jordan River
Jabbok River
GAD
Aphek
Tappuah
EPHRAIM
AMMON
Gath
Upper Beth Horon
DAN
Gezer
Bethel
Ai
Gilgal
Kiriath Jearim
Gibeon
Jericho
Jarmuth
BENJAMIN
Heshbon
Azekah
Kephirah
Jerusalem
Beth Jeshimoth
Mt. Nebo
Medeba
Libnah
Adullam
REUBEN
JUDAH
Lachish
Eglon
Hebron
Kedemoth ?
Dibon
Makkedah
En Gedi
Wilderness of Judah
Arnon River
Debir
Dead Sea
MOAB
Hormah?
Arad
SIMEON
EDOM

marches around the city without attacking (6:1-3). Surely, this marching intimidates and unnerves Jericho's citizens. Finally, on the seventh day, Israel marches out to conquer. Joshua tells the people that all Jericho's wealth is "sacred to the Lord and must go into his treasury" (6:19, NIV). No individual may keep spoils of war. He also reminds them to spare Rahab (6:17). The priests sound the trumpets, the army shouts, and Jericho's walls collapse (6:20). Exposed, the city lies defenseless. Yahweh gives Israel the city, Rahab is rescued, and Joshua's fame spreads (6:21-27). Israel has captured a strategic, well-watered city in the heart of Canaan. They now have a base for further operations.

During the battle, however, a man named Achan takes some gold, silver, and clothing for himself (7:1,20-21). When Israel tries to capture their next objective, a tiny place called Ai, they do not succeed (7:2-5). Amazed and worried, Joshua asks God why they have been defeated (7:6-9). Yahweh directs him to Achan. Achan eventually confesses (7:20-21). When given the death penalty, Achan does not complain (7:25-26). Rather, he obediently gives glory and praise to Yahweh (7:19). Apparently, he realizes he must suffer the consequences of disobeying the covenant. With this problem corrected, Israel now finally overruns Ai (8:1-28). To remind the people of their obligations and potential blessings, Joshua leads them long miles northward for a covenant renewal ceremony at Gerizim and Ebal (8:30-35) before returning to resume the battle. Hopefully, covenant breaking will not halt their progress again.

Events now work together to hand Israel another major victory. Because of the Jews' success, many cities unite to fight them (9:1-2). The Gibeonites, who live just west of Jericho, have a different plan. They attempt to fool the Israelites into thinking they are a distant nation by dressing in old clothes and carrying moldy bread (9:3-13). They even say that they have come from afar to serve Yahweh (9:9). Without asking God, Joshua makes an alliance with them (9:14-15). Too late, Israel learns its error, but they are now bound by their oath. They cannot destroy Gibeon, though they do make the Gibeonites their servants (9:16-27).

Soon, several kings march against Gibeon because of their treaty with Israel (10:1-5). Of course, the Gibeonites ask Israel for help (10:6). Joshua seizes this chance to defeat many armies at once (10:7-8). Israel marches all night and surprises their opponents at dawn (10:9-11). To give the people a complete victory, Yahweh answers Joshua's prayer and makes the sun stand still so the enemy cannot flee by night (10:12-14). This miracle emphasizes the idea that Yahweh "was fighting for Israel!" (10:14, NIV). God does whatever is necessary to help Israel inherit their land. Even mistakes like trusting the Gibeonites can lead ultimately to great victories.

From his base in the center of the region, Joshua now moves south and north. Makkedah, Libnah, Lachish, Eglon, Hebron, Debir, and other southern towns are taken. Southern Canaan now belongs to Israel (10:29-43). Next, Joshua attacks in the north. Major places such as Hazor fall. Once again, a group of nations fight Israel, which only makes Joshua's task easier. Joshua soon has control of the region's biggest cities (chap. 11). Most of the conquest is now complete (chap. 12). At least, the prominent population centers have been subdued.

The text claims that all these victories fulfill God's earlier promises (11:15,23). Joshua simply carries out what Moses commanded. Yahweh has fought for Israel, which is why they have beaten so many powerful foes (10:42). Unlike their predecessors, this generation of Israelites follows the Lord's directions. They are faithful to their covenant Master. They receive the promised rest (11:23).

Joshua 13—22: The Promised Land Divided

At first glance Joshua 11:23 and 13:1 appear to contradict one another. The first text says Joshua took the whole land, while the second notes that in Joshua's old age large portions of land were yet unconquered. What 11:23 probably means is that Canaan's power bases no longer exist. All major military centers have fallen. Thus Israel now *only* has to disperse, defeat all smaller towns, and settle in their proper places. The most difficult task is over. Now a new challenge awaits. Joshua with Eleazar, the priest, divides the land among the tribes and tells them to displace the remaining Canaanites (Josh. 13—21). He even allows the tribes whose inheritance lies beyond the Jordan (compare Num. 32) to go home (Josh. 22). Their obligation to help the other tribes become established in Canaan has been fulfilled, but trouble lurks for the future. Phinehas has to mediate a solution to an animated argument over altar rights among tribes east and west of the Jordan (chap. 22).

Perhaps more than any other Israelite, Caleb has earned his inheritance. Like Joshua, he has suffered in the desert despite his desire to invade the land. Thus, his conquest of Hebron is a high point in the story (14:6-15). Even at eighty-five years of age, he is ready to fight (14:10). This remarkable man, like his friend Joshua, plays a key role in Israel's success because of his long-term faith in God.

Joshua 23—24: Renewing the Covenant

His life's work nearly done, Joshua leads Israel in a covenant renewal ceremony one last time. He first encourages the leaders, just as Moses encouraged him (23:1-11; compare Deut. 31:1-8). He tells them they will inherit the land if they obey God's law, for God will continue to fight for them. On the other hand, disobedience will bring destruction (23:12-16). Clearly, the blessings and curses outlined in Deuteronomy 27—28 remain in effect. Israel has a permanent relationship with Yahweh.

Joshua leads the people in a simple, yet vital, ceremony. He begins by retelling their national story (24:1-13). Starting with Terah, Abraham's father, Joshua describes how Israel went from serving other gods to worshiping Yahweh. This story includes Israel's journey from slavery in Egypt to freedom and prosperity in Canaan. Given this great past, Joshua challenges the people to serve Yahweh in the present and future. As all great leaders must, Joshua sets an example for his followers. Regardless of what others decide, he says, he and his family will serve God (24:14-15).

Quickly the nation praises God and agrees to keep the covenant (24:16-18). They realize that the Lord has given them the land (24:18). Joshua then probes the depth of their commitment. He says they cannot serve God; their rebellion will cause Yahweh to punish them (24:19-20). Still they persist. They state emphatically, "We will serve the Lord" (24:21, NIV). So Joshua writes the covenant "in the Book of the Law of God" (24:26, NIV). He has done all he can to pass on Abraham's promises and Moses' standards.

When Joshua dies, he is buried in his family's inheritance in the north (24:29-30). Joseph's bones, which were carried from Egypt (compare Ex. 13:19), are also buried in the promised land (24:32). This burial particularly stresses the importance of the promised land. The land belongs to all people of faith, and it symbolizes the permanence of God's love for Israel. The leaders who succeed Joshua continue to help the people follow Yahweh (24:31). Yet the comment that Israel served God as long as Joshua and his contemporaries lived leads to a question. Will Israel obey Yahweh when these giants die? Leadership remains a major issue.

Conclusion

Like Moses, Joshua is a unique individual. He is both warrior and spiritual leader. At times he is afraid, yet he overcomes these fears to win great victories. Though he could seek prestige for himself, he constantly praises the Lord and honors Moses' memory. By blending these qualities, Joshua is able to raise Israel to new national greatness. He is the person who finally fulfills the land promise. Abraham's descendants have a homeland. How long they keep it depends on their obedience to the Lord. Only time will tell if Israel will continue to uphold the standards of Joshua's generation.[1]

Questions for Reflection

1. How does the conquest of Canaan fulfill God's promises to Abraham?
2. What leadership characteristics does Joshua exhibit?
3. Is Israel's conquest strategy too harsh?
4. What is the importance of Joshua's distribution of the land to the tribes?

Note

1. Theological commentaries on Joshua include M. H. Woudstra, *The Book of Joshua,* The New International Commentary on the Old Testament (Grand Rapids: Eerdmans, 1981); and Trent C. Butler, *Joshua,* vol. 7 in *Word Biblical Commentary* (Waco, Tex.: Word Books, 1983). A commentary for laity is Dan G. Kent, *Joshua, Judges, Ruth,* vol. 4 in *Layman's Bible Book Commentary* (Nashville: Broadman Press, 1980). See also Trent C. Butler, *Understanding the Basic Themes of Joshua* (Dallas: Word Publishing, 1991).

5
Judges: *Chaos in the Promised Land*

Plot: Chaos reigns because Israel disobeys the covenant and because they have no king. God allows other nations to oppress Israel so they will repent. When Israel turns back to God, they are rescued from their enemies by civil and military leaders called "judges." Repeatedly, however, they fall back into their sinful habits, and they even rape and kill one another.
Major Characters: Othniel, Ehud, Deborah, Barak, Gideon, Abimelech, Jephthah, Samson, Micah, an unnamed Levite
Major Events: Joshua's death, Deborah and Barak's victory, Gideon's defeat of the Midianites, Jephthah's victory over Ammon, Samson's battles with the Philistines, the rape and murder of a Levite's concubine, and the decimation of the tribe of Benjamin

Introduction

Judges is a unique book. It tells some of the most gruesome stories in the Bible. At the same time it stresses single-minded worship of Yahweh. Many colorful characters appear, most of whom have obvious character flaws. Yet God uses these individuals to govern and deliver Israel. Given these seemingly contradictory facts, what is Judges's main purpose?

Normally, it is wise to let a book speak for itself. That is, readers should study a text and then decide what it means. Because of its seemingly offensive stories, though, it is proper to announce Judges's theme now. Both in 17:6 and 21:25, the book's last verse, the text declares its main idea (compare 18:1). This book describes what happens when everyone does what is "right in his own eyes" (KJV). When the covenant is ignored and when there is no king (powerful leader), chaos results. People offer human sacrifices (11:30-40). Women are raped and dismembered (19:1-29). Relatives kill one another in civil wars (chap. 20). Readers should not think Judges's author favors such actions. Rather, the writer paints such gruesome pictures to warn future generations against lawlessness.

Despite its gloomy theme, Judges often uses humor and absurd situations to tell its story. In this way the book avoids wallowing in the sordid past. These devices also allow the author to discuss positive, or at least neutral, events as well. As with all historical stories, how Judges tells its story determines the force of the literature.

It is difficult to tell how much time unfolds in Judges. Of course, scholars disagree about the book's chronology, given these events' nearness to the exodus (compare chap. 2). Other factors also affect an understanding of the text's sequence of events. For instance, neither date for the exodus is reached by adding the years mentioned in the Judges.[1] Therefore, several scholars believe that many of the judges' careers overlap.[2] This idea makes sense because the judges govern various parts of Israel, fight enemies from several foreign countries, and live in many different Israelite towns. Too, the twelve tribes operate more as individual states than as a unified nation. Clearly, some overlap of ministries is likely.

Ultimately, either of the two possible dates for the exodus, plus the times of wilderness wandering and conquest, provides a reasonable setting for Judges. Both possibilities allow for the work of the judges to occur. Either date fits the general biblical description of this chaotic time in Israel's history. It is logical, then, to interpret the book in its general historical context and hope further archaeological data will help establish a more precise dating.

Certain sociological factors impacted Israel during this era.[3] First, new enemies moved into the region. Among others, the Philistines rose to prominence. Second, new weapons were developed. Iron slowly replaced bronze as the metal for war instruments. Nations who possessed iron weapons defeated those who did not (compare 1 Sam. 13:19-22). Israel was slow to produce iron implements of their own. Third, vast migrations of peoples occurred. No major power ruled the area, so various people groups came in and out of Canaan. Some of these groups raided Israel's settlements. Fourth, Israel was extremely disorganized. With no central government or standing army, Israel was vulnerable to every moderately strong power in the region. Besides all these difficulties, the covenant people had spiritual problems, as we shall soon see. The stage is set, then, for a chaotic situation.

Judges 1:1—2:5: The Roots of Chaos

Israel continues to conquer Canaan after Joshua's death. Judah leads the way (1:1-2), and several other tribes capture their portion of the promised land (1:3-36). Despite their success, however, Israel never completely displaces the Canaanites. Many people groups are allowed to remain, and these are forced to work for Israel (compare 1:28,29,33,35).

Unfortunately, Israel's unwillingness and inability to drive out their enemies causes problems. When the Canaanites are spared, their gods are also spared. Israel, thereby, breaks their covenant agreement with Yahweh (compare Deut. 20:16-18). Because the people worship these gods, God says Israel will be defeated by the enemies they spared (2:1-3). God will not tolerate disobedience and idolatry. To remind Israel of their covenant obligations, the Lord will allow their enemies to oppress them. Israel weeps at Yahweh's decision, but they know it is fair (2:4-5).

This short section serves two important functions. First, it reminds the reader of God's love for the people and Israel's past victories. Things have gone well for Israel since they left the desert because they have kept the covenant (2:1-3). Second, it hints at trouble on the horizon. If Israel has powerful enemies and worships idols, how can they flourish in the land? Must they endure another wilderness-type experience?

Judges 2:6—16:31: Living in Chaos

After everyone of Joshua's generation dies, a new, unfaithful generation emerges. The leadership crisis leaves this group knowing "neither the Lord nor what he had done for Israel" (2:10, NIV). They, therefore, plunge Israel into a *sin cycle* that lasts throughout Judges. Because they do not appreciate Yahweh, they worship Canaanite gods (2:11-13). So God sends nations that defeat Israel to encourage the people to change (2:14-15). Once in trouble, Israel eventually asks for Yahweh's help (2:15). Out of kindness, the Lord then sends judges, or military leaders, to defeat the oppressing, punishing nation (2:16-18). The people serve God while the judge lives, but they turn away when he or she dies (2:19). Their rebellion starts the cycle all over again. Covenant breaking, thereby, causes Israel to flounder in the land of promise (2:20-23).

Othniel acts as the nation's first deliverer (3:7-11). Israel angers the Lord by serving the Canaanite fertility gods Baal and Asherah (3:7). The Canaanites, like Israel, were farmers and herdsmen. They depended on the land's fertility for support. According to Canaanite belief, Baal and his wife Asherah caused crops to grow and animals to bear young. Because of its emphasis on fertility, Baal worship had strong sexual overtones. Some Baal worshipers even had sexual relationships at worship centers with prostitutes dedicated to Baal.

Clearly, Baal worship violates the Israel-Yahweh covenant. Thus, Yahweh allows Cushan-Rishathaim, a king of a migrating people, to oppress Israel (3:8). When Israel cries out to God, though, Othniel, Caleb's nephew, saves them (3:9; compare 1:13). God's Spirit empowers him to defeat the enemy, and the land enjoys peace for forty years (3:10-11). Then Othniel dies, and the sin cycle begins once more (3:11). This short text introduces a process that recurs repeatedly.

The second judge story combines humor and irony as the sin cycle is repeated. Once again, Israel sins; and, once again, they are punished, this time by Moab for eighteen years (3:12-14). Israel's new deliverer, Ehud, is "a left-handed man" (3:15, NIV). Ancient cultures considered left-handed persons crafty and skillful. Ehud's enemy is Eglon, the extremely fat king of Moab (3:17).

As a defeated nation, Israel has to pay whatever taxes Moab sets. This "tribute" money is brought regularly by Israel's leaders (3:15). Ehud decides to bring Eglon a special gift. He straps an eighteen-inch knife to his right thigh and helps carry the tax money to Eglon (3:17-18). Once in the king's presence, Ehud finds a way to clear the room, leaving himself alone with Eglon. He tells the king he has a secret message for him, which causes Eglon to dismiss his attendants (3:19). Indeed, once they are alone, Ehud increases Eglon's interest by saying the message is from God (3:20). What does God want to tell Eglon?

Now irony, revenge, and humor take over the story. Ehud has a message all right. According to him, God tells Eglon to die, for he plunges his knife into the king's huge stomach (3:21). Apparently used to right-handed men, Eglon does not see Ehud's left-handed attack. Eglon is so fat that all eighteen inches of the blade disappear into him (3:22). The flesh even covers the handle, so Ehud does not bother (or is too disgusted) to retrieve his weapon (3:22).

The oppressor is dead, but the humor has just begun. Ehud slips out of the room, locking the door behind him (3:23). Soon Eglon's attendants return. Finding the lock bolted, the servants decide the king must be using the rest room (3:24). They are embarrassed to do so, but they finally unlock the door (3:25). While they have been pondering Eglon's bathroom habits, Ehud has snuck away and formed an army to fight Moab (3:26-28). Israel then routs a leaderless Moab, and the land has peace for eighty years (3:29-30). This story is just the first of many times Judges describes an Israelite victory and also laughs at the defeated foe.

After Ehud dies, Israel sins again (4:1). This time Jabin, king of Hazor, oppresses Israel (4:2). His commander, Sisera, though, is the main enemy (4:2). Sisera has nine hundred iron chariots at his disposal, so he easily dominates Israel for two decades (4:3). When the people cry to God, two leaders emerge: Deborah, a prophetess, and Barak, a military leader (4:4-8). Deborah tells Barak to fight Sisera because Yahweh is ready to deliver Israel (4:6-7). He is unwilling unless she goes with him (4:8). Deborah agrees to accompany Barak, but predicts a woman will get the credit for the victory (4:9-10).

Ironically, Deborah will not be the only honored woman. As promised, Barak destroys Sisera's army, yet Sisera himself escapes to what he believes is a friendly family (4:11-16). He is taken in by Jael, the wife of Heber, one of Sisera's allies (4:17). Because Heber is his friend, Sisera is probably relieved when Jael greets him. She invites him into her tent and even tells him to have no fear (4:18).

Jael treats Sisera in a motherly fashion. She calms his fears and tucks him in for a nap (4:18). Like a child, Sisera asks for a drink before he sleeps (4:19). Like a mother, she gives him warm milk, which makes him even drowsier (4:19). Before he falls asleep, Sisera makes Jael promise to turn away anyone looking for him (4:20). Yet, unlike a caring mother, Jael takes a hammer and drives a tent peg through the sleeping Sisera's head (4:21). Of course, he dies.

Eventually, Barak comes by Jael's tent looking for Sisera. Jael stops Barak, invites *him* into the tent, and reveals Sisera nailed to the floor (4:22). Israel has been delivered by a crafty, *motherly* woman, her hammer, and her tent peg. To commemorate the event, Deborah and Barak write a song about their conquest (Judg. 5). Once more, Israel has gotten help in some odd ways with unusual weapons.

By now, readers know Israel will sin again, so it comes as no surprise when Midian oppresses the Jews (6:1). Midian was another large people group that moved in and out of the region. They came, raped the land, and moved on (6:2-6). Israel is virtually helpless to stop Midian and is reduced to hiding in mountain hideouts and caves (6:2). Clearly, they need a new national savior who will help them keep the covenant and defeat Midian (6:7-10).

Again, Yahweh chooses an unlikely hero, the son of a Baal worshiper. When God's angel approaches Gideon, the future judge is threshing wheat in secret, hoping to keep it from the Midianites (6:11-12). The angel says Yahweh is with Israel and calls Gideon a "mighty warrior" (6:12). Gideon's response lacks tact. He replies that God's presence and help are hardly evident. Indeed, he concludes that "Yahweh has abandoned us and put us into Midian's hands" (6:13).

Now the Lord enters the conversation. Yahweh tells Gideon to deliver Israel. Gideon doubts his own abilities, so he asks Yahweh for some special signs. He prays that God will make some lamb's wool wet and the ground dry one morning, and then make the opposite happen the next day (6:36-40). God performs this sign. Gideon, who has already desecrated Baal's altar (6:25-32), accepts the Lord's challenge to lead Israel.

Gideon needs an army to defeat Midian. So he gathers a fighting force of 32,000 warriors (7:3). Yahweh states that the army is too big! If they win the battle, they will give themselves the credit (7:2). Therefore, Gideon says that anyone who is afraid may leave. About 22,000 take this chance to go (7:3). This humorous scene over, God claims Gideon still has too many soldiers (7:4). A strange test depletes the ranks to 300 men. All who drink water from their palms are chosen, while those who duck their heads into a stream are sent home (7:5-6). Gideon is left with 300 soldiers who lap their water like dogs (7:7). This mighty fighting force will conquer Midian.

Since he is vastly outnumbered, Gideon needs a resourceful strategy. He arms his soldiers with trumpets, torches, and jars. In the middle of the night the Israelites blow the trumpets, break the jars, and lift the torches (7:19-20). Normally, armies had only a few trumpeters; so when the awakened Midianites hear three hundred trumpets, see the lights, and hear jars breaking, they panic. They run in terror and even kill one another in the dark (7:21-22). Soon, Gideon chases them, calls more troops into action, and completely devastates the Midianites (7:24-25). This hated enemy has finally fallen.

Because of his leadership skills, Israel asks Gideon to be their king (8:22). He declines this honor, but he does have them contribute gold to make an idol (8:23-27). He also sets up a royal life-style (8:29-30) and names a son Abimelech, meaning "My father is king." The idol is kept in Gideon's town, and many people begin worshiping it there. In this way Gideon maintains a certain control, albeit illegitimate, over the nation. Despite this episode, however, Gideon has a generally positive ministry. Israel commits worse sins of idolatry after he dies (8:33-35).

Two judges in the middle of the book demonstrate how horrible the sins become. Abimelech, one of Gideon's seventy sons, murders all but one of his brothers (9:5). He gathers an army of mercenaries that terrorizes northern Israel (compare 9:42-45). Unlike most other judges, Abimelech's life has no redeeming value. He is a totally self-serving man, one who truly does whatever is right in his own eyes.

The second of these judges, Jephthah, delivers Israel from Ammon, an enemy who will plague them for years. As usual, the people have begun worshiping other gods (10:6). This time, Yahweh sends armies from east and west to punish Israel (11:4-13). After a long battle Jephthah defeats Ammon. To secure victory, he vows to sacrifice to the Lord the first thing "out of the door" of his house when he returns home (11:30-31). Perhaps he thought an animal would emerge first, since they were normally stabled in homes during this era.[4] Much to his surprise, however, his only child, a daughter, comes to meet him (11:34). Because of his vow, he offers her as a sacrifice (11:39).

Does Yahweh approve of such actions? Of course not! Genesis 22 has already prohibited human sacrifice. Killing children and siblings does not honor God despite the beliefs and practices of Israel's neighbors. Again, it is important to remember Judges's theme. Unthinkably immoral things happen when all the people do what is right in their own eyes.

Perhaps more than any other character in the book, Samson embodies the mistake of living by human standards. Samson does whatever he wishes at all times, and thereby squanders his great potential. Like other important biblical characters, he has an unusual birth. His parents are unable to have children (13:1-3). Yet God tells them they will have a son. Since this will be a special child, he must serve God. Samson will be a Nazirite, which, according to Numbers 6:2-21, means he must not drink strong wine, cut his hair, touch dead bodies, or eat unclean food. All other parts of the law apply to him as well. Yahweh promises to use this child to deliver Israel from the Philistines, who have been oppressing them.

Contrary to Moses' law (Ex. 34:11; Deut. 7:3), Samson decides to marry a Philistine woman (14:1-2). Israelites could marry foreigners who followed the Lord (compare Ruth); but marriages with idol worshipers, such as the Philistines, were forbidden. Samson's parents warn him against this union (14:3), but he persists. He says, "She is right in my eyes" (14:3), an obvious reference to the book's main theme. Samson will do what he thinks best, despite what the Lord and his parents say. God will wrench some good from Samson's disobedience (14:4), however, as He does many times in Judges.

Samson and his parents eventually go to Philistia to make the marriage arrangements (14:5). While on the way, Samson kills a lion with his bare hands (14:6). This event demonstrates Samson's great strength, as will many similar episodes later. Going home, Samson finds honey in the lion's carcass. He eats a little, then gives some to his parents, but he does not tell them where he got it. Again, Samson has broken Moses' law. Nazirites were supposed to avoid dead bodies of all kinds (Num. 6:6), so once more he does as he pleases.

During his wedding feast Samson asks his guests a riddle and bets thirty linen garments they cannot solve it (14:12-13). Based on the lion and the honey, he says, "From the eater comes something to eat, and from the strong comes something sweet" (14:14). The guests ponder the puzzle for three days, then threaten to burn the bride, her parents, and their home if she does not give them the answer (14:14-15). She gets him to tell her only after much nagging and whining, but he tells her (14:17). Thus, the guests solve the riddle, and Samson loses his bet (14:18). To collect the garments, Samson, empowered by God's Spirit, kills thirty Philistines and takes their clothes. Then he goes to his father's house (14:19), too angry at his wife to return to her.

Killing these Philistines is just the first time Samson punishes the Philistines. Because he stays away for some time (15:1), his wife is given to another man (14:20; 15:2). Angered at the Philistines, Samson ties torches to three hundred foxes and sets them loose in Philistine grain fields (15:4-5). Their crops destroyed, the Philistines retaliate by burning Samson's "wife" and her father (15:6). Samson's anger boils over, and he kills many Philistines (15:8). When they come to retaliate, Samson slaughters one thousand of them with the jawbone of an ass (15:13-17). He is clearly God's instrument for punishing Philistia, and he acts as judge over Israel for twenty years (15:20).

Two more incidents that revolve around Samson's relationship to women now follow. Both episodes put him in danger. He escapes once, but not twice. Philistine women will finally bring about his downfall.

In the first story, Samson visits a prostitute in Gaza, a Philistine city (16:1). The people wait for dawn so they can kill him. He fools them, though, by leaving early. On his way out he rips the doors of the city gates from their place and carries them out of town (16:2-3). Once more, despite his questionable morals, Samson escapes.

Finally, Samson goes too far. He loves another Philistine woman, named Delilah (16:4). She plots to betray him to the Philistines for 1,100 shekels of silver, a huge amount of money (16:5-6). Day after day, she probes the source of his strength. Time after time, he lies to her. Each time he gives an answer, the Philistines come against him; yet each time, he overwhelms them (17:6-14). As with his wife, Samson finally tells his secret after extensive nagging (16:15-16). Samson reveals that he is a Nazirite. His hair has never been cut, and it is the source of his strength (16:17). He has broken every other Nazirite vow and survived. However, when Delilah cuts his hair—the one Nazirite commandment explicitly named at the announcement of his birth (13:5)—Samson becomes weak. Lulled to sleep in Delilah's lap, he awakes without hair. Sadly, he does not know God has left him (16:20). The Philistines blind him, chain him, take him to prison, and use him as a beast of burden (16:21-22).

Samson dies killing Philistines. On one of their great feast days the Philistines worship Dagon, their god (16:23). They send for the supposedly broken Samson to prove their god's power (16:23-24). While they celebrate his pain, Samson avenges himself. He asks God for one last gift of power and uses it to topple the arena's pillars, killing himself and the whole crowd (16:25-29). Thus, Samson manages to destroy many more in death than he did in life (16:30).[5]

Perhaps more than any other judge, Samson illustrates Israel's attitude during this era. Like the people, Samson does whatever is "right in his own eyes" (KJV). Despite his Nazirite vows, he repeatedly follows his own appetites. Certainly, God uses him to punish the Philistines. At times Samson does honor the Lord. He personifies Israel as a whole, being a rather inconsistent follower of God.

Judges 17—21: The Consequences of Living in Chaos

After Samson's death, Israel's spiritual condition worsens. Idolatry becomes common. Chapters 17—18 describe the career of a "young Levite" who stops serving the Lord. For a salary, room, and board he agrees to serve as priest for a family that worships idols (17:1-13). When some Israelites ask him if God wants them to conquer two undefended cities, he says, "Go in peace. God has approved your plan" (18:6). They go and do overthrow the towns (18:7-13). Because of his successful prediction, the warriors determine to make the Levite their priest. They steal the Levite and his master's idols, offer the Levite a raise and promotion, and take him with them to their town (18:13-29). The Levite then leads them to worship these idols (18:29-31). Without question, Israel worships however they wish, just as they act however they wish.

The final story in Judges is horrible. Its events are so repulsive that the author begins it by carefully explaining that at that time "Israel had no king" (19:1, NIV). The story ends with the observation that "In those days Israel had no king. Everyone did what was right in his own eyes" (21:25; compare 17:6; 18:1). These events do not please God. The whole episode illustrates the consequences of Israel's disobedience.

A Levite from northern Israel takes a concubine from the southern town of Bethlehem (19:1). She runs away to return home (19:2), so the Levite goes south to retrieve her. With the reclaimed woman, he begins the journey home (19:3-10). They stop in Gibeah, a town in Benjamin's territory. It was customary for inhabitants of Israelite towns to offer visitors a place to stay, but no one invites them in (19:11-15). Finally, an old man asks them to stay with him (19:16-21).

During the night a group of men surround the house. They demand that the Levite be sent out so they can have sex with him (19:22). To quiet (and maybe shame) the crowd, the old man offers his daughter as a sex object (19:23-24). The men refuse, so the Levite sends his concubine into the street, where she is raped and abused until morning (19:25). Her body weakened, she only has enough strength to crawl to the house's doorway (19:26-28). Her master exhibits no concern for her. As he leaves in the morning, he finds her at the door and says, "Get up. Let's go" (19:28)—but she has died. To protest her death, he cuts her body into twelve pieces and sends a portion to each tribe of Israel (19:29-30).

This grisly gift causes Israel to gather and ask what has happened (20:1-3). The Levite describes his concubine's death (20:4-7), which makes them decide to confront "Gibeah of Benjamin" (20:8-11, KJV). When commanded to hand over the rapists/murderers, however, the Benjamites refuse, a decision that begins a civil war (20:12-14). Rather than the guilty parties involved, all Israel will suffer for the woman's murder.

Benjamin has only 26,000 soldiers, but many of them are expert stone hurlers (20:14-16). Therefore, Benjamin's army can stay inside Gibeah and kill their enemies as they invade. The other tribes have 400,000 foot soldiers (20:17), a seemingly unbeatable force. Because of their stone throwers, Benjamin wins the first battle. Israel loses 18,000 men trying to conquer Gibeah. On their second attempt, though, Israel nearly obliterates Benjamin. They kill 25,100 Benjamites (20:35,46), slaughter their animals (20:48), and burn their towns (20:48). Only a few men survive.

Israel has paid a high price for doing what is "right in their own eyes." Over 40,000 men have died. An innocent woman has been raped and killed. Her body has been dismembered, yet her killers have been protected. Without obedience to the covenant, or a king to enforce civil laws, such atrocities occur.

Judges concludes with a humorous episode that eases some of the reader's disgust with the events in chapters 17—20. Since the men from Benjamin have been guilty of rape and all kinds of sexual abuses, the other tribes vow not to let their daughters marry them (21:1). How, then, will Benjamin get wives? They cannot intermarry indefinitely. Some relief comes when Israel conquers a neighboring city and gives its daughters to the Benjamites for wives (21:6-12), but more women are still needed (21:13-18).

One last effort nets the required number of women. An annual festival is planned in Shiloh. The girls from Shiloh dance in this festival. The men from Benjamin are told to hide in the vineyards near Shiloh, wait for the girls to dance by the road, and then grab one for a wife (21:19-24). Each man, therefore, catches a wife! Of course, this method of choosing a wife is not God's will. The story sounds absurd and exhibits irony. In this way it is humorous. Because it is a result of sin, though, it is also tragic. These events only happen because the people are doing what is "right in their own eyes" (21:25).

Conclusion

Judges illustrates the consequences of lawlessness and poor leadership. Covenant breaking leads repeatedly to punishment. Often, Israel has no leadership, and at other times their leaders do not serve God wholeheartedly. No one like Joshua emerges. This spiritual and political vacuum must be filled, or Israel will never become a great nation. What will God do to address these problems?[6]

Questions for Reflection

1. What positive lessons can we learn from a chaotic era like that of the judges?
2. In what ways are the judges role models for us?
3. Is life as repetitious and cyclical as Judges portrays its period of history?

Notes

1. J. Alberto Soggin, *Judges,* trans. John Bowden (Philadelphia: Westminster Press, 1981), 8-9.
2. Soggin, 10-11.
3. Compare John Bright, *A History of Israel,* 2d ed. (Philadelphia: Westminster, 1972), 166-75.
4. This idea comes from Kenneth E. Bailey, "The Manger and the Inn: The Cultural Background of Luke 2:7," *Theological Review II* 2 (1979): 33-44.
5. I take this comment to be a negative comment.
6. See also Arthur E. Cundall, "Judges" in *Tyndale Old Testament Commentaries,* vol. 7 (Downers Grove, Ill.: Inter-Varsity, 1968), 15-215; Robert G. Boling, *Judges*, vol. 6A in *The Anchor Bible* (Garden City, N.Y.: Doubleday, 1975); Dan G. Kent, *Joshua, Judges, Ruth,* vol. 4 in *Layman's Bible Book Commentary* (Nashville: Broadman Press, 1980); Leslie Hoppe, *Joshua, Judges,* vol. 5 in *Old Testament Message* (Wilmington, Del.: Michael Glazier, Inc., 1982).

6
1 and 2 Samuel: *A Kingdom in the Promised Land*

Plot: God establishes Israel in Canaan by giving them a king. After Samuel closes the era of the judges and Saul serves as Israel's first king, David leads the people to possess fully their inherited land.
Major Characters: Samuel, Saul, Jonathan, David, and Absalom
Important Minor Characters: Hannah, Eli, Abner, Joab, Nathan, Uriah, and Bathsheba
Major Events: Samuel's career, Saul's rise and fall, David's emergence, God's promise of an eternal kingdom to David, David's adultery with Bathsheba, and Absalom's revolt

Introduction

Much of the chronological confusion that surrounds the events from the exodus through the judges disappears when 1 and 2 Samuel begins. Because of the comprehensive analysis of Israel's kings in 1 and 2 Samuel, 1 and 2 Chronicles, and 1 and 2 Kings, as well as the existence of evidence from other nations, most of the incidents in the rest of the Old Testament can be dated with some precision. Historians can at least fix times for events within ten years of their occurrence.

The Books of Samuel cover, roughly, at least 1070-970 B.C. Samuel leads Israel for a *minimum* of twenty years (1 Sam. 7:2); Saul probably rules for about forty years (1 Sam. 13:1); then David becomes king near 1010 B.C. These dates are approximate but adequate for our study. Israel undergoes many changes in this era. Their government, religion, and societal structure are all altered by what happens.

1 Samuel 1—7: Samuel's Career

Israel's woes continue at the start of 1 Samuel. They still have no king, and the people do not obey God's command. Something is needed to break the endless cycle of sin, punishment, and oppression. Judges has already hinted at a temporary solution in 17:6 and 21:25. If Israel had a king, perhaps law and order would exist and the nation would serve Yahweh. Moses also mentioned this possibility in Deuteronomy 17:14-20. These hints become a reality in 1 and 2 Samuel. Despite the problems a monarchy brings, such as taxation and oppression, Israel chooses to become a kingdom instead of a loosely organized group of clans.

Before the first king arises, however, a last great judge and prophet named Samuel ministers to the people. This individual helps Israel make the transition from one era to another. He is the last judge, and he also crowns the first king. His flexibility, piety, and zeal make him one of Israel's best leaders. Though he does not want the people to crown a king, his ministry helps make the monarch a success.

Like Isaac, Moses, Samson, and other important characters, Samuel's birth occurs under unusual circumstances. His mother, Hannah, cannot conceive (1:2). To make matters worse, her husband has another wife who has had children (1:2). This rival wife taunts Hannah unmercifully (1:6). Hannah prays at Shiloh, Israel's worship center at that time, for God to open her womb (1:9-11). She promises to give the child to God if she bears a son (1:11). Because "her lips moved, but her voice was not heard" (1:13, KJV), Eli, the priest, thinks she is drunk; so he rebukes her. Once she explains her situation, though, he blesses her (1:17). Eventually, she does conceive and give birth to a son she names Samuel (1:19-20).

True to her word, Hannah dedicates Samuel to God's service. She takes him to Shiloh, where he works alongside Eli (1:21-28). Eli's own sons are corrupt men who take choice portions of meat from the sacrifices (2:12-17) and sleep with women who serve in the sanctuary (2:22). Clearly, these men cannot lead Israel when Eli dies. Samuel must fill this role. A prophet reveals that Eli's family will lose their privilege of ministering in God's house (2:27-36).

While Samuel is young, God chooses him to be a prophet. During the night Yahweh calls Samuel's name three times (3:1-8). Each time the boy goes to Eli, thinking the old man has asked him to come. Finally, Eli realizes God is speaking to Samuel and tells him to answer the Lord and listen for a message (3:9). Samuel obeys but hears a horrible promise. Yahweh says Eli's sons will be judged for their deeds and Eli will be punished for not stopping their sins (3:11-14).

Samuel hesitates to give Eli this news, yet he does so at Eli's urging (3:17-18). Because God speaks to Samuel, he eventually becomes known as "a prophet of the Lord" (3:20) who truly possesses and preaches God's word (3:21; 4:1).

Samuel's predictions about Eli's family come true when Israel loses a battle with the Philistines. In one skirmish Israel suffers 30,000 casualties, a number that includes Eli's sons (4:1-11). Not only does Israel take heavy losses, they also lose the ark of the covenant—the symbol of Yahweh's presence—to Philistia (4:11). When he hears his sons are dead and the ark has been captured, Eli falls over, breaks his neck, and dies (4:18). Israel is humiliated again as it was in Judges. Sin has led to defeat and oppression by another nation.

Humor takes over the story at this depressing point. The Philistines store the ark in the temple of Dagon, their god, to show his superiority over Yahweh. After one day, however, the Philistines find Dagon bowing down to the ark (5:1-3)! Yahweh clearly rules Dagon. On the second day Dagon bows before the Lord again, and this time his head and hands are severed (5:4-5). Dagon has no power or wisdom. Only Yahweh is real. God sends a plague on every town where the Philistines store the ark (5:6-12). Again, God proves that all idols are worthless. Yahweh directs history and controls nature.

Like their god, the Philistines also suffer humiliation by the Lord. Because they have the ark, God causes mice and tumors (or hemorrhoids) to afflict them. Eventually, they send the ark back with golden replicas of the mice and tumors (6:1-18). The mighty Philistines are reduced to surrendering to rodents and hemorrhoids! Their pride in Dagon and themselves has diminished.

Twenty years after these events (7:2), Samuel rallies Israel. He challenges the people to destroy their idols and serve the Lord (7:2-4), much as Joshua did in his day (Josh. 24). Samuel prays for the people and offers sacrifices on their behalf at Mizpah (7:5-9). The Philistines hear that Israel has gathered to pray, so they plan an attack (7:10); but God helps Israel overcome them (7:11). Throughout the next several years Israel has few problems with the Philistines (7:13-14). Samuel judges Israel, and the land has rest (7:13-17). Of course, this sequence of events mirrors the cycle so prevalent in Judges.

Samuel is a great leader. He is prophet (3:19-20), priest (7:9), and judge (7:15) at the same time. He pushes the nation to keep its covenant obligations to God (7:2-4) and intercedes for the sinful people (7:5-6). In short, he is an ideal judge. No other judge surpasses him in moral and ethical excellence. Yet, despite his efforts, Israel will ask for, and receive, a totally different kind of leader. After decades as a confederacy, Israel will become a kingdom, an event that God uses to plant the people firmly in the promised land.

1 Samuel 8—15: Saul, the First King

When Samuel gets old, he appoints his sons judges over Israel (8:1-2). Unfortunately, they, like Eli's sons, are different from their father. They accept bribes and make justice impossible (8:3). Israel seems destined to start the sin cycle all over again. This discouraging possibility makes the reader wonder if Israel will *ever* be secure in their homeland. How long will this hopeless situation continue?

Israel's elders suggest a solution to the nation's difficulties. They claim that Israel needs a king "like the other nations" have (8:5). Presumably, the elders think a king could bring economic and military stability to Israel. Too, they have been defeated repeatedly by foreign kings, so they probably want to copy what they believe is a successful pattern. Regardless of their reasoning, this request marks a major turning point in Israel's history. Israel will no longer operate as a *theocracy,* or group ruled by God alone. Now they will have a human master as well.

Samuel does not agree with the elders and seems hurt by their actions (8:6). God tells him, though, that Israel rejects the Lord's rule, not Samuel's (8:7). This request is simply a new stage in the nation's long history of rebellion against the Lord (8:8). Given this reality, God simply commands Samuel to warn the people what serving a king will be like (8:9). Thus, Samuel says the king will draft some of Israel's sons and daughters into the army (8:10-12). He will also have some young people serve in his court (8:13) and will tax the nation (8:14-18). Despite everything the prophet says, Israel still demands a king, so the Lord decides to grant their wish (8:19-22).

Saul soon emerges as Israel's first king through a rapid series of events. Saul is tall and generally physically impressive (9:2). He is very unassuming, though, and has no idea he will become king. Some donkeys belonging to Saul's father (Kish) are lost, so Kish sends his son and one of his servants to find them (9:3). The two men are unable to find the donkeys, so the servant suggests they consult Samuel, who, through his prophetic powers, may be able to tell them where the animals have gone (9:3-14).

Before Samuel meets Saul, the Lord tells the prophet that the new king will come to him the next day (9:15-16). When Saul actually approaches Samuel, the Lord says, "Look. There is the man I mentioned to you. He will govern my people" (9:17). Samuel quickly identifies himself as the prophet, reveals the donkeys have been found, and, most importantly, says that Saul will satisfy Israel's desire for a king (9:19-20). Stunned, Saul replies that he comes from an insignificant family in Israel's smallest clan (9:21). Samuel has surely made some mistake!

Saul is named king three times, once in private and twice in public. In private Samuel pours oil on Saul's head and declares him God's anointed leader (10:1). Many subsequent kings will also be anointed with oil to signify their status. Further, Samuel tells Saul God's Spirit will come upon him as a sign of the Lord's approval of his ministry (10:6). This prediction soon comes true (10:9). After Saul leaves Samuel, he meets a group of prophets. God's Spirit comes upon him and causes him to prophesy (10:10-11). This event demonstrates that God has indeed made Saul king.

The first public announcement of God's choice reveals Saul's shyness. Samuel calls Israel together at Mizpah (10:17). After an elaborate process of elimination, Samuel declares Saul king, but the new monarch is nowhere to be found (10:20-22). Despite the earlier assurance of God's favor Saul has hidden himself among the baggage (10:22-23). This lack of self-confidence will lead to even more bizarre behavior later in the story. For now, Samuel presents Saul to the people, gives him a copy of God's rules for kings (perhaps Deut. 17:14-20), and dismisses the group (10:24-25). Most of the nation accepts Saul's leadership, but some wait to see if he can really defeat Israel's enemies (10:27).

A second public confirmation of Saul's authority comes after his initial success in battle. Ammonites surround an Israelite town and demand surrender (11:1-2). The city calls for help (11:3-5). Greatly moved by God's Spirit, Saul gathers a mighty army, then slaughters the Ammonites (11:6-11). Now all Israel declares Saul king in a ceremony at Gilgal (11:12-15).

God has given Saul a great start for his kingdom. Again, the Lord makes good come out of Israel's lack of faith. Samuel says the monarchy will work as long as the king and the people follow the Lord (12:1-24), but, he warns, "Yet if you persist in doing evil, both you and your king will be swept away" (12:25, NIV). As always, God's fullest blessings only come when Israel obeys the covenant.

After this positive start Saul seems to have a great future. All Israel rests secure. Unfortunately, this situation does not last long. Once more Saul fights the Philistines. His son Jonathan, who becomes a major character later, attacks the Philistines before Israel's army can withstand a counterattack (13:3-4). Saul summons more troops, but the enemy musters a larger force (13:5-6). Israel's men become afraid, and some hide in caves, rocks, pits, and cisterns, while others desert (13:6-7). Clearly, Saul has serious problems.

Apparently, Saul could not start the battle without God's approval. To demonstrate this approval, Samuel was supposed to come and

offer sacrifices. Samuel had promised to arrive in seven days but is late (13:8). With his army scattering, Saul offers the sacrifice, an act

only priests were to perform (13:10). Just as he finishes, Samuel appears and corrects him (13:10-12). Samuel declares that because of this mistake Saul's kingdom will not endure (13:13-14). This prediction means none of Saul's sons will rule Israel. God would have established Saul forever (13:13), but his disobedience disqualifies him (13:14; 12:25). Samuel says a man after God's own heart will lead Israel. Who is this person?

Even after this episode, Saul continues to rule Israel. He and his son Jonathan lead the people in a decisive victory over Philistia (13:16—14:52). Jonathan's bravery provides the impetus for this success. He attacks the enemy with only one man to help him (14:1-14), then leads a general attack when the Philistines panic (14:15-23). In every way he proves himself a worthy man of high character. He would have made an excellent king if his father had not sinned.

One more sad episode causes Yahweh to reject Saul altogether. God decides to allow Israel to defeat the Amalekites, an old enemy (15:1-3). Samuel tells Saul that all the Amalekites and their animals must be killed. These are basically the same rules of war God gave Joshua. Unlike Joshua, however, Saul kills the people, but spares Agag, their king, and keeps the best animals for spoil (15:4-9). Only the weak and worthless animals are destroyed. Saul has disobeyed a second time.

God reacts strongly to Saul's actions. The Lord is sorry He made Saul king (15:10-11). Therefore, Samuel goes to Saul and confronts him. With great pride Saul, who has already made a monument to honor himself (15:12), greets Samuel. The king says he has kept God's command (15:13). Samuel answers, sarcastically, "Then why do I hear bleating sheep and lowing cattle" (15:14). Saul claims the animals are for a sacrifice to God (15:15). Samuel's reply is telling. He informs Saul that the Lord desires obedience more than sacrifices (15:22) and declares God has rejected Saul as king (15:23). Despite Saul's pleas for forgiveness, Samuel offers him no comfort. He merely tells him the kingdom will pass "to one better than you" (15:28, NIV). Samuel relents and joins Saul in worship, but he never promises Saul can remain king (15:30-31).

In light of the faults of other leaders God leaves in place, why is Saul rejected? After all, David, his successor, sins greatly, as we shall see. Men like Gideon and Samson are far from sinless. Though no perfect answer can be given, perhaps it is helpful to compare Saul's rejection with Moses' punishment. Both men are chosen by God, and both men have some success. Yet both disobey God in areas of wor-

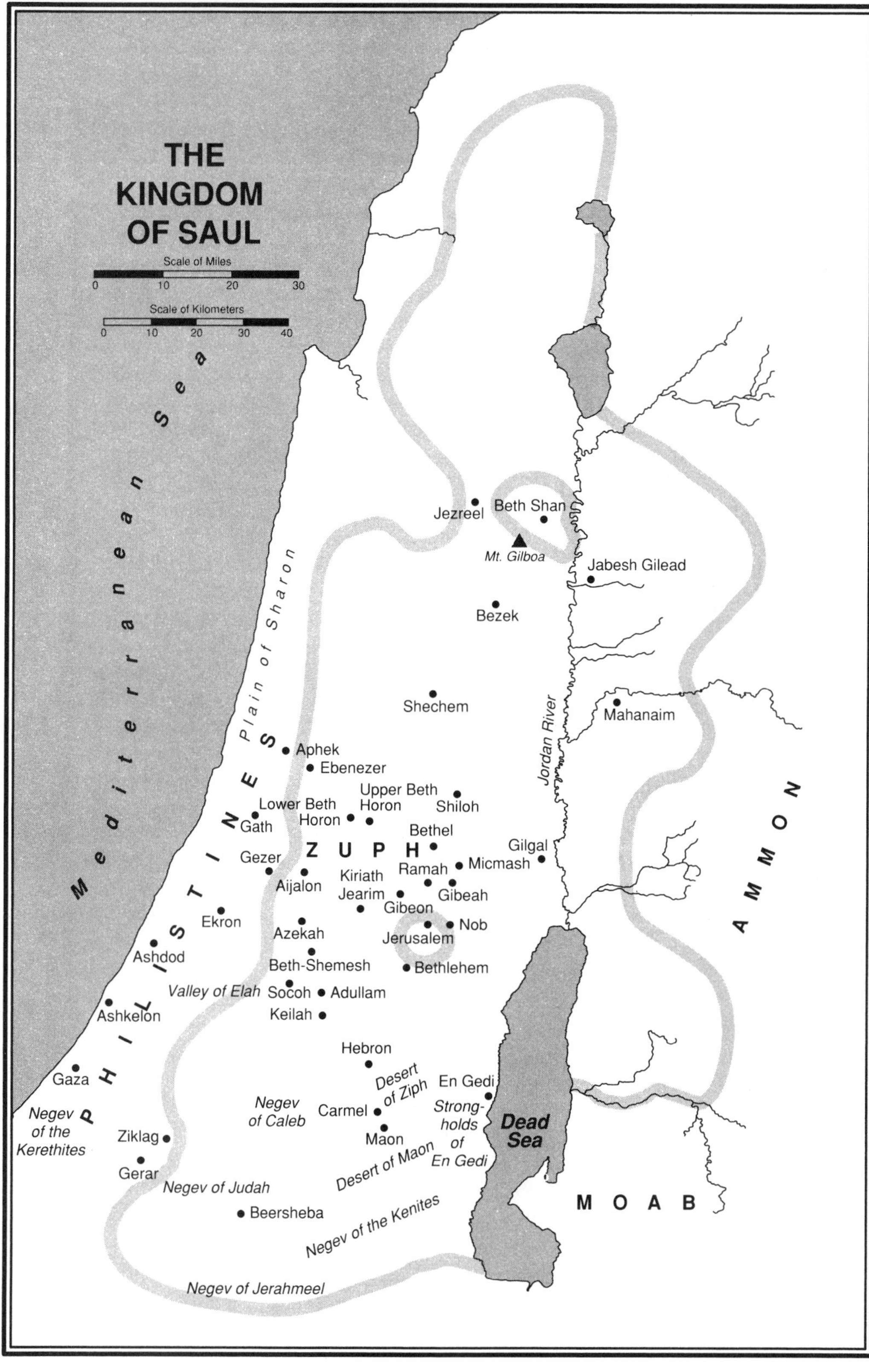

THE KINGDOM OF SAUL
Scale of Miles
0 10 20 30
Scale of Kilometers
0 10 20 30 40
Mediterranean Sea
Plain of Sharon
PHILISTINES
ZUPH
AMMON
MOAB
Jezreel
Beth Shan
Mt. Gilboa
Jabesh Gilead
Bezek
Shechem
Mahanaim
Jordan River
Aphek
Ebenezer
Upper Beth Horon
Shiloh
Lower Beth Horon
Gath
Bethel
Gilgal
Gezer
Micmash
Ramah
Aijalon
Kiriath Jearim
Gibeah
Gibeon
Nob
Ekron
Azekah
Jerusalem
Ashdod
Beth-Shemesh
Bethlehem
Valley of Elah
Socoh
Adullam
Ashkelon
Keilah
Hebron
Gaza
Desert of Ziph
En Gedi
Negev of the Kerethites
Negev of Caleb
Carmel
Strong-holds of En Gedi
Dead Sea
Ziklag
Maon
Gerar
Desert of Maon
Negev of Judah
Beersheba
Negev of the Kenites
Negev of Jerahmeel

ship. Both also disobey direct commands of the Lord. Both fail to *honor* Yahweh. The swiftness of these punishments reveal how seriously God takes worship and His word.

1 Samuel 16—31: The Rise of a New King

The events in 1 Samuel 15 prompt some important questions. For example, if Saul does not rule (13:14), who will lead the people? Who is this new king who has a heart like the Lord's? Given Saul's military victories, how can the new person (15:28) be better than his predecessor? Will this king bring a long-term solution to Israel's seemingly endless leadership crisis? Will Israel keep their covenant with Yahweh? What will happen to Saul? Other issues arise, but these questions are sufficient. Israel stands at an important crossroads in their history.

Once more, God initiates the solution to Israel's problems. Yahweh instructs Samuel to travel to Bethlehem, where he will meet a man named Jesse and his sons. One of the young men will be Israel's next king (16:1). Samuel goes to Bethlehem and invites Jesse's family to offer sacrifices with him (16:2-5). Thus, Samuel sees all but one of Jesse's sons. The oldest, Eliab, impresses the prophet, but the Lord warns him not to look at appearance and height. Indeed, God says, "The Lord does not view things like men do. Men look at outward appearances, but the Lord looks at the heart" (16:7; compare 13:14). Seven sons eventually pass before Samuel, yet none of them is God's choice (16:8-10).

Finally, the youngest son, David, who has been watching the sheep, meets Samuel (16:11). He is a handsome young man (16:12). God commands Samuel to anoint him king, just as he had anointed Saul earlier (16:12). When the prophet anoints him, God's Spirit rushes upon David (16:13). Whereas Yahweh had once empowered Saul to rule (10:6,10; 11:6), now David receives this strength. In fact, the next verse states that God's Spirit leaves Saul and is replaced by an "evil spirit from the Lord" (16:14, NIV) that "falls upon" or "terrorizes" him. Placed together, verses 13 and 14 clearly indicate that a change in God-appointed and approved leadership has occurred.

Because of its strangeness, an explanation of 16:14 is necessary. Readers may fear that this text means that God deserts, then terrorizes, people who disobey. Five points help ease such concerns. First, the passage *does* emphasize that God punishes sin. Not even believers can sin without experiencing the Lord's gracious discipline. Second, the passage's main purpose is to note the change in leadership, as had been noted. Third, the "evil spirit" was not a demon or other frightening being since Saul's servants speak of it without fear in

16:15-16. Music soothes this "spirit," which may indicate that Saul suffers from a mild form of manic-depression. Fourth, the author of 1 Samuel wants readers to know that God rules history. Whatever happens to Saul is controlled by a merciful Yahweh. Fifth, 1 Samuel never says Saul was eternally damned for his sin. Ultimately, however, no perfect answer exists. It is important, then, to interpret the text in the light of all Scripture. God loves all people, including Saul. Further, the Lord does not punish unjustly. Finally, sin does have consequences. A loving, just God does what is best at all times.

Though David has been named king by Yahweh, he cannot rule until Saul either resigns or dies. Saul never considers abdicating, so only his death can bring David to the throne. Until then, David must bide his time. God will guide David, but this in-between period of time causes David, and the reader, a great deal of tension and frustration.

David soon rises to prominence. He first enters Saul's court as a musician. Saul's servants suggest that a harpist be secured who will play during the king's bouts of depression (16:15-16). They pick David because of his musical skill (16:17-18). Saul likes David's work, so he keeps him in his service (16:23), and David becomes a fixture in Israel's power structure.

Another, more dramatic, event establishes David as a national hero. Israel and Philistia are at war again (17:1-3). This time, Philistia has a "champion named Goliath," a massive man nine feet tall whose spear shaft looks like a "weaver's rod" (17:4-7). Goliath taunts Saul's army, daring any of them to fight him. Which champion wins will decide the battle (17:8-10). Because of Goliath's size and strength, no Israelite will challenge him (17:11)—not even David's brothers (17:12-13).

Family obligations (17:14-15) prevent David from being a member of Israel's standing army. His father, worried about his oldest sons, sends David to see how they are doing (17:17-19). When David reaches camp, he hears Goliath defy Israel and sees Israel's soldiers run in fear (17:20-24). Angered, David decides to fight the giant (17:32). Despite Saul's and his brothers' attempts to discourage him (17:28,33), David does not change his mind. He has killed bears and lions in the past and expects to kill Goliath now (17:34-37).

With only a shepherd's staff, a sling, and five smooth stones, David meets Goliath (17:40). The giant curses David "by his gods" and promises to feed his flesh to the birds and beasts (17:41-44). David counters by claiming that Yahweh will give him the victory (17:45-47). More is at stake in the text now than a mere battle. The power of Israel's God has become the issue.

The conflict ends quickly. David kills Goliath by hitting him in the forehead with the first stone. Then he cuts off Goliath's head with the Philistine's own sword (17:48-51). Israel's whole army now routs the enemy (17:51-54). David becomes a war hero. Women sing about his exploits:

> "Saul has slain his thousands,
> and David his tens of thousands" (18:7, NIV).

When Saul hears this music, however, he becomes jealous and fears that David will replace him (18:8). God has given David great popularity, which will help him assume the throne later; yet at the moment this popularity brings him serious problems.

Partly because of his jealousy and partly because of his emotional imbalance, Saul takes desperate measures to eliminate David. First, Saul twice tries to kill David with a spear while he plays the harp (18:10-11). Second, Saul tries to have David killed in other ways. He offers David his daughter in marriage but requires that David kill a hundred Philistines as a wedding present, hoping the Philistines will destroy him (18:17-27). Because these attempts fail, Saul hates David even more, especially since David's popularity grows (18:28-30). Third, despite Jonathan's protests, Saul again attempts to strike David with a spear (19:1-10). Finally, Saul sends men to kill David while he sleeps (19:11-17). David escapes with his wife's help.

Throughout this whole terrifying time Jonathan supports David. He challenges his father's treatment of David, which makes Saul hurl a spear at *him* (20:33). Jonathan warns David to flee before Saul's murderous plans succeed (20:42). Jonathan befriends David even though this support means he will not follow his father on the throne (20:31). In fact, Jonathan looks forward to David becoming king and hopes to serve alongside his friend (20:16-17; 23:17-18). Few Old Testament characters display Jonathan's courage, humility, and loyalty.

Once he leaves Saul's court, David is forced to live like an outlaw.[1] His life becomes a process of avoiding one peril after another. For example, he flees to Gath, Goliath's hometown, where he is immediately recognized as Philistia's old enemy (21:10-11). To escape, he acts like a madman (21:12-15). Too, Saul chases David and on one occasion nearly catches him (23:7-29). David gathers a small army of outcasts and misfits (22:1-2), while Saul murders those who help or support David even if the supporters are priests (21:1-9; 22:6-23). Twice David has an opportunity to kill Saul but refuses to do so (chaps. 24; 26). Still, Saul hates David. Discouraged, David decides his only hope for survival lies in becoming an ally of the Philistines; so he serves Achish, the son of the king of Gath (27:1-12). When will David become king? Ironically, the Philistines eventually help David's cause. Not only do they protect David from Saul, they also remove Saul as well.

When chapter 28 begins, Israel and Philistia are at war again. Since David and his followers live in Philistia, his Philistine benefactor tells him he will have to fight against Israel (28:1). David agrees (28:2), which seemingly ends his future as Israel's king. After all, how could the nation ever accept a leader who had killed his own people? A crisis has developed.

Meanwhile, Saul has become a desperate man. Samuel has died (25:1; 28:3), and God's Spirit has left Saul. The king has no way to ask Yahweh how to fight the Philistines (28:4-6). Against Moses' law (Lev. 19:31) and his own earlier orders (28:3), Saul decides to seek help from a medium (28:7). He asks the medium to bring Samuel back from the grave, and she does (28:8-14). When Samuel actually appears, the medium becomes terrified, so perhaps she was not used to being successful in her trade. Saul asks Samuel how the battle will go (28:15). Samuel's reply drains all Saul's strength. Samuel informs him that David has been chosen king and that Saul and his sons will join him in the grave the next day (28:16-19). Whatever his other faults, Saul is not a coward. He fights the battle despite knowing he will die. Still, Saul has broken God's rules again. He believes in God and wants God's help, but he does not obey the Lord.

Just before the great battle, the Philistine officers do not allow David to fight with them (29:1-11). This decision keeps him from killing his own people. Thus, he can still become king. While David stays near the battle front, however, Amalekites raid his camp. All wives and children are kidnapped (30:1-3). Unlike Saul, David receives a word from God, who tells him to pursue the enemy (30:6-8). Also unlike Saul, David attempts to annihilate the Amalekites (30:17) and, thereby, manages to regain everything that was taken (30:18).

While David wins his skirmish, Israel gets crushed by the Philistines. Many Jews including Saul's sons—even Jonathan—die (31:1-2). Archers wound Saul himself (31:3). Because he is near death, Saul asks his armor-bearer to kill him, lest the enemy abuse him (31:4). The armor-bearer refuses, though, so Saul falls on his own sword (31:4). Israel loses the war, their king, and most of his heirs in one day. With Saul dead, David has a clearer path to the throne.

It is difficult to assess Saul's life and work. On the one hand, he helps establish Israel as a legitimate nation. Israel no longer fears every enemy. On the other hand, though, he disobeys God, which brings consequences for himself, his family, and the whole nation. He could have had a permanent kingdom. Instead, he becomes jealous, vengeful, and petty. In many ways, then, Saul is a hard man to characterize. He is inconsistent at best, yet his demise is regrettable.

2 Samuel 1—10: David Builds a Kingdom

David does not rejoice when he learns of Saul's and Jonathan's deaths. A young Amalekite brings David the news and even claims that he killed Saul (1:1-10). He tells this lie hoping David will reward him. David's reaction surprises the messenger. First, David and his followers mourn for Saul and Jonathan (1:11-12). Then, David has the Amalekite executed for claiming to have killed Israel's king (1:13-16). David refused to kill Saul because Saul was the anointed king (chaps. 24; 26), so he condemns the man for supposedly murdering Saul. Finally, David sings a lament for the dead (1:17-27). He especially mourns the loss of his loyal friend Jonathan (1:26).

Saul's death does not automatically allow David to rule Israel. Judah makes him their king (2:1-7), but the other tribes support Ish-bosheth,[2] one of Saul's surviving sons (2:8-9). Because of this division, two factions emerge in Israel: one follows David while the other favors Ish-bosheth. Both sides have armies. Abner leads Ish-bosheth's forces, and Joab leads David's. These armies fight regularly, leading to many deaths. On one notable occasion Abner kills one of Joab's brothers (2:10-32).

This conflict continues for several years (2:10-11; 3:1). Two murders finally allow David to take the throne, though he has nothing to do with either one. Abner breaks with Ish-bosheth because the king accuses Abner of sleeping with one of Saul's concubines (3:6-7). This accusation raises the issue of Abner's loyalty, since the person who controls the royal harem controls the kingdom. Angered at the king, Abner decides to help David (3:8-11). The two men meet, and Abner arranges for David's power base to grow (3:12-21). After Abner leaves, however, Joab avenges his brother's death by murdering Abner (3:22-27). David mourns Abner's death (3:31-38). He declares his own innocence (3:28) and deplores Joab's act (3:29), yet he does not replace Joab.

Ish-bosheth is murdered next. While the king sleeps, two men kill and decapitate him (4:5-7). Like the Amalekite, they think David will reward them (4:8). Indeed, he rewards them the same way he did the Amalekite—he has them executed (4:9-12). Again, David refuses to agree with murder. This event leaves him as the only serious contender for the throne.

At last, all twelve tribes anoint David king (5:1-5). It has taken a long time for God's promises to come true, but they do materialize. God remains faithful. Now, David consolidates his power in three important ways. First, he conquers Jerusalem (5:6-14). Thus he unites the nation by establishing a permanent capital. He now has a solid political base. Second, he defeats the Philistines (5:17-25). Ridding Israel of this old foe establishes his military power. Third, he brings the ark of the covenant to Jerusalem, displaying his religious commitment (6:1-23). Each of these achievements helps make him the undisputed authority in the land. For now, Israel's nagging, long-term problems have been solved. Because they have a good leader, they follow Yahweh and defeat their enemies. No ruler since Joshua has done so much for the people.

To demonstrate approval of David's work, the Lord makes him an astounding promise. This pledge is linked to those made to Abraham and represents a high point in the Old Testament story. The episode begins when David desires to build a temple for the Lord (7:1-2). He believes it wrong that he has a nice home while God's ark sits in a tent (7:2). At first, Nathan, the king's prophet, encourages David to build (7:3), but God instructs Nathan to tell David not to construct a temple (7:5-13). David's son will build the house of worship (v. 13). What, then, can David do for God?

Yahweh appreciates David's gesture. Instead of asking David to build God a house, the Lord promises to build *David* a house (7:11). What kind of house? A royal house that consists of David's descendants! David's son will follow him on the throne and construct the temple (7:12-13). God will then "establish the throne of his kingdom forever" (7:13, NIV). Incredibly, David will never lack a son to rule Israel, for God's love will never leave David's house, as it did Saul's (7:14-15). Yahweh concludes by saying: "Your house and your kingdom will endure forever before me; your throne will be established forever" (7:16, NIV). This promise overwhelms David (7:18-29). God has made him the father of an eternal household.

What does this passage mean? Why is it significant for the rest of the Old Testament? Like Abraham, David has been promised special descendants. God will use the children of both men to bless the world. Even more importantly, the rest of the Bible argues that 2 Samuel 7:1-17 means that the messiah, Israel's savior, will come from David's family. Isaiah, Jeremiah, Micah, and the other prophets look for an ideal *son of David* who will serve the Lord and rule justly. Many psalms, such as Psalm 110, express belief in the same things, as do the gospel writers (compare Matt. 1—2). Therefore, this promise serves as a theme that unites the Old and New Testaments because it eventually leads to Jesus Christ. The promises to Abraham of heir, covenant, and land continue to shape the Old Testament but are now joined by the theme of the eternal nature of David's kingdom. Like the promises to Abraham, this new idea will grow and take clearer shape as the biblical story unfolds. Only after the earthly kingdom disintegrates will the deeper meaning of the promise become apparent.

After the great promise David continues to prosper. Enemies are defeated (8:1-14; 10:1-19). David creates an organizational structure for his kingdom (8:15-18). He also shows kindness to the son of his old friend Jonathan (9:1-13). Yahweh blesses everything the king does. His life has reached a high level of success.

2 Samuel 11—19: David's Sin and Its Consequences

At the pinnacle of his career David stumbles and falls. He sins in a way that causes himself, his family, and his kingdom serious problems. These difficulties begin when David stays at home instead of going with his army to war (11:1). With this added leisure time, he has the luxury of looking at his capital at night (11:2). One night, he sees a beautiful woman bathing (11:2). He inquires about her identity, perhaps to find out if she is married. If she is unmarried, he can add her to the harem. His messengers tell him, however, that her name is Bathsheba and that she is married to Uriah, one of David's best warriors (2 Sam. 23:39). Despite this knowledge the king sends for Bathsheba and sleeps with her (11:4).

Unfortunately, David sleeps with her when she is most likely to conceive (11:4). She informs David she is pregnant (11:5), so David attempts to conceal the affair. He brings Uriah home from the war, hoping he will lie with his wife (11:6-8). Uriah refuses to go home, though, since his fellow soldiers are still in the field (11:11). His first plan ruined, David gets Uriah drunk and then sends him to Bathsheba (11:12-13). Uriah still does not sleep with his wife (11:13). Finally, David has Joab make sure Uriah dies in battle (11:14-25). Then, he marries Bathsheba (11:26-27). David has covered his sin. Or has he?

Obviously, David has sinned significantly. He has compounded adultery with murder and lies. By not going to war, he has placed himself above his soldiers (compare Deut. 17:20). Likewise, adding another woman to his already-substantial harem (2 Sam. 3:1-5) breaks Moses' commands for kings (Deut. 17:17). Of course, the Ten Commandments prohibit murder and adultery (Ex. 20:13-14).

God soon confronts David for his actions, since this whole sordid episode "displeased the Lord" (11:27, NIV). Once more Nathan enters the story, this time to challenge and correct David with a remarkable parable (12:1-6). He reminds David how well God has treated the king (12:7-8) and states that David has despised the Lord (12:9-10). David repents, but he must face the consequences of his actions. Even David's sins must be punished. Two awful results will soon occur: the son Bathsheba bore (11:27) will die (12:14), and David will someday have someone sleep with his wives "in broad daylight" (12:11-12). Despite David's prayers his son dies (12:18). After a time the couple has another son—Solomon (12:24-25)—who will ease the loss of the first child. The reader should also expect the other punishment to happen sooner or later.

Sadly, the person who will lie with David's harem comes from his own family. Prior to this, Amnon, one of David's sons, falls in love with his half-sister Tamar. Her full brother's name is Absalom. Rather than marry Tamar, Amnon lures her into a room, rapes her, then sends her away (13:1-15). David hears about the rape and gets angry (13:21), but he does nothing. Perhaps the memory of his own sin paralyzes him.

Absalom waits two years for David to punish Amnon, then takes matters into his own hands. He kills Amnon and runs to another country (13:23-37). David grieves for Amnon (13:37); he wants Absalom to return (13:38-39), but he *does* nothing. Joab finally brings Absalom back (14:23); yet David refuses to see him for two, long years (14:28,33).

Meanwhile, Absalom plots to overthrow his father. Through shrewd political maneuvering, he manages to gain the people's favor (15:6). He promises the average person justice, equality, and hope (15:1-5), and he recruits some of David's top advisors for his conspiracy (16:15-23). At the peak of his popular support he revolts against David, drives his father from Jerusalem, and sleeps with the royal concubines in full view of the people (15:7—16:23). Absalom has seemingly become king, and Nathan's prediction of David's punishment has come true.

With help from Joab and Hushai, an old royal advisor who stays in Jerusalem to give Absalom bad advice, David overcomes Absalom. Hushai tells Absalom not to pursue David immediately, which gives the king and his followers time to rest and regroup (17:1-29). The next day, Joab leads David's army against Absalom. Though David asks Joab to spare Absalom, Joab makes sure he dies (18:1-15). With their leader dead, the rebels soon surrender (18:16-17). When he learns of his son's death, David mourns, even to the point of wishing he had died for him (18:33). Wisely, Joab counsels the king to stop weeping, lest his army desert him (19:1-8). Finally, David gathers himself and leads his men back to Jerusalem (19:8-43). His sin with Bathsheba has brought death, misery, and civil war; yet God pardons him and allows him to remain king. The Bible rarely offers a more striking portrayal of the effects of sin, punishment, and God's ultimate forgiveness.

2 Samuel 20—24: David's Last Years

David's final years are marked by more turmoil. A man named Sheba leads a rebellion that leaves only Judah supporting the king (20:1-3). As in the Absalom revolt, Joab rescues David (20:7-22), though once again he murders an innocent man in the process (20:9-10). He has become so valuable to the king that David allows him to remain head of the army. War continues with the Philistines (21:15-22), and Saul's sins continue to haunt Israel (21:1-14).

Through all these difficulties God keeps the promise to David that he and his descendants will remain on the throne. David's failings do not negate Yahweh's faithfulness, and the king praises the Lord's goodness (22:1—23:7). Whatever his other flaws, David rarely forgets how he rose from shepherd to king. He is not guilty of ingratitude.

One last, rather difficult, story ends 2 Samuel. For some unstated reason, Yahweh becomes angry at Israel, and, therefore, "incited David against them" by ordering him to take a national census (24:1, NIV). David commands Joab to number the people with the counting of warriors in mind (24:2). Even Joab, who is hardly a moral giant, thinks this plan is wrong (24:3). Apparently, Joab thinks David fears another rebellion or has grown proud. Joab loses the argument, so the project proceeds (24:4-9). After the census is taken, David feels guilty and learns that God will now punish the nation (24:10-11). Thousands of people die in a plague before the Lord relents (24:12-17). David admits his sin and asks God to punish him, not the people. Thus, this odd punishment stops as it began—with no explanation. After the plague David worships Yahweh. He purchases a threshing floor, offers sacrifices there, and receives God's forgiveness (24:18-25). So the book ends with David in God's favor.

Conclusion

God's promises to Abraham have basically been fulfilled. His heirs have become a great nation. His descendants have a homeland and possess a covenant with Yahweh. Israel even seems to have solved its leadership crisis. God's promise to David provides them with stable leadership. After decades of floundering in a sin cycle, Israel appears to be beginning a great new era in their history. Yahweh continues to bless the people, correct their faults, and turn their errors into benefits.[3]

Questions for Reflection

1. How do you explain God's choice and ultimate rejection of Saul?
2. If you had been living in Samuel's day, would you have favored kingship as the political system for Israel? Why?
3. In what ways is David a man after God's own heart?
4. How do you explain God's wrath against Israel in 2 Samuel 24?

Notes

1. John Bright, *A History of Israel,* 2d ed. (Philadelphia: Westminster, 1972), 188 and following.

2. This name means "man of shame" and was probably given him by David's supporters.

3. For commentary on 1 and 2 Samuel see Ralph W. Klein, *1 Samuel,* vol. 10 in *Word Biblical Commentary* (Waco, Tex.: Word Books, 1983); P. Kyle McCarter, Jr., *1 Samuel,* vol. 8 in *The Anchor Bible* (New York: Doubleday, 1980); P. Kyle McCarter, Jr., *2 Samuel,* vol. 9 in *The Anchor Bible* (New York: Doubleday, 1984); A. A. Anderson, *2 Samuel,* vol. 11 in *Word Biblical Commentary* (Dallas: Word Books, 1989).

7
1 and 2 Kings: *Losing the Land*

Plot: Israel slowly, yet persistently, slides from the glories of Solomon's reign to idolatry, division, destruction, and exile. A few outstanding prophets and kings prolong this process but are unable to stop it.
Major Characters: David, Solomon, Rehoboam, Jeroboam, Omri, Ahab, Jezebel, Elijah, Elisha, Jehu, Uzziah, Hezekiah, Manasseh, and Josiah
Major Events: David's death, Solomon's temple construction, the division of the kingdom, Ahab and Jezebel's conflict with Elijah, Elisha's ministry, the fall of Samaria, the Sennacherib crisis, and the destruction of Jerusalem

Introduction

First and Second Kings presents a dazzling array of characters and events while analyzing hundreds of years of history. Thus, most readers need some help in keeping the people, facts, and figures in 1 and 2 Kings straight in their minds. Otherwise, they become discouraged, wonder how these *historical books* could possibly apply to today's world, and stop reading. Basically, if the books' plots, themes, and characters are kept in focus, then the text makes sense.

Starting with David's death, 1 and 2 Kings describes the death of Israel as a nation. The first sign of illness appears when Solomon, David's son, begins to worship idols. When he dies, a second sign emerges. The nation divides into two parts: North and South. David's sons rule one region while other individuals reign over the other. Two hundred years after the division, a third sign of illness becomes apparent when Assyria, a powerful nation, destroys Northern Israel. Finally, the nation dies altogether when Babylon, yet another enemy, conquers Southern Israel and levels Jerusalem. Therefore, these books tell the horrible story of Israel's demise. Every event in the story either accelerates or slows the nation's end.

Several important characters dictate the plot. David links 1 and 2 Kings with 1 and 2 Samuel. Solomon helps fulfill God's promises to David in 2 Samuel 7:1-17, yet he also sins in a way that hastens Israel's ruin. Rehoboam and Jeroboam tear the kingdom into two pieces, and Jeroboam creates a new religion. Ahab and Jezebel lead the nation away from God. Hezekiah, Josiah, and six other faithful kings attempt to make the nation repent and seek Yahweh but ultimately fail to do so.

Perhaps the prophets are the books' most impressive characters. Elijah and Elisha play the most important roles in the story. Still, other prophets like Ahijah and Micaiah also try to turn Israel back to Yahweh. All these good prophets remind Israel of their covenant obligations. They stand against the kings who dishonor God and mislead the people. Many times the prophets are persecuted, yet they are never silenced.

Two other *characters* deserve mention. Though not individuals, Assyria and Babylon make a huge impact on the story. Assyria destroys the northern part of Israel, and Babylon devastates what remains. Both nations hover over the story's action, waiting for the chance to attack. When they complete their work, 2 Kings 17:23 declares that they have done *God's* work. Israel's sins have been punished in the manner dictated by Deuteronomy 27—28.

Certain themes in 1 and 2 Kings clarify the plot and characterizations. Most of these ideas come from Deuteronomy. First, God expects Israel to obey the stipulations of the covenant. Even the kings must act according to the rules in Deuteronomy 17:14-20 as did Joshua. Above all, idolatry must be avoided, and the law, followed. Second, God rules history. Kings and nations are controlled by their Creator. Third, prophets arise and preach repentance to a sinful nation (Deut. 18:14-22). Fourth, the temple is built, fulfilling 2 Samuel 7:1-17 and establishing Jerusalem as the central place of worship (Deut. 12:4-6). Sacrifices can be offered only at this special site. Fifth, God will forgive and restore Israel when they sin (1 Kings 8:46-53; 2 Kings 25:27-30). These ideas appear in the books of Joshua, Judges, and Samuel, so the author of 1 and 2 Kings helps interpret the book by offering readers some familiar concepts.

Almost four centuries pass in 1 and 2 Kings. David dies about 970 B.C. Solomon reigns forty years, then the nation divides. The Northern Kingdom lasts until 722 B.C., and the South falls in 587 B.C. Other dates are important and will be mentioned, but these are the ones most necessary for understanding the story. In fact, 722 and 587 are vital for grasping the rest of the Old Testament since the prophets either announce, experience, or comment on these events. Likewise, most of the writings relate to David, Solomon, or the fall or rebuilding of the nation.

What kind of history, then, does 1 and 2 Kings present? One factor dominates the books' opinion of all kings, nations, and events. If the kings serve the Lord and do not worship idols, they are good kings. If they offer sacrifices only in Jerusalem, they are even better. If they destroy idols and bring spiritual renewal, they receive the author's complete approval. Failure in any of these areas leads to national catastrophe. In other words, no factor—economic, military, or otherwise—affects Israel's destiny as much as their relationship to God. This world view causes the author to write a *sacred history* that warns future generations of Israelites against repeating the same mistakes.

1 Kings 1:1—12:24: The Rise and Fall of Solomon's Family

Just as Joshua's death links Joshua and Judges and Saul's does the same with 1 and 2 Samuel, here David's death provides a transition between 1 and 2 Samuel and 1 and 2 Kings. David has grown old now and cannot even stay warm with the help of a beautiful young woman named Abishag (1:1-4). Given his condition, a new king must soon take the throne. As when Saul died, this current situation causes rivalry and upheaval. David's son Adonijah proclaims himself king with support from Joab and other prominent leaders (1:5-9). Nathan the prophet, on the other hand, wants Solomon to replace David (1:10).

A serious struggle results. Sensing that Adonijah will become king unless drastic measures are taken, Nathan counsels Bathsheba to remind David of his promise to her that Solomon will succeed him (1:11-14). This news may surprise readers, since the promise is not mentioned earlier. Bathsheba reminds David of the pledge, as does Nathan (1:15-27). One last time, the king rouses himself for political action. He instructs Nathan, Zadok the priest, and Benaiah, a great warrior (2 Sam. 23:20), to put Solomon on David's mule, anoint him king, and to proclaim that Solomon is David's choice (1:32-35). When these orders are carried out, the people accept Solomon as king (1:43-48). Adonijah, Joab, and their allies are now at Solomon's mercy (1:49-53). David's ability to name his own successor reveals that his popularity and political savvy have not disappeared over the years.

With death approaching, David advises Solomon in three areas. First, he encourages Solomon to follow God and obey the covenant (2:2-3). Yahweh will then bless Solomon and keep the promises made in 2 Samuel 7 (2:3-4). Second, David tells his son to execute Joab and some men who aided Absalom's revolt (2:5-6,8-9). This advice reveals a flaw in David. He never punished Joab or the others, but he asks Solomon to do so. Third, the king asks Solomon to reward some old friends (2:7). David's counsel is wise. Solomon must learn to trust God, distrust his enemies, and honor his allies. Probably no one in Israel's history understood how to balance these aspects of leadership better than David.

With David's death (2:10-12) an era has passed. Israel now clearly favors having a king. The nation has a solid economy, fighting force, and system of justice. Its days as a group of tribes that fears every new enemy are over. This imperfect ruler, who follows Yahweh and yet sins greatly, has achieved something of a political miracle. At the same time he has given worship added status by bringing the ark to Jerusalem, listening to the prophets, and supporting the priests. Next to Abraham and Moses, David is the most influential person in the Old Testament.

Solomon quickly follows David's political advice. He lets Adonijah live until he makes a heavy-handed attempt to get the throne by asking to marry Abishag, David's last concubine (2:13-21). Again, whoever possesses the harem rules the land (compare 2 Sam. 3:7; 16:21-22), so his request lacks subtlety and wisdom. Solomon has him killed (2:22-25). Joab soon dies too. Though Joab runs to the tabernacle for sanctuary, Solomon has him put to death (2:28-35). Finally, Solomon executes Shimei, a man who opposed David during the Absalom revolt (2:36-46). Now, Solomon has no rivals to the throne or rebels to stir dissent against him.

Except for a few significant exceptions, Solomon also follows David's spiritual counsel during the early years of his reign. He does marry Pharaoh's daughter, and he does offer sacrifices outside of Jerusalem (3:1-3). These tendencies lead to greater problems later but have yet to hamper Solomon. At this stage he asks God to give him wisdom to rule the people, for he realizes he is young and inexperienced. God answers this prayer and promises to make the king rich and famous (3:10-14). Soon, he is able to settle seemingly impossible disputes (3:16-28), organize an effective governmental structure (4:1-19), and establish a powerful, even opulent, royal court (4:20-28). His wisdom becomes known throughout the region (4:29-34). He writes numerous proverbs and songs and acquires a vast knowledge of botany and biology. Yahweh has indeed kept His promise to Solomon, just as He kept those made to David.

Solomon demonstrates his love for God by building the temple. Since Israel has no experience in such projects, Solomon enlists Hiram, king of Tyre, to help with construction (5:1-6). Hiram provides Solomon the necessary cedar and pine logs for the temple (5:7-12). To secure workers, Solomon conscripts men "from all Israel" (5:13). Over thirty thousand men labor during the seven years it takes to finish the building (5:13-18; 6:38). Eventually, the people resent this policy of drafting workers for royal building projects (12:4), but for now they do not protest.

Temple construction begins in the fourth year of Solomon's reign, or about 966 B.C. (6:1). By modern standards the temple was not very big, only thirty feet wide, ninety feet long, and forty-five feet high. Hundreds of modern and not-so-modern churches are larger. What makes the temple so stunning is its interior and furnishings. Inside, the stone walls are covered with cedar, and the cedar, with gold (6:14-22). Ornate carvings adorn the sanctuary as well (6:23-35). All the utensils for worship are finely crafted and made of precious metals (7:13-51). With all other items in place Solomon brings the ark of the covenant, which houses Moses' tablets, to the temple (8:1-9). Yahweh expresses approval of the temple by sending a "cloud of glory" (8:10-12).

Several theological themes emerge from the temple's completion. First, Moses' prediction that God would choose a central place for worship has come true (Deut. 12:4-6). All sacrifices must take place here, or God will not accept them. Second, God's promises to David continue to materialize. David's son rules Israel and has, indeed, built a temple for the Lord (2 Sam. 7:13). Third, God lives with the people in the promised land. Yahweh continues to keep the covenant made years ago. Fourth, Israel can have sins forgiven by sacrificing here. Fifth, Israel stands at the midpoint of their history. Struggling for land and survival lies behind them; exile waits in the future. Never again will Israel have such a king, such a worship center, such influence, or such peace. God's promises to Abraham and David have been kept.

Before the priests offer the first sacrifice in the new temple, Solomon prays. He asks God to keep the promises made to David (8:25-26), to hear Israel's prayers (8:27-30), to judge the wicked (8:31-32), and to bless the foreigner who accepts Israel's God (8:41-43). Most importantly, he prays that Yahweh will forgive the people when they sin (8:33-40,46-53). He asks that even if Israel goes into exile as a punishment for their iniquities that God bring them back to the land (8:46-51). In other words, he prays with Deuteronomy 27—28 in mind. After this prayer, sacrifices and a festival conclude the dedication ceremonies (8:62-65). Then God promises to do as Solomon has asked if the people will obey the covenant (9:1-9).

Solomon undertakes other building projects. He builds a palace for himself that requires thirteen years to complete (7:1-12). Obviously, it is larger and probably more expensive than the temple. Later,

Solomon rebuilds towns (9:17) and constructs store cities and ships. He even builds a palace for his Egyptian wife (9:10-24). His fame spreads still farther (10:1-13), and he becomes extremely rich (10:14-29). It appears that Solomon serves and pleases God.

Beneath the surface several of Solomon's practices erode his moral strength. As he gets older, Solomon collects seven hundred wives and three hundred concubines, many from idol-worshiping countries (11:1-3). Most of these marriages with foreign women were politically motivated. They kept peace between Solomon and his neighbors. Eventually, Solomon worships his wives' gods and even builds worship places for them (11:4-9). He no longer serves God alone, which means he has broken the covenant and must face punishment (11:9-12). Love of women, coupled with excessive wealth, has led to his downfall. God tells him that the kingdom will be divided into two parts (11:11). Solomon's descendants will only rule because of Yahweh's promises to David and love for Israel (11:12-13).

Various individuals rebel against Solomon in his last years (11:14-24). The most significant foe is Jeroboam, one of Solomon's officials (11:26-28). Just as Yahweh used Samuel to anoint David, so now the Lord sends a prophet, Ahijah, to inform Jeroboam that he will rule ten tribes in Israel (11:29-31). At least eight more times in 1 and 2 Kings, prophets will make strategic predictions.[1] God promises to make Jeroboam's kingdom as permanent as David's if he will obey the covenant (11:37-39). Like Saul, Solomon becomes so jealous of this young man that he attempts, unsuccessfully, to kill him (11:40).

Like his father, Solomon exerted great influence on Israel's history and heritage. He raised the kingdom to new heights, both militarily and economically. Building the temple aided Israel's worship. Unlike David, however, he served other gods. Whatever his other faults, David never committed idolatry. Though wise and the author of wisdom literature (4:29-34), Solomon foolishly forsook the covenant that undergirded the nation and the monarchy.

After Solomon dies, his son Rehoboam assumes leadership (12:1). Led by Jeroboam, the people ask him to relieve the burdens of taxation and forced labor that Solomon created (12:2-4). Foolishly, Rehoboam threatens the people. He tells them he will be much harsher than his father (12:5-15), causing all but Judah and Benjamin to follow Jeroboam (12:16-21). This division occurs according to the prophet Ahijah's word (11:30-31; 12:22-24). Solomon's house has fallen from its great heights. Solomon's sons will rule only a small portion of what he had governed. In contrast to his father, Rehoboam becomes neither wise, rich, nor powerful and proves unable to reunite the nation (14:21-31).

Kings of Israel (North)*	
Jeroboam I	930-909 B.C.
Nadab	909-908 B.C.
Baasha	908-885 B.C.
Elah	885-884 B.C.
Zimri	885 B.C.
Tibni	885-880 B.C.
Civil Unrest	885-880 B.C.
Omri	880-874 B.C.
Ahab	874-853 B.C.
Ahaziah	853-852 B.C.
Joram	852-841 B.C.
Jehu	841-814 B.C.
Jehoahaz	814-798 B.C.
Jehoash	798-782 B.C.
Coregency	793-782 B.C.
Jeroboam II	782-753 B.C.
Zechariah	753-752 B.C.
Shallum	752 B.C.
Menahem	752-742 B.C.
Pekahiah	742-740 B.C.
Pekah	740-732 B.C.
Hoshea	732-722 B.C.

* All dates approximate

Kings of Judah (South)*	
Rehoboam	930-913 B.C.
Abijah	913-910 B.C.
Asa	910-869 B.C.
Coregency	872-869 B.C.
Jehoshaphat	869-848 B.C.
Coregency	853-848 B.C.
Jehoram	848-841 B.C.
Ahaziah	841 B.C.
Athaliah	841-835 B.C.
Joash	835-796 B.C.
Amaziah	796-767 B.C.
Coregency	792-767 B.C.
Azariah/Uzziah	767-740 B.C.
Coregency	750-740 B.C.
Jotham	740-731 B.C.
Coregency	735-731 B.C.
Ahaz	731-715 B.C.
Hezekiah	715-687 B.C.
Coregency	697-687 B.C.
Manasseh	687-642 B.C.
Amon	642-640 B.C.
Josiah	640-609 B.C.
Jehoahaz	609 B.C.
Jehoiakim	609-598 B.C.
Jehoiachin	598-597 B.C.
Zedekiah	597-587 B.C.

* All dates approximate

Now two kingdoms exist. Until 2 Kings 17 the story includes two kings, two capitals, and two religions. Yet they share the same destiny—destruction. Most of the material in 1 Kings 12:25—2 Kings 10:36 deals with the Northern Kingdom. All of 2 Kings 18—25 discusses the Southern Kingdom. Still, some overlap occurs, so perhaps the following chart will help readers keep the kingdoms separate.

Name	Capital	Size	Economic Status
Israel/ Northern Israel	Samaria	10 Tribes	Fairly Wealthy
Judah/ Southern Israel	Jerusalem	2 Tribes	Struggling

1 Kings 12:25—15:34: The Rise and Fall of Jeroboam's Family

As soon as he becomes king, Jeroboam disobeys God. He realizes that it is not politically wise to allow his people to travel south to Jerusalem to worship. Therefore, he breaks the covenant in the most flagrant way possible. He starts a new religion, one that serves his interests instead of God's or the people's. This alternative religion reverses Moses' teachings. Instead of shunning idols, Jeroboam makes two golden calves and teaches the nation that *these* gods delivered Israel from Egypt (12:28-30; compare Ex. 32). Instead of insisting on worship in Jerusalem, he builds local shrines in two different locations where the calves can be worshiped (12:29-31). Rather than making only Levites priests, he allows anyone who wishes to lead worship at the shrines (12:31). Finally, he institutes rival festivals to those held in Jerusalem (12:32-33).

Two prophets denounce Jeroboam's actions. The first, an unnamed individual, appears at the king's altar and declares that it "will be split apart and the ashes on it will be poured out" (13:3, NIV). He also predicts a king named Josiah will someday destroy this cult altogether (13:2). Jeroboam raises his hand to give the order to seize the prophet, but his hand shrivels up (13:4). The prophet prays for him, restoring the hand; yet Jeroboam never repents.

An informative story about prophecy appears next. God has told the unnamed prophet to go home a certain way (13:10). A second prophet meets him, invites him to his house, and lies to him, saying God has told him to invite him (13:11-19). Because the first prophet

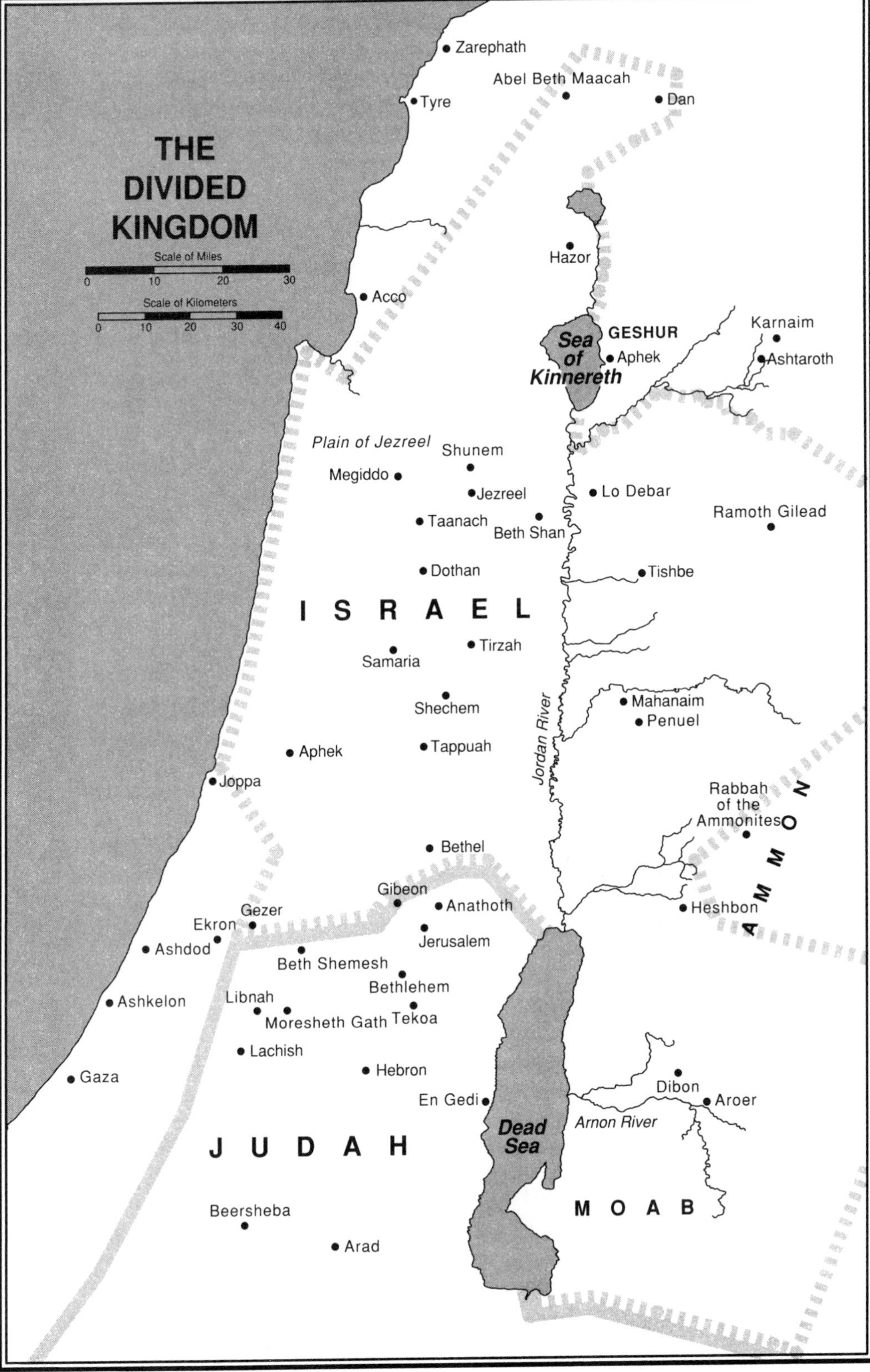
THE DIVIDED KINGDOM
Scale of Miles
0
10
20
30
Scale of Kilometers
0
10
20
30
40
Zarephath
Abel Beth Maacah
Tyre
Dan
Hazor
Acco
GESHUR
Sea of Kinnereth
Aphek
Karnaim
Ashtaroth
Plain of Jezreel
Shunem
Megiddo
Jezreel
Lo Debar
Ramoth Gilead
Taanach
Beth Shan
Dothan
Tishbe
ISRAEL
Tirzah
Samaria
Shechem
Mahanaim
Penuel
Jordan River
Aphek
Tappuah
Joppa
Rabbah of the Ammonites
AMMON
Bethel
Gibeon
Anathoth
Gezer
Ekron
Jerusalem
Heshbon
Ashdod
Beth Shemesh
Bethlehem
Ashkelon
Libnah
Moresheth Gath
Tekoa
Lachish
Hebron
Gaza
Dibon
En Gedi
Aroer
Dead Sea
Arnon River
JUDAH
MOAB
Beersheba
Arad

goes home with the second, he is killed by a lion (13:20-26), while the lying prophet survives (13:27-32). Two lessons are taught here. First, both good and bad prophets exist during this time, just as Moses and Balaam lived at the same time. Second, God's prophets must do what God says. Otherwise, they lose their credibility.

Jeroboam has already met the second prophet who criticizes him. Ahijah, who declared God's choice of Jeroboam, has grown old. The king sends his wife to the prophet to learn what will happen to the king's sick son (14:1-5). Ahijah says that Jeroboam's idolatry and evil have caused God to reject him and his household (14:6-9). Yahweh will destroy Jeroboam's sons so that they will never rule Northern Israel (14:10-11). A later king will wipe them out (14:14). Worse still, because his people accept Jeroboam's religion, the whole nation will eventually go into exile (14:14-16). Both Jeroboam and the nation he created are doomed.

In the south in Judah, things are a bit better. Abijah, Rehoboam's successor, does not follow the Lord (15:1-8); but his son Asa does (15:9-11). Asa leads a religious reform that includes purging the land of Baal worship and restoring the temple (15:11-15). Still, Asa never defeats Northern Israel during his forty-one year reign (15:9-10,16-22). The largest portion of the old nation remains more powerful.

God's word about Jeroboam's descendants soon comes true. Nadab, his son, follows him on the throne (15:25-26), but Baasha kills Nadab and his whole family (15:27-28). Baasha is no more righteous than Jeroboam or Nadab, however, so a prophet (Jehu) announces his coming destruction as well (16:1-4). Jeroboam's power has ended, and he is now remembered only as the man who led the people astray. In fact, he becomes the book's example of what it means to sin against God (compare 15:34; 16:7,19; etc.).

1 Kings 16:1—2 Kings 10:36: The Rise and Fall of Omri's Family

Late in Asa's career, a new and powerful king named Omri arises in Northern Israel. He follows a series of rulers who overthrow the current king and then govern for relatively short periods of time (16:8-20). Though a date is difficult to determine with absolute accuracy, Omri comes to power between 885 and 880 B.C., fights other leaders for several years, and only has total control of Northern Israel for about seven years (16:21-23). Despite this short reign, Omri achieves a great deal. He stabilizes the government and builds a capital city called Samaria (16:24). His son Ahab succeeds him so his descendants may govern Northern Israel for some time. Omri arranges a marriage between Ahab and Jezebel, the king of Tyre's daughter, bringing peace between these neighbor nations (16:31). Indeed, Omri is so impressive a king that other countries called Northern Israel "The house of Omri" long after his death.[2]

Nowhere is the difference between the perspective of secular history and 1 and 2 Kings more apparent than in their opinions of Omri.[3] Secular history portrays him as an able and effective monarch. In contrast, 1 Kings 16:25-26 denounces him for practicing Jeroboam's illegitimate religion. Thus, his idolatry overshadows everything else he accomplishes and merely helps hasten the death of the nation. Despite this negative assessment, or perhaps because of it, Omri's sons' careers dominate the story until 2 Kings 10.

Even before the text describes the events of Ahab's reign, the author says Ahab "did more evil in the eyes of the Lord than any of those before him" (16:30, NIV). Why is he so evil? First, he continues to perpetuate Jeroboam's religion (16:31). Second, Ahab marries Jezebel of Tyre, a woman who worships Baal (16:31). Third, he spreads Baal worship (16:32-33). All these sins bring Northern Israel closer to ruin.

God responds to Ahab's sin by sending a prophet to oppose him. This strategy unfolded in a smaller way when Ahijah and the unnamed prophet confronted Jeroboam (1 Kings 13—14). Now, however, the conflict between the king and Yahweh's prophets controls the plot. Elijah, Micaiah, and Elisha withstand Ahab and his sons until no one from Omri's family rules Northern Israel.

Elijah bursts on the scene in 17:1. Because of Ahab's sins, the prophet says there will be no rain "except at my word" (17:1, NIV). During this drought, God provides for Elijah through miraculous means (17:5-6) and through the hospitality of a widow (17:7-17). Elijah demonstrates his prophetic powers by multiplying the widow's food sources (17:14-16) and raising her son from the dead (17:17-23). This last miracle causes the woman to declare, "Now I know that you are a man of God, and the word of God in your mouth is true" (17:24). Her words echo Moses' standards for a prophet: doing God's work and speaking God's word accurately (Deut. 18:14-22). Elijah qualifies as a God-sent prophet on both counts.

Three years of drought pass, and the resulting famine becomes severe (18:1-2). Finally, Elijah meets with Ahab, who calls the prophet the "troubler of Israel" (18:17). Elijah says the king—not the prophet—troubles Israel, because Ahab and his father have rejected God and served Baal (18:18). To illustrate God's power and Baal's nonexistence, Elijah proposes a cosmic duel. He and Baal's prophets will pray on Mount Carmel. Whichever deity answers with fire from heaven is sovereign (18:19-24) and deserves to be worshiped. The king and people agree to this contest.

Four hundred and fifty prophets of Baal—all supported and fed by Jezebel (18:19)—oppose Elijah. They place a bull on an altar and ask Baal to consume it. For half a day they pray, shout, and dance (18:25-26). Baal does not answer. Now Elijah taunts his foes. He suggests that Baal may be asleep, or busy, or even using the bathroom (18:27).[4] They respond with even more frenzied activity, including cutting themselves with knives. This lasts until late afternoon (18:28-29), but no answer comes.

Elijah takes over. He has the altar soaked with water three times (18:30-35). If fire falls from heaven, it will have to burn up a soggy sacrifice. Next, he prays that God will prove His power and vindicate Elijah's ministry (18:36-37). Without delay, fire descends from heaven, burns the sacrifice, scorches the earth, and evaporates the water (18:38). In response, the people confess that the Lord is God (18:39). Baal, who supposedly rules nature and makes crops grow, has been proven a fraud. Elijah directs the people to kill Baal's prophets (18:40). Having achieved this victory, Elijah now predicts rain (18:41-45). God controls all of nature. Only Yahweh can cause rain or drought. Baal has no power at all.

Needless to say, Jezebel does not appreciate the death of her prophets, so she threatens Elijah's life. Jezebel must have been a powerful and resolute woman, for her threat causes Elijah to run deep into the desert. He has gotten fire from heaven, but he is afraid of the queen (19:3-8). Elijah eventually hides in a cave and complains to God about his situation (19:10). Yahweh promises to protect him and gives him three tasks. He must anoint Hazael king of Syria, Jehu king of Israel, and Elisha to be prophet in his place (19:15-17). Once Elijah emerges from the cave, he does make Elisha his successor (19:19-21). Elisha eventually performs the other tasks.

Syria, a northern neighbor, wages war constantly against Ahab and his successors. God allows Ahab to defeat Syria and its king Ben-Hadad (20:1-31). Like Saul, however, Ahab spares the enemy king (20:32-34). A prophet condemns this action as detrimental to the people's future (20:35-43). He also predicts that the Syrians will someday kill the king (20:42). Even when God blesses Ahab, the king refuses to obey the Lord.

A naked act of oppression causes Yahweh to remove Ahab and Jezebel. Ahab wants to buy a field, but the owner refuses to sell (21:1-3). The king goes home and pouts (21:4). Jezebel discovers why he is sulking and moves into action. She gets him the land by hiring some men to tell lies about the owner, then has him executed (21:7-14). The owner dead, Jezebel takes the field (21:15-16). Such actions were not unusual for foreign kings, but Israel's rulers were supposed to act differently. Israel's land belonged to the twelve tribes (Josh. 13—

21), not to kings. Elijah tells Ahab that this murder will be punished. Ahab and Jezebel will die where their victim died, and dogs will lick up their blood (21:19). What is more, Ahab's descendants will be cut off (21:20-24). His deeds have led to this awful punishment (21:25-26). He repents, so God postpones the punishment (21:28-29); but Jezebel offers no apology.

Three years pass before the first part of Elijah's prophecy against Ahab and Jezebel comes true. For once, both halves of Israel decide to fight together, this time against Syria (22:1-3). Ahab's fellow king, Jehoshaphat, asks Ahab to consult the prophets before they go to war. Four hundred false prophets tell the rulers they will win the battle (22:4-6). Jehoshaphat remains unconvinced, so Ahab sends for Micaiah, a true prophet imprisoned (22:8-9) for opposing Ahab. Micaiah predicts disaster for Israel and death for Ahab (22:10-17), accusing the other prophets of being liars (22:18-28). Ahab disguises himself in battle but dies nonetheless (22:29-40). The words of God's prophets never fail.

Jehoshaphat and Ahab are very different kinds of men. Ahab expands baalism, while Jehoshaphat rids "the land of . . . male shrine prostitutes" (22:46, NIV). Jehoshaphat values the opinions of the prophets, but Ahab asks them to tell him what he wants to hear. Neither man eliminates the local shrines, the "high places." Therefore, though one man harms Israel more than the other, both contribute to the nations' ultimate downfalls.

The prophets continue to play a major role in the plot during 2 Kings, where Elisha replaces Elijah as God's most prominent representative. After predicting Ahab's successor's (Ahaziah) death (2 Kings 1), Elijah himself goes to heaven in a chariot of fire (2:11-12). Before this event, however, Elisha asks to receive a "double portion" of Elijah's spirit, a request God grants (2:9-10). Thus, God will enable him to perform even more miracles than Elijah, a man who has earned a reputation as one of Israel's greatest prophets. In fact, as centuries passed, Elijah became the *model* for godly prophets (compare Mal. 4:1-6). How, then, will Elisha demonstrate this "double portion" of power?

As the story unfolds, Elisha performs an amazing variety of miracles. The wonders have practical, personal, physical, political, and military value. For example, Elisha heals water (2:19-21), helps a widow pay her debts by multiplying oil she sells (4:1-7), feeds a large crowd with only a few loaves of bread (4:38-44), and makes a lost axhead float (6:1-7). All these actions have very practical, everyday implications. His most famous personal miracle occurs when he calls bears out of the woods to maul some young men who insult him (2:23-25). He also heals other people, as when he raises a friend's son from the dead (4:8-36) and cleanses the Syrian Naaman's leprosy (5:1-26).

Elisha's political and military miracles typically either help rescue Northern Israel from an enemy or appoint a new ruler for Northern Israel or Syria. These incidents prove once more that Yahweh rules history. Whether in the case of the Moabite rebellion (3:1-27), the trapping of the Syrian army (6:8-23), or the unusual defeat of Syria (6:24—7:20), the prophet creates military victories caused by Yahweh's power. Similarly, his prediction that Hazael will succeed Ben-Hadad as king of Syria (8:7-15) and his anointing of Jehu to destroy Omri's final descendants (9:1-13) demonstrate God's rule over rulers. God's prophet simply conveys the Lord's decisions.

Without question, Elisha proves a worthy successor of Elijah. God used these men to encourage Israel to repent. They validate their claim to speak for God by performing extraordinary acts. Although Elijah captured the imaginations of more later readers than Elisha, in many ways Elisha's career surpasses his. Future biblical prophets follow their examples, especially in the messages they preach.

About ten years after Ahab's death, Omri's descendants cease ruling Northern Israel, just as Elijah had promised (1 Kings 21:17-22). In 842 B.C. Elisha appoints Jehu, Northern Israel's army commander, king (9:1-13). Jehu immediately kills both the king of Northern Israel (Joram) and the king of Southern Israel (Ahaziah; 9:14-29). Next, he orders Jezebel slain, who remains proud and defiant to the end (9:30-37). Then, he slaughters all the remaining descendants of Omri (10:1-17). Finally, he lures the priests of Baal to a temple and executes them all (10:18-27). Thus, Omri's house finally falls. Jehu does not worship idols, yet he does not follow the Lord's law carefully either (10:28-31). Spiritually speaking, an idolatrous king has been replaced by a lukewarm follower of Yahweh. Destruction still awaits both kingdoms.

Seven decades (about 885-815 B.C.) unfold between Omri's rise to power and Jehu's death. During these years both halves of Israel fail to serve God wholeheartedly. Northern Israel worships Baal. They also continue to practice Jeroboam's religion. Led by Omri's family, the nation sinks farther into sin and, therefore, moves closer to punishment. Southern Judah does not transgress as much but still tolerates idolatry. Not even God's prophets can stop this moral decay.

2 Kings 11—17: The Decline and Fall of Northern Israel

Northern Israel's descent towards exile now quickens. Four of Jehu's descendants govern after him. None of them serve Yahweh fully, for not one turns from "the sins of the house of Jeroboam"

(13:6; 14:11,24; 15:9). The third of these kings, Jeroboam II, enjoys military and economic success (14:28). First and Second Kings' author, though, assesses him by spiritual standards. He fails in this area. To punish Northern Israel, and perhaps to warn them of coming defeats, God allows Syria to oppress them (13:3; 14:26-27). They get some relief (13:10-25) but no lasting victory.

Five more kings serve before Northern Israel's destruction in 722 B.C. The first, Shallum, is assassinated by Menahem, who replaces him (15:13-16). During Menahem's ten-year reign, Assyria becomes a major threat to the whole region. Coming from present-day Iraq, the Assyrians marched overland towards Israel about 740 B.C.[5] Led by Tiglath-Pileser III (745-727),[6] this fierce army threatened all of Palestine and even Egypt. To remove this threat, Menahem pays Tiglath a huge sum to stay away (15:19-20). This respite proves temporary. The Assyrians remain a threat to Northern Israel's safety.

After an uneventful two-year reign, Pekahiah is murdered by Pekah (15:23-26).[7] Assyria again threatens the nation, and this time the king refuses to pay them to leave. Therefore, Tiglath conquers portions of Northern Israel, then deports some Jews to Assyria (15:29). The covenant curses of Deuteronomy 27—28 have begun to take effect. Parts of Israel have gone into exile. Still, time remains for repentance. The whole nation does not have to disappear. God continues both to punish Israel and allow room for mercy and forgiveness.

Unfortunately, Northern Israel refuses to seek God. Hoshea becomes their last king when he assassinates Pekah (15:30). His nine-year tenure leads to religious and political disaster. He continues Pekah's policy of not cooperating with Assyria (17:4). Therefore, Shalmaneser V, Assyria's king, attacks Northern Israel and lays siege to Samaria (17:5). Shalmaneser dies before Samaria surrenders, so in 722 B.C. Sargon finishes the conquest. Many Jews are killed and enslaved. Others are deported to Assyria (17:6).

Everything Moses and the prophets have warned about has come true. Israel's idolatry (17:8-12), disregard of the covenant and of the prophets (17:13-15), and participation in pagan religious rites (17:16-17) have angered God (17:18). The ten northern tribes cease to function as a nation (17:18). Judah and Benjamin will soon join their relatives in exile, since they are no more righteous than the north (17:19-20). Once more, the prophets' predictions prove true (17:23). Political mistakes were made, of course, but the spiritual errors cause Northern Israel's downfall. Again, 1 and 2 Kings present Yahweh as the Lord of history and the covenant God of Israel.

From 812-722 B.C., Judah has slightly better leadership than Northern Israel. For example, Joash repairs the temple (12:1-18).

His son, Amaziah, also does "right in the eyes of Yahweh" (14:3), though both men fail to remove the places outside Jerusalem where sacrifices are made. Other kings, though, are like those in Northern Israel. For instance, Ahaz worships idols (16:2-4) and robs the temple to pacify the Assyrians (16:8-18). Judah's death takes longer but is as certain as Northern Israel's.

2 Kings 18—25: The Decline and Fall of Southern Israel

Before Southern Israel (Judah) disintegrates, however, two significant kings try to lead religious renewal. The first king is Hezekiah, who, though estimates vary, probably reigned about 715-687 B.C.[8] The author of 1 and 2 Kings gives him almost unqualified praise. Hezekiah's faith is like David's, for he worships only Yahweh and destroys all idols (18:3-5). He obeys Moses' law (18:6). Because of this faithfulness, God blesses him in many ways.

Early in his reign Hezekiah abandons his father Ahaz's policy of paying tribute money to Assyria (v. 7). Assyria leaves Jerusalem alone when they destroy Northern Israel (18:9-12); however, they return eight years later because he withholds the money (v. 14); so the Assyrians attack and capture all the nation's fortified towns except Jerusalem (18:13). Hezekiah then decides to send payment again. Like Ahaz, he strips the temple to get enough silver and gold to buy off his enemy (18:13-16).

This concession does not fully satisfy Assyria's king. He sends an army to Jerusalem and demands surrender (18:17). The Assyrians even claim Yahweh has sent them (18:22-23). Fearing all is lost, Hezekiah goes to the temple to pray (19:1). He also sends his aides to get Isaiah the prophet's advice (19:2-4). The king asks the Lord to defeat the Assyrians, but he bases his request on concern for God's honor (18:14-19). Much like David before his encounter with Goliath, Hezekiah asks that those who abuse God's name be humbled. Isaiah gives Yahweh's startling answer. Sennacherib, Assyria's king, will hear a rumor, leave Jerusalem, and die at home (19:5-7). God keeps this promise by killing 185,000 Assyrian soldiers at night (19:35-36), causing Sennacherib to withdraw. Assassins murder him in Assyria (19:37). Yet another prophet has mediated Yahweh's control of world events.

Only one episode mars Hezekiah's career. After God heals him of a serious illness (20:1-11), the king of Babylon sends some envoys to ask about Hezekiah's health (20:12). Hezekiah shows them everything in his palace and kingdom (20:13). When they leave, Isaiah tells the king that Babylon will conquer Jerusalem someday (20:14-

18). This threat reminds readers one more time that all Israel will eventually go into exile.

Two evil kings precede Israel's last good king. Manasseh, though Hezekiah's son, leads the people to worship many idols (21:1-3). He also puts altars "to all the starry hosts" (21:3, NIV) in the temple courts, engages in occult practices, and offers human sacrifice (21:4-7). Obviously, he breaks Moses' law (21:8). Prophets warn him, then state that his actions confirm God's decision to destroy Israel for its sins (21:10-15). Unfortunately, this poorest of all kings rules fifty-five years (21:1), the longest tenure in the country's history. Amon follows him but only lasts two years. Then Amon's eight-year-old son takes his place (21:19-26).

Josiah governs in Jerusalem for thirty-one years (about 640-609). Others run the government while he is a child. When he becomes an adult, though, he makes his own decisions. He decides to serve Yahweh and to lead his people to do the same, so he has the temple repaired (22:3-7). During this effort the high priest finds a copy of "the Book of the Law" (22:8, NIV). When he hears the law, Josiah realizes that God must be ready to punish Israel (22:9-13). Perhaps he heard at least part of Deuteronomy 27—28. He consults a prophetess, Huldah, who tells him the nation will perish but that the disaster will occur after his death (22:15-20).

While he lives, Josiah directs a vigorous religious reform movement in Jerusalem. As Joshua had done, Josiah leads the nation in a covenant renewal ceremony (23:1-3). He stops idol worship, removes the pagan altars from the temple area, desecrates the high places, and destroys sites used for human sacrifice and astrology (23:4-14). Witches and spiritists cease to function (23:24). He also defiles Jeroboam's old altar, directly fulfilling the unnamed prophet's earlier prediction (1 Kings 13:2-3). Perhaps most significantly, he orders the people to observe the Passover, a much-neglected festival (23:21-23). Without question, Josiah is the greatest reformer the nation ever produced. The writer of 1 and 2 Kings finds no fault with his life and work.

Josiah dies tragically in 609 B.C. In 612 B.C., Egypt's king passes through Judah to fight Babylon and nip their relentless onslaught in the bud. Babylon defeated Assyria, thus replacing them as the region's most powerful oppressor. Josiah marches against Egypt but is killed (23:29-30). Israel's last great hope for staving off exile can no longer save the people. Judgment is now inevitable.

A series of ineffective and irreligious kings follow Josiah. Jehoahaz serves for only three months before the Egyptians put their own puppet king, Jehoiakim, on the throne (23:31-35). Jehoiakim reigns eleven years (609-598) and merely continues the slide into sin and punishment (23:36-37). He is forced to serve Babylon and give them tribute money. When he refuses for a time, the Babylonians oppress Israel (24:1-6). This episode is just a hint of what is to come. After Jehoiakim's death, Jehoiachin governs for three months before the Babylonians replace him with Zedekiah (24:8-17). Clearly, Israel's government has become unstable because of constant pressure from Babylon.

Zedekiah acts as Israel's last king (597-587). He serves Babylon quite obediently for nearly a decade but finally rebels (24:18-20). His action constitutes political suicide. Babylon's army surrounds Jerusalem, cuts off all food and water, and eventually takes the city (25:1-4). Zedekiah is forced to watch the Babylonians kill his sons, then has his eyes gouged out (25:7). Jerusalem's walls are toppled; the temple is looted, then burned (25:8-17). Many Israelites are led to exile in Babylon (25:18-21).

This defeat completes the loss of the promised land. What Joshua won and David developed, Israel has now lost. Abraham's heirs have lost their land because they broke their covenant with the Lord. God delayed punishment as long as possible. The people have no one but themselves to blame for this catastrophe.

Does Israel have any hope for the future? The text suggests that they do. Thirty-seven years after his exile, Jehoiachin receives special honor in Babylon (25:27-30). Though only a brief passage, this story suggests that God is not finished with Israel. Promises made to Abraham and David remain in effect. Hope lives, even in exile. It will take the rest of the Old Testament, though, to explain how these promises are kept.

Conclusion

Our study of what happens in the Old Testament is now complete. We know how human sin led to God's promises to Abraham and how those promises structure the Pentateuch. Further, we have seen how Israel's covenant breaking causes them to lose the land. Finally, we have discovered a new promise, this time to David. In the midst of losing the land, Israel received a pledge of an eternal kingdom (2 Sam. 7:1-17). Promise, fulfillment, despair, and hope have intertwined. As we move on to the Latter Prophets and the Writings, all these elements of the Old Testament story will grow in importance. They are also the keys to reading the remaining books with understanding.[9]

Questions for Reflection

1. Explain several ways that Solomon's activities break the Sinai covenant.
2. Why is idolatry such a serious offense in Kings?
3. Describe the importance of the prophets' work in Israel's history.
4. List the three most significant kings in Israel's history and explain why you think they are important. Do your choices agree with the author of 1 and 2 Kings?
5. Do you consider 1 and 2 Kings depressing books? Do they find any redeeming value in Israel's history?

Notes

1. Gerhard von Rad, *Studies in Deuteronomy,* trans. David Stalker (London: SCM Press, 1963), 78-81.

2. John Bright, *A History of Israel,* 2d ed. (Philadelphia: Westminster, 1972), 237.

3. Bright, 237-38.

4. This interpretation of 18:27 agrees with a number of scholars who believe "gone on a journey" is a euphemism.

5. Mordechai Cogan and Hayim Tadmor, *2 Kings* (New York: Doubleday, 1988), 14.

6. Tiglath rules Assyria during these years.

7. According to 2 Kings 15:27, Pekah rules twenty years. This figure probably includes several years that he ruled in Gilead before governing the whole nation.

8. Compare Cogan and Tadmor, 15-16, but note Bright's opposing position, 277 and following.

9. See the following commentaries for further study: Richard Nelson, *First and Second Kings,* Interpretation (Atlanta: John Knox, 1987); John Gray, *I & II Kings,* 2d ed., Old Testament Library (Philadelphia: Westminster, 1970); Simon J. DeVries, *1 Kings,* vol. 12 in *Word Biblical Commentary* (Waco, Tex.: Word Books, 1985); T. R. Hobbs, *2 Kings,* vol. 13 in *Word Biblical Commentary* (Waco, Tex.: Word Books, 1985).

THE ASSYRIAN EMPIRE
Black Sea
Sinope
Tieum
CIMMERIANS
Byzantium
Chalcedon
Astacus
Abydos
Cyzicus
PHRYGIA
Gordion
TUBAL
Kanish
MESHECH
Lesbos
Sardis
LYDIA
Samos
Miletus
Phaselis
Taurus Mountains
CILICIA
Tarsus
RHODES
CRETE
CYPRUS
Mediterranean (Western) Sea
URARTU
Lake Van
Lake Urmia
Tabriz
Caspian Sea
Meshed
ASSYRIA
MEDIA
Iranian Desert
Dur Sharrukin
Nineveh
Haran
Gozan
Carchemish
Calah (Nimrud)
Asshur
Tigris River
Nuzi
Arpad
Aleppo
Qarqar
Hamath
Arvad
Euphrates River
Akkad?
Rhagae
Herat
Ecbatana
Kashan
Isfahan
Yazd
Sippar
Cuthah
Babylon
Borsippa
BABYLONIA
Nippur
Larsa
Erech
Ur
CHALDEANS
ELAM
Susa
Kerman
Persepolis
Tadmor
SYRIA
PHOENICIA
Sidon
Tyre
Damascus
Samaria
Jerusalem
AMMON
MOAB
EDOM
Raphia
Brook of Egypt
Kadesh Barnea
Sela
Elath
Pelusium
Sais
Tanis
Migdol
Bubastis
On
Memphis
EGYPT
Herakleopolis
Hermopolis
Siut
Abydos
Thebes
Syene (Elephantine)
ETHIOPIA
Red Sea
Dumah
Arabian Desert
Tema
Dedan
Persian Gulf
SCALE OF MILES
0 100 200 300
SCALE OF KILOMETERS
0 100 200 300 400 500

Part III
The Prophets

Introduction

Human beings love to ask: Why? Small children raise this question constantly as they grow. Young people seek reasons for accepting traditional beliefs. Adults also ask: Why? They do this especially when tragedy strikes. Israel's prophets predict, then experience, their country's horrible destruction. Thus, they ask several questions about this tragedy. Why does this punishment happen? Why are wicked countries like Assyria and Babylon allowed to defeat God's people? Why do the people refuse to follow Yahweh? Why must the righteous suffer with the wicked?

These are logical questions, since 1 and 2 Kings offer fairly general reasons for Israel's downfall. Those books claim idolatry causes God to punish the people and focus on how the kings lead the nation into sin. The prophets appear, of course, but their impact on the last two centuries of Israel's history is not explained fully. In Isaiah, Jeremiah, Ezekiel, and the Twelve (Minor Prophets), the prophets denounce Israel's sin in great detail. They warn the nation to change. They counsel kings. Despite all the tragedies they experience, though, they also envision a great future for Israel and their enemies. In short, 1 and 2 Kings offer a broad analysis of Israel's downfall while the Prophets give the topic extensive treatment.

Who were the prophets? What were their main tasks? Two Hebrew words for *prophet* help answer these questions. The first term *ro'eh* means "seer" and indicates that prophets could "see" things other people missed. They could "see" how the future would unfold based on what the covenant taught. Chiefly, they could "see" that Assyria and Babylon would conquer Northern and Southern Israel if the people did not repent.

The second word *nabi'* means "to bubble forth." It probably means the prophets had urgent messages that spilled out of them. These messages were usually about contemporary evils. The prophets tell Israel to keep the covenant. They stress kindness to the poor and helpless, justice in the courts, and loyalty to marriage vows.

A careful reading of Old Testament prophecy indicates that the vast majority of time the prophets speak about everyday matters. Perhaps as much as 90 percent of prophecy deals with moral problems we still face today. Only 10 percent (or so) of prophecy predicts the future. Most of these predictions, such as the birth of Jesus, have already been fulfilled. Therefore, it is best to read prophecy as warnings against sin, rather than as blueprints for the future. The prophets do speak of the end times, but it is most certainly not their main emphasis.

Introduction to Reading Prophecy

Most readers need some help to understand prophecy. After all, stories are fairly rare in these books. Poetic speeches replace prose narratives as the main type of writing. Characters appear, yet have different functions than those in Genesis—2 Kings. Still, many of the themes from the Law and Prophets remain. Too, readers know the historical events the prophets discuss. Most importantly, the covenant remains the basis of God's relationship to Israel. Therefore, many readers do have to learn some new skills to grasp prophecy, but they already possess knowledge that makes the process easier. Themes, characters, and historical events still create interesting plots.

B. D. Napier notes seven themes that dictate action and argumentation in prophecy. These concepts emerge from Israel's history. He claims the prophets teach "that Israel now stands between Egypts, that what she was she will be again."[1] God chooses and saves Israel, judges their sin, but plans to redeem them once more. So a constant cycle, much like the one in Judges, emerges in prophetic literature from the following concepts:

1. "Thus says Yahweh": Word and symbol
2. "Out of Egypt I called my son": Election and covenant
3. "They went from me": Rebellion
4. "They shall return to Egypt": Judgment
5. "How can I give you up?": Compassion
6. "I will return them to their homes": Redemption
7. "A light to the nations": Consummation[2]

These ideas can be compressed into three main emphases: sin, punishment, and restoration. Each naturally follows the other. God has loved and redeemed Israel, so the Lord sends the prophets to condemn Israel for breaking the Mosaic covenant. God has been faithful, but the people are corrupt and ungrateful. Therefore, as Deuteronomy 27—28 warns, Israel is punished by going into exile.

God waits before allowing Assyria and Babylon to conquer Israel. Though the people are given time to repent, only a few ever change. Judgment comes, then, because of the nation's stubbornness, not God's harshness. Despite this rebellion, however, Yahweh promises to restore the nation.

Sin, punishment, and restoration crisscross the prophetic literature, helping the reader follow the text's argument. When confused, one can normally determine which of these three ideas is being stressed and understand the book again. When most readers learn to recognize these fundamental notions, they begin to enjoy prophecy.

Most scholars stress the sin and punishment aspects of prophecy. This tendency is legitimate, since the prophets do constantly expose Israel's covenant breaking and its consequences. However, it is important to remember that God always punishes as a last resort and only to create a brighter future for Israel's faithful. All three themes are necessary to the prophets' preaching about Israel's covenant with Yahweh.

Prophecy's story line closely parallels Israel's history. For example, Isaiah and Jeremiah warn the people of the coming Assyrian and Babylonian invasions brought on by national sin. Both men observe, and Jeremiah experiences, the punishment of Israel's refusal to repent. Ezekiel dreams of Israel's return to their homeland. Hosea—Micah chronicles Israel's sin. Nahum, Habakkuk, and Zephaniah describe the sin's punishment. Haggai, Zechariah, and Malachi participate in Israel's restoration. History and literature merge in these and other ways in the books.

Five important characters appear in prophecy: God, the prophets, the remnant, the rebels, and the nations. Obviously, God is the major character. Yahweh acts as father, king, lover, friend, or judge, depending on the main theme a book is presenting. The prophets themselves interact with the Lord and convey God's messages to the people. Sometimes the prophets obey God perfectly; at other times they resent God's demands on their lives. Israel splits into two separate groups. One, the faithful remnant, keeps the covenant and honors Yahweh. The other, the rebels, constantly breaks virtually every covenant command. Finally, the nations outside Israel constitute a character group. Normally, they threaten Israel's future. Despite their harsh activities, however, God includes them in the restoration to come. How these characters relate to one another helps reinforce prophecy's emphasis on sin, punishment, and restoration.

As the introductory chapter in this book states, most prophecy is written in poetry. Three kinds of poetry are common: synonymous, antithetical, and synthetic.[3] In the first, the author states an idea in one line, then reemphasizes the same idea in the next line. For instance, Isaiah 1:2 says, "Hear, O heavens! / Listen, O earth!" Such poetry forces the reader to focus on the author's point. Ideas become impossible to avoid. The second type presents opposite but complementary comments in succeeding lines. Isaiah 1:3 reads:

> an ox knows his master,
> the donkey his master's manger,
> but Israel does not know,
> my people do not understand.

Both ideas make the same point: Israel foolishly disobeys God. The last type of poetry uses several successive lines to make a point. Isaiah 1:4 cries,

> Alas, sinful nation,
> a people loaded with guilt,
> a brood of evildoers,
> children given to corruption!

Readers are systematically convinced of a truth. One word picture after another assaults the imagination until the awfulness or greatness of the message becomes apparent.

Authors of prophecy develop these poetic forms into a variety of literary forms. Isaiah, Jeremiah, and Zephaniah create dialogues between God, the prophets, and the people. Something like early ancient Greek drama results. Habakkuk uses poetry to describe an interior struggle he has with God. Amos, Hosea, and others forge forceful poetic sermons. Zechariah and Ezekiel present their dreams for Israel's future. Clearly, then, prophetic poetry is dynamic. Once its principles are grasped, readers gain new and exciting insights into ancient and modern life.

Hebrew prophecy interprets Israel's history. It explains *why* the nation fell from the heights of David and Solomon's era to the depths of exile. It thereby warns future generations to avoid the mistakes of the past. At the same time, prophecy fills later generations with hope. Israel's best days lie in the future. Indeed, all nations can anticipate great blessings. Unfortunately, these glorious days will come after terrible punishment. Why God works this way unfolds in Isaiah, Ezekiel, Jeremiah, and the Twelve.[4]

Basic Elements of Prophecy

Books	Isaiah, Jeremiah, Ezekiel, The Twelve
Characters	Yahweh, Prophets, Israel's Faithful, Israel's Disobedient, the Nations
Plot	Israel's history from 742-420 B.C.

Themes	Sin, Punishment, Restoration
Literary Type	Poetry, some Narrative

Notes

1. B. D. Napier, "Prophet," *Interpreter's Dictionary of the Bible,* 5 vols. (Nashville: Abingdon, 1962-76), 3:911.

2. Napier, 910-19.

3. These categories were first suggested by Robert Lowth, *Lectures on the Sacred Poetry of the Hebrews*, trans. G. Gregory (Andover: Codman Press, 1829).

4. For further introduction to prophecy, see Carl E. Armerding, W. Ward Gasque, eds. *A Guide to Biblical Prophecy* (Peabody, Mass.: Hendrickson Publishers, 1989); C. Hassell Bullock, *An Introduction to the Old Testament Prophetic Books* (Chicago: Moody Press, 1986); William A. Vangemeren, *Interpreting the Prophetic Word* (Grand Rapids: Academic Books, 1990); Joseph Blenkinsopp, *A History of Prophecy in Israel* (Philadelphia: Westminster, 1983); Claus Westermann, *Basic Forms of Prophetic Speech,* trans. Hugh Clayton White (Philadelphia: Westminster, 1967); David L. Petersen, *The Roles of Israel's Prophets,* Journal for the Study of the Old Testament Supplement Series 17 (Sheffield, England: JSOT Press, 1981); James M. Ward, *The Prophets,* Interpreting Biblical Texts (Nashville: Abingdon Press, 1982); J. Lindblom, *Prophecy in Ancient Israel* (Philadelphia: Fortress, 1962); Bernhard Lang, *Monotheism and the Prophetic Minority,* The Social World of Biblical Antiquity Series 1 (Sheffield, England: The Almond Press, 1983).

Dates of the Prophets*	
Amos	760 B.C.
Hosea	750-725 B.C.
Jonah	750 B.C.
Isaiah	740-687 B.C.
Micah	701 B.C.
Zephaniah	630-620 B.C.
Jeremiah	627-587 B.C.
Nahum	612 B.C.
Habakkuk	610-600 B.C.
Ezekiel	593-571 B.C.
Obadiah	587 B.C.
Haggai	520 B.C.
Zechariah	520 B.C.
Malachi	450 B.C.
Joel	?

* All dates approximate

8
Isaiah: *Prophet of Sin and Salvation*

Plot: Israel's sin causes Yahweh to send Assyria to punish the people. Isaiah predicts the future Babylonian invasion as well. After their punishment, however, Israel will be redeemed by the coming son of David.
Major Characters: Isaiah, Yahweh, Ahaz, Hezekiah, Israel's Remnant, Assyria, and Babylon
Major Events: Isaiah's call, Ahaz's fear of Samaria and Syria, Assyria's invasion of Israel, and Babylon's future invasion of Judah

Introduction

Isaiah lived during the difficult days described in 2 Kings 16—20. While he ministers, Assyria grows in power, conquers Samaria, and seriously threatens Jerusalem. Isaiah confronts King Ahaz for making an alliance with Assyria (7:1-14). He also counsels Hezekiah to trust Yahweh to repel the Assyrians and anticipates the Babylonian invasion (chap. 39). All told, his life and words comment on Israel's history from about 742 to 538 B.C.

Partly because of the Book of Isaiah's fantastic theological and historical scope, scholars debate whether the prophet Isaiah actually wrote the entire prophecy. Though some commentators questioned the book's authorship earlier, intensive discussion of the issue began in the nineteenth century.[1] Numerous writers noted that Isaiah 1—39 focuses on the Assyrian threat while chapters 40—66 emphasize the Babylonian conquest. They also claimed that Jerusalem is intact in 1—39 but destroyed in 40—66. Further, Cyrus, who rules Persia and allows the Jews to return home after 539 B.C., is mentioned by name in Isaiah 44:28 and 45:1. Finally, these scholars believed that the first half of the book stresses sin and punishment, yet the second half promises restoration. These and other reasons led them to suggest two (or more) authors of Isaiah: one who lived about 740 to 700 B.C. and one who lived about 550 to 500 B.C.

Of course, not every scholar accepted this conclusion.[2] Opponents argued that Assyria and Babylon are mentioned in both halves of the book. They noted that Jerusalem is threatened *and* intact in 1—39 and 40—66. As for the mention of Cyrus, they said Isaiah simply predicts Israel's future in these texts. Sin, punishment, and restoration are common prophetic themes, they claimed, so the presence of these ideas in any part of the book would not be unusual.

Old Testament experts continue to research and discuss Isaiah's authorship.[3] Opinions on the topic will doubtlessly continue to be published. As in the matter of the Pentateuch's authorship, first-time readers of the Old Testament need to be aware of the issue. Still, beginning students ought to master the basics of prophetic literature and the content of Isaiah before making decisions about scholarly debates. Scholars on both sides of the issue acknowledge that Isaiah presents a unified message.[4] Students need to examine this message as a first step to further analysis.

Isaiah 1—12: Sin and the Messiah

Like Elijah, Elisha, Micaiah, and the other earlier prophets, Isaiah knows Israel has broken its covenant with God. According to Isaiah, Israel acts like a rebellious child, or stupid animal, because they do not obey the Lord, their maker (1:2-3). Thus, Israel is evil, corrupt, and guilty (1:4). God's people have become like Sodom and Gomorrah (1:10). This immorality has occurred despite the Lord's constant attempts to change their actions (1:5-9,18-20). Every level of society—rich, poor, rulers, or servants—shares the guilt (1:23). What will Yahweh do to correct this situation?

Three courses of action will be taken. First, God will send a day of judgment to punish the people. This "Day of the Lord" will remove sin from the land (2:6-22). Whether referred to as "the last days" (2:2), "that day" (2:11), or "the day of the Lord" (2:12), this event means the same thing. Israel will be devastated (3:1—4:1), its rulers humiliated (5:8-13), and its population deported (5:26-30). Though these divine actions seem harsh, they are only taken after Israel has had time to repent. They will also lead ultimately to Israel's restoration (4:2-6). The "day" will cleanse Israel, leaving a righteous minority called "the remnant" (4:3) to begin anew. Most of the prophets share Isaiah's convictions about the Day of Yahweh.

God's second action is less dramatic, yet very important. Warning always precedes punishment in the Old Testament, so Yahweh chooses prophets to remind the people of their covenant obligations.

Isaiah 6 describes Isaiah's call to ministry. God appears in a vision as seated on a throne attended by angels who declare, "Holy, holy, holy is the Lord of hosts; the whole earth is full of his glory" (6:3, NRSV). Sensing God's purity and greatness, Isaiah realizes his own humanity and sinfulness (6:4-5). When he confesses his sin, God forgives him and explains Isaiah's ministry. The prophet must preach against the nation's sin (6:9-10). He must not, however, expect to convince them to reform (6:11-13). Indeed, Isaiah will preach until only a small portion of Israel remains (6:13). Certainly, he does not relish his task, but he agrees to do as God commands (6:8,11).

Yahweh's third action develops from the promise made to David in 2 Samuel 7:1-17. Eventually, a righteous "son" of David will arise, lead the people to serve God, and end the people's punishment. Isaiah tells Ahaz, a rather inconsistent Davidic descendant, that "the virgin shall conceive and give birth to a son" whose presence will mean God is with the people (7:14). The king receives this amazing promise as a pledge of protection. He fears Samaria and Syria will punish him for supporting Assyria. This child apparently comes from David and Ahaz's family, for Matthew 1:22-23 applies this promise to Jesus' birth. Sometime after Assyria punishes Israel (8:1-10), God will send a person from David's family who will rule in wisdom, power, and peace (9:2-7). Indeed, this individual will initiate an era of unprecedented peace (11:1-9). He will also gather all of Israel's exiles, who will then constitute the remnant that rebuilds the nation (11:10-16). Only this leader can guarantee Israel's future.

Each part of this three-pronged strategy receives major treatment in the other prophetic books. The promise of David's son, though, impacts the whole Bible. As Israel moves closer to destruction, the prophets claim that only this individual can save the nation. Likewise, after destruction the prophets look to this savior to rebuild Israel. Of course, the New Testament teaches that Jesus fulfills Isaiah's predictions about this person, and that Jesus will judge the world on the day of Yahweh. Obviously, then, Isaiah 1—12 contributes a great deal to biblical theology.

Isaiah 13—27: Sin and the Nations

Yahweh rules all nations, according to Isaiah. At times the Old Testament stresses Israel so much that readers forget that, since God created all nations, all peoples are under Yahweh's control. Isaiah 13—27 reminds us that all individuals and countries are accountable to God and that Yahweh loves all nations. Isaiah 13—27 chastens ten nations besides Northern and Southern Israel. Most of these, such as Moab, Edom, and Philistia, are Israel's traditional, neighboring enemies. Others, though, such as Syria, Assyria, and Babylon, appear because they are Israel's most consistently powerful enemies.

God announces Babylon's fate first, followed by Assyria's (chaps. 13—14). Babylon was a significant nation for hundreds of years. From the time of their great law-giving king Hammurabi (variously dated between 1800 and 1500), until Persia conquered them in 539 B.C., the Babylonians maintained a high profile in the ancient world. They were not always militarily powerful but could always rise given the chance. Of course, their most famous deed in Scripture was destroying Jerusalem in 587 B.C. Isaiah predicts both Jerusalem's fall (14:3) and Babylon's defeat (13:17-22). Babylon's oppression of Israel and other nations (14:3-8) and pride (14:13-15) leads to their destruction.

Assyria receives shorter treatment (14:24-27). This mighty conqueror will be crushed (14:25). This is not a new theme. Isaiah has already said that after Assyria smashes Israel (8:1-10) they will be judged by God (10:5-19). Yahweh had sent Assyria to punish sinful countries, yet the punisher turned into a cruel destroyer (10:7). Assyria ceases to be military power after Babylon defeats them in 612 B.C., so Isaiah's prediction comes true.

After predicting that Moab will be decimated "in three years" (16:14), Isaiah turns again to the greatest threats to Israel's security. Syria, Israel's constant foe in 1 and 2 Kings, will disappear. Damascus "will become a heap of ruins" (17:1). Why? Because they have not served the Lord (17:10). Syria had heard Yahweh through Elisha, yet they did not put away their idols.

Ethiopia and Egypt will share Syria's fate. These two lands are linked because an Ethiopian (Cushite) ruler led Egypt during Isaiah's lifetime.[5] God asks Isaiah to perform special acts that portray Cush and Egypt's future. The prophet walks naked and barefoot for three years, which means these nations will go naked and barefoot into exile (20:1-6). This prediction intends to warn Israel against hoping Egypt and Cush will defeat Assyria (20:5-6).

Despite their coming defeat, though, Yahweh has special plans for Cush and Egypt. After the day of the Lord, Ethiopians will worship God in Jerusalem (18:1-7). Even more incredibly, Egypt and Assyria will worship Yahweh together (19:19-23). Indeed, then Israel, Assyria, and Egypt will be equals (19:24). All will be God's people (19:25). Clearly, the day of judgment seeks to restore *all* nations to the Lord. God rules history so salvation can reach all races.

Further messages against Babylon (21:1-10) and Israel (chap. 22) appear next and are joined by condemnations of Edom (21:11-12), Arabia (21:13-17), and Tyre (chap. 23). With Israel and most of its neighbors denounced, Isaiah now summarizes the horrors of judgment day. It will be a day of distress for all people (24:1-3). The earth will dry up and wither, causing great human suffering (24:4-16). It will be, then, a time of terror (24:17-18). God will punish all disobedient peoples (24:21-23).

What will result from this horrible day? The salvation of the just and the restoration of Israel! Isaiah praises God for saving "the poor" and "the needy" (25:4). Further, he thanks Yahweh for restoring Jerusalem and letting the city live in peace (26:1-15). Finally, Isaiah rejoices in the regathering of Israel's exiles from the defeat of 722 B.C. (27:12-13). Clearly, the day of the Lord will ultimately benefit Israel. Salvation can only emerge after sin has been purged from the land. It will also benefit the nations, since only punishment will lead them to accept Yahweh's rule (19:19-25).

Isaiah 28—35: Sin and the Fall of Israel

Yahweh's patience now begins to fade. Despite offers of forgiveness, Northern and Southern Israel continue to refuse to repent. Samaria will soon fall, and Judah is also in danger. Assyria's massive army threatens the whole land. Judah looks to Egypt for help, but their only real ally now is the Lord. Six times Yahweh warns the people of "woes" to come (28:1; 29:1; 29:15; 30:1; 31:1; 33:1). Failure to repent will bring judgment (chap. 34), though this punishment will eventually work to the faithful's advantage (chap. 35).

Northern Israel teeters on the brink of destruction in 28:1-4. Led by drunkards, the nation has no future. The priests have no respect for God's word, which causes them to teach improperly (28:9-10). Political leaders have, likewise, assured the country's downfall. Destruction occurs in 722 B.C.

Jerusalem acts no better. Its leaders have made a "covenant with death" (28:15,18), which probably refers to their pro-Egypt alliance. They think this great killer can kill Assyria. God rejects this notion. Lies, injustice, and improper alliances will be swept "away" on the day of the Lord (28:14-22). Soon Jerusalem will be encircled by enemy armies (29:5). God will deliver them temporarily (29:5-10), but the people still honor the Lord with their mouths, not their hearts (29:13). They commit sins they believe God cannot see (29:15). Such "stubborn children" will not escape discipline (30:1).

Isaiah particularly despises Israel's reliance on Egypt. He warns that trusting in Pharaoh can only lead to disgrace (30:1-5). God alone can defeat Assyria (31:1-9). Only the righteous king introduced in chapters 1—12 can lead the nation back to God (32:1-8). Jerusalem should repent, for Yahweh wants to forgive them (30:18). God wants to give them the covenant blessings outlined in Leviticus 26 and Deuteronomy 27—28 (30:19-26).

Unfortunately, Southern Israel seems determined to repeat Samaria's mistakes. Thus, Judah will be judged along with the other sinful nations (chaps. 33—34). God will destroy the heavens and defeat the world's peoples (34:1-15). Nothing will remain except a small remnant of land and people (34:16-17). These few survivors will return to Jerusalem, rejoicing in the Lord's salvation (35:10). God will strengthen the weak (35:3), encourage the fearful (35:4), open blind eyes (35:5), and heal lame limbs (35:6). It is tragic that only judgment can make such blessings possible.

Isaiah 36—39: Jerusalem's Reprieve

By Isaiah 36, Northern Israel has already fallen. In 701 B.C., Assyria attacks and conquers all Judah's fortified cities (36:1). Only Jerusalem remains, and it is under siege (36:2-3). This situation has already been described in 2 Kings 18—19, so the reader knows what will follow. What is important, then, is to observe how this material fits into Isaiah's overall message. As in 2 Kings, the story demonstrates God's mercy and Hezekiah's good leadership. Jerusalem's deliverance allows the people time to repent.

Besides offering Jerusalem a reprieve from judgment, chapters 36—38 validate Isaiah's earlier predictions about Assyria. After the Assyrians promise to destroy the city (36:4-22), Isaiah reassures Hezekiah (37:1-13) and denounces the enemy (37:21-35). Yahweh then kills 185,000 Assyrian soldiers (37:36-37) and sends Sennacherib home to die (36:38). Punishment has begun to overtake the great conquering power and will continue to do so until Babylon crushes Assyria in 612 B.C.

Some of Isaiah's messages of hope were misunderstood later in Israel's history. When offering Hezekiah hope, Yahweh declares, "I will defend this city and save it, / for my sake and for David my servant's sake!" (37:35). In the next century, during Jeremiah's time, the people claim this promise is unconditional. That is, they believe Jerusalem will never be conquered, no matter what the people do (compare Jer. 7:1-15). This interpretation twists Isaiah's words. He speaks to a specific situation—the Sennacherib crisis. He does not intend to offer comfort to those who disregard God's word.

Chapters 38—39 provide a transition to the next major section of the book. God loves and heals Hezekiah (38:1-22), just as He loves and defends Israel in 37:35-38. When Hezekiah shows the envoys from Babylon his kingdom, though, the issue of Southern Israel's future emerges again. Isaiah says Babylon will destroy Jerusalem someday (39:1-8). The book has offered virtually no hope that the people will repent. Thus, judgment may fall at any time.

Isaiah 40—55: Salvation and the Servant of God

Isaiah 1—39 constantly warns Israel to repent or face exile. At no time does the book describe the actual destruction of Samaria or Jerusalem. By chapter 36, Northern Israel has indeed fallen, but the text does not mention the event. Likewise, chapter 39 predicts Babylon's 587 B.C. victory over Jerusalem, yet the prophecy never depicts this tragedy. Rather, the book presents both nations as exiled in chapters 40—66, then offers comfort to its readers. Comfort emerges from two ideas: the renewal of the nation after the day of the Lord and the work of a "servant of the Lord" who leads the people to serve God.

Isaiah 40 speaks as if the day of Yahweh has already passed. God tells the prophet to "comfort" Israel by telling them they have "received from the Lord's hand double for all [their] sins" (40:1-2, NIV). Yahweh further promises to build a smooth highway for all the exiles who will return home (40:3-5). Isaiah questions these promises. He reminds the Lord that the nation has been reduced to faded grass and ruined flowers because of God's withering wind of punishment (40:6-7). Nonetheless, he hopes in God (40:8). Based on Yahweh's power and goodness (40:9-11), Isaiah tells the people about all who hope in God:

> They will soar on wings like eagles;
> they will run and not be weary,
> they will walk and not faint (40:31).

How will this salvation occur? First, God will send a nation "from the East" to punish Babylon (41:1-4). This threat agrees with earlier statements about Babylon's future (compare 13:1—14:23; 21:1-10). As time passes, Persia becomes the foe from the east. Led by Cyrus the Great, Persia overwhelms Babylon in 539 B.C. The prophecy even identifies Cyrus by name in 44:28 and 45:1. Babylon's demise will signal a new and better day for Israel (41:8-10).

Second, a "servant of God" will arise to bring the nation back to God. This person acts as a spiritual counterpart to Cyrus's political activity. Who is the servant? At first the text calls Israel God's servant (41:8). As the prophecy unfolds, however, the servant passages seem to describe an individual.

Bernhard Duhm notes that at least four major "servant songs," or poems, exist in Isaiah 40—55.[6] Each one contributes to the servant's portrait. Isaiah 42:1-7 describes the servant as one chosen and empowered by God (42:1), humble (42:2), an encourager (42:3-4), a "light to the Gentiles" (42:6), and a healer of the blind (42:7). This person's work is sorely needed, since Israel is spiritually blind (42:18-22). Next, Isaiah 49:1-7 says the servant speaks God's word (49:2), restores Israel to God (49:5), and reaches out to the Gentiles (49:6). This passage follows a series of texts that promise Israel a bright future but that also note the nation's continuing stubbornness (chaps. 43—48).

Two more "songs" reveal that the servant will turn Israel by suffering for the nation. While the nation remains stubborn, the servant preaches God's word (50:4), sustains the weary (50:4), suffers unjustly (50:6), and trusts in Yahweh's salvation (50:8-9). Finally, Isaiah 52:13—53:12 explains how the servant revives the people. The servant bears the nation's sicknesses, sorrows, and sins (53:4-6). Despite great affliction, the servant never opens his mouth (53:7-9). God crushes the servant (53:10), yet promises he will have offspring and "divide spoils" later (53:10-12). These actions lead to glory for Jerusalem (chap. 54). All who are thirsty for spiritual water can now come to God and drink (chap. 55).

The New Testament writers state that the servant songs are pictures of Christ's life, death, and resurrection. For instance, Matthew 12:15-21 claims that Jesus' humility fulfills Isaiah 42:1-4. Paul partly bases his ministry to the Gentiles on 49:6. Most of all, the early church believed 50:4-9 and 52:13—53:12 describe Christ's death. Philip proclaims this viewpoint to the Ethiopian eunuch (Acts 8:32-33). Luke quotes 53:12 to explain why Jesus dies alongside thieves (Luke 22:37). Clearly, early believers used these texts as the foundation for their teachings on the cross.

Israel's salvation in chapters 40—55 parallels its sources for redemption in chapters 1—12. In the earlier passages, the cleansing day of Yahweh and the coming Davidic king constitute the people's means of hope. Similarly, the day of the Lord and the work of the servant redeem Israel in chapters 40—55. Hope seems more certain in chapters 40—55, though, since the defeats of 722 B.C. and 587 B.C. lie in the past. Punishment has already eliminated many wicked people, which paves the way for a better nation led by a better leader.

Isaiah 56—66: Future Glory for God's People

Isaiah continues to offer hope in the book's final chapters. This hope is based on Yahweh's promise of swift salvation for Israel (56:1) and on the Lord's pledge to redeem people from all nations (56:3,6-8). Regardless of race, those who obey God will ascend God's "holy mountain" (56:7). Whoever disobeys, though, can only expect punishment (56:9—57:13). Thus, in chapters 56—66 salvation and hope exist for all who will respond to God's offer of forgiveness.

The choice between repentance and rebellion becomes even more evident as the prophecy continues. For example, in 57:14-21 God declares healing for the "contrite and lowly in spirit" (57:15), but announces, "There is no peace . . . for the wicked" (57:21). How will the people be healed? By mourning and fasting for their sin (58:1-14) and by confessing their injustice, dishonesty, and treachery (59:1-15). Then Yahweh "will come to Zion" (59:20), place God's Spirit in the people (59:21), and glorify Jerusalem as never before (60:1-22). Indeed, God will be the city's "everlasting light" (60:21), and the people will multiply (60:22). Jerusalem will never again appear empty and godforsaken.

If these assurances are not sufficient, the Lord offers further incentives to repent and believe. Some Israelites may feel too weary and discouraged to respond to Yahweh. To empower these hurting people, the Lord pledges good news, healing, freedom, comfort, and joy (61:1-3). The pitiful remnant will look like a radiant bride (61:10). Again using wedding imagery, Yahweh promises to make devastated Jerusalem a beautiful city once more (62:1-12).

How will God achieve such miracles? As in Isaiah 2:6-22, the day of judgment will eliminate Israel's wicked enemies and evil citizens (63:1-6). After this event the righteous remnant of believers will praise God's deeds and rebuild the nation (63:7—64:12). Yahweh will respond by forgetting Israel's sinful past (65:1-10). Those who reject the Lord will be destroyed (65:11-12), while Yahweh's "servants" will receive amazing blessings (65:13-16). In fact, these faithful will enjoy life in a re-created heaven and earth (65:17). The time of perfect peace introduced in Isaiah 11:1-9 will actually occur (65:20-25). Sin, which has marred creation since Genesis 3:1-20, will lose its power.

Isaiah concludes with one last call to decision. Yahweh *will* bless Jerusalem (66:1-2). Those who refuse to accept the offer of forgiveness *will* suffer punishment (66:3-4). It is better for Israel, then, to allow Yahweh to perform this miracle. They should become the citizens of the "new earth" (66:22). Any other decision is foolish with salvation so accessible.

Conclusion

Isaiah is a perfect book to begin the Latter Prophets for a number of reasons. First, it unfolds during the crisis years of Hezekiah's reign, which allows Isaiah to discuss why Northern Israel falls to Assyria. Second, it explores extensively Israel's sin, punishment, and restoration. Thus, prophecy's major themes are introduced. Third, its careful analysis of Israel's sin produces a solid rationale for the nation's judgment. Clearly, Isaiah answers many *why* questions, yet more explanation is needed. In particular, the destruction of Jerusalem itself demands attention.[7]

Questions for Reflection

1. What parts of Isaiah's preaching are meant to encourage the people?
2. What do you learn about Jesus' life and work from Isaiah?
3. What does Isaiah teach about God's sovereignty?

Notes

1. Note S. R. Driver, *An Introduction to the Literature of the Old Testament* (1891; reprint, Gloucester, Mass.: Peter Smith, 1972), 206 *ff.*; G. A. Smith, *The Book of Isaiah*, The Expositor's Bible (New York: Harper, 1928); and John Skinner, *The Book of the Prophet Isaiah*, Century Bible (Cambridge: Cambridge University Press, 1896-98).

2. Note J. A. Alexander, *A Commentary on the Prophecies of Isaiah* (New York: Scribner's, 1846).

3. Note John A. Hayes and Stuart A. Irvine, *Isaiah the Eighth-century Prophet: His Times and His Preaching* (Nashville: Abingdon, 1987), who argue that Isaiah has more than two authors but that chapters 1—33 are all from eighth-century Isaiah.

4. Compare John N. Oswalt, *The Book of Isaiah, Chapters 1—39*, New International Commentary on the Old Testament (Grand Rapids: Wm. B. Eerdmans, 1986); and John D. W. Watts, *Isaiah 1—33,* vol. 24 in *Word Biblical Commentary* (Waco: Word, 1985).

5. Otto Kaiser, *Isaiah 13—39: A Commentary*, trans. R. A. Wilson, Old Testament Library (Philadelphia: Westminster, 1974), 112.

6. Bernhard Duhm, *Das Buch Jesaja* (Göttingen: Vandenhoeck and Ruprecht, 1892).

7. See also Trent C. Butler, *Isaiah*, vol. 10 in *Layman's Bible Book Commentary* (Nashville: Broadman Press, 1982); Page H. Kelley, "Isaiah," in *The Broadman Bible Commentary,* vol. 5 (Nashville: Broadman Press, 1971), 149-374; S. H. Widyapranawa, *The Lord Is Savior,* International Theological Commentary Isaiah 1-39 (Grand Rapids: Wm. B. Eerdmans, 1990); George A. F. Knight, *Servant Theology,* International Theological Commentary, Isaiah 40-55, rev. ed. (Grand Rapids: Wm. B. Eerdmans, 1984); George A. F. Knight, *The New Israel,* International Theological Commentary, Isaiah 56-66 (Grand Rapids: Wm. B. Eerdmans, 1985); Claus Westermann, *Isaiah 40-66,* (Philadelphia: Westminster, 1969).

9
Jeremiah: *Prophet of Sin and Punishment*

Plot: God chooses Jeremiah to announce Southern Israel's sin and ultimate destruction. Not even Jerusalem will survive. Jeremiah often dreads his gloomy task, but he faithfully calls the nation to repentance. After defeat, Israel will someday be restored.
Major Characters: Yahweh, Jeremiah, and Baruch
Minor Characters: Israel's kings—especially Jehoiakim and Zedekiah, Pashur, Hananiah, and Nebuchadnezzar
Major Events: Jeremiah's call, Jeremiah's "temple" sermon, Jeremiah's disputes with God, Jerusalem's fall, and Jeremiah and the people's exile

Introduction

Jeremiah's ministry occurs during difficult and depressing times. Southern Israel—all that remains of united Israel—deteriorates morally and politically. Eventually Babylon conquers the land. Despite all Jeremiah's warnings, the people choose to disobey the Lord. The kings are no better than their subjects. Sadly, Jeremiah is dragged into exile with those he sought to help. Only a few bright spots dot this otherwise gloomy prophecy.

According to 1:1-3, Jeremiah becomes a prophet in 627 B.C. and continues until after Jerusalem's destruction in 587 B.C. Thus he works during the reigns of the following kings:

1. Josiah (640-609), a good king who leads the great reform described in 2 Kings 22 but is killed in battle by Egypt (2 Kings 23:29-30);
2. Jehoahaz (609), who rules only three months before being deposed by Pharaoh;

3. Jehoiakim (609-598), an enemy of Jeremiah, who favors Egypt over Babylon. Babylon takes some young people, including Daniel, into exile in 605 B.C.;
4. Jehoiachin (598-597), who rules only three months before surrendering and being taken captive by the king of Babylon. In 597 B.C. Babylon loots the temple and again carries some Israelites into exile along with Jehoiachin and his family;
5. Zedekiah (597-587), an inconsistent man who seeks Jeremiah's advice yet fails to serve God. The Babylonians capture and destroy Jerusalem in 587 B.C.[1]

Obviously, two conclusions emerge from this list. First, Israel is caught between Babylon and Egypt. These two superpowers use Israel as a battleground. Second, Israel's political situation is chaotic. Changing monarchs leads to diverse policies. Instability results.

Babylon replaces Assyria as Israel's greatest enemy. In 612 B.C., the Babylonians and the Medes capture Nineveh, the Assyrian capital. Assyria regroups and allies itself with Egypt. Babylon defeats both nations at Carchemish in 605 B.C., which makes it the dominant power in the region. Unfortunately, Israel seems always to back the losing army.[2]

Throughout his long career, Jeremiah counsels the people to repent and keep the covenant. Only then can they remain in the land. James Leo Green observes that some form of the word *repent* appears 111 times in the book, and that Jeremiah teaches that repentance will be painful.[3] Despite its painfulness, though, the process of change must take place. Otherwise, God will allow Babylon to overwhelm Jerusalem. Punishment will follow sin unless repentance becomes evident.

Scholars disagree over who wrote Jeremiah and why it is in its present form.[4] Unlike most biblical books, Jeremiah does not unfold in chronological order. Instead, it announces its historical framework in 1:1-3, then "jumps around" according to the theme being stressed. Despite its unusual sequencing, the prophecy has unity of purpose. Because of its odd format, perhaps the following outline will help beginning readers:

1. Jeremiah 1: Introduction to the Prophecy
2. Jeremiah 2—29: Israel's Sin
3. Jeremiah 30—33: Israel's Restoration
4. Jeremiah 34—51: Israel and the Nations' Punishment
5. Jeremiah 52: Conclusion

Seen this way, the book stresses prophecy's main themes: sin, punishment, and restoration. To do so, the book highlights Jeremiah's conflicts with God and his human enemies. Jerusalem's destruction is the event that holds the book together.

Jeremiah 1: Introduction to the Prophecy

Virtually every important aspect of the book appears in this opening chapter. Readers should, then, pay especially close attention to these verses. Jeremiah's historical setting (1:1-3), major themes (1:4-16), and main characters (1:17-19) are all introduced.

Readers often skim introductory passages like 1:1-3 hurriedly, believing the book's message unfolds in later material. By doing so, however, they miss several vital details. First, Jeremiah's hometown and family do not mark him for greatness. Anathoth is a small town in Benjamin, Israel's smallest tribe. Second, his family are priests. If he condemns any religious practices, his own relatives may be displeased. Third, that the "word of the Lord" (1:2) comes to him sets him apart as a faithful preacher of God's word.

Besides these important items, Jeremiah's historical framework emerges in 1:2-3. Though scholars debate the issue,[5] the text says he begins to prophesy in Josiah's thirteenth year, or about 627 B.C. He continues until 587 B.C. when Babylon destroys Jerusalem. Josiah's reform (about 622 B.C.) occurs after Jeremiah's call to ministry, so not even that event changes the people permanently.

Virtually all Jeremiah's preaching concerns events between the defeats of 722 B.C. and 587 B.C. Southern Israel has every opportunity to see what happened to Samaria and change (note 3:8-11), but they never repent. Because the people fail to learn from history, they suffer disgrace and exile.

With Jeremiah's historical context in place, the text now announces its major themes. In 1:4-10, Jeremiah's reluctance to become a prophet becomes apparent. Because of youth and inexperience, he feels he cannot preach (1:6). To reassure him, God says that Jeremiah was born to be a prophet (1:5). Further, Yahweh promises to be with him and will even tell him what to say (1:9). Clearly, God will help him in every aspect of his work. Several times in the story Jeremiah will feel inadequate for his task, and each time the Lord will enable him to continue.

Next, three word pairs introduce the three major aspects of his preaching (1:10). Jeremiah's messages attempt:

> to pluck up and to tear down,
> to destroy and to overthrow,
> to build and to plant (1:10).

The first pair means he will preach against sin, the second that he will announce judgment, and the third that he will promise restoration after punishment. Like all prophets, then, Jeremiah will stress sin, punishment, and restoration. He will do so, however, during a time when punishment means the end of the nation.

Jeremiah's book receives its structure from these three themes. Basically, chapters 2—29 comprise the pluck-up-and-break-down section. The prophet faithfully warns the nation of their sins' consequences. Next, chapters 30—33 discuss the build-and-plant concept. After defeat, Israel will serve the Lord once again. Finally, chapters 34—51 describe killing and destruction quite vividly. Babylon invades the land and eventually subdues it. Like chapter 1, the final chapter is summary in nature.

Where will Jeremiah get the authority to preach these themes? According to 1:11-12, God will be "watching" over the words and make sure they come true. Like a boiling pot, Israel's sins will soon spill over into judgment (1:13-16). Jeremiah can be sure that Israel's enemies will win. Though not a pleasant message, it will be an accurate one. Jeremiah will speak God's word, so he will have God's authority.

Jeremiah will have many enemies who will try to stop his ministry (1:17-19). Indeed, four foes are mentioned: kings, priests, officials, and people (1:18). Though this list seems broad, each category is defined in the book. To encourage the prophet, God declares that Jeremiah is fortified, like iron and bronze, and well able to defeat his enemies (1:18). Yet Yahweh says Jeremiah's struggles with his enemies will be fierce. They will "fight," or make war against him. God even promises to rescue the prophet, which evidently means Jeremiah will suffer some setbacks. Still, God's presence and power will sustain him.

After chapter 1 readers have learned of Jeremiah's prophetic call (1:5), basic message (1:10), and human obstacles to the fulfillment of his task (1:17-19). Jeremiah's fear of his task has also become clear, and God has promised him survival and success. Nothing essential about his life and work remains unexplained. All that is needed is for the career itself to unfold.

Jeremiah 2—29: Israel's Rebellion against God

Jeremiah 2—29 presents a comprehensive picture of Israel's sins. This emphasis begins when God dialogues with the prophet in chapters 2—20. Yahweh convinces Jeremiah that the nation in general deserves punishment and helps the prophet survive the first threats against his life. Then the text shifts to the sins of various specific groups, such as the kings, prophets, and priests in chapters 21—29.

These groups attempt to silence Jeremiah's critical sermons but always fail to do so. Their rank rebellion against God seals Israel's doom.

God carefully instructs Jeremiah before sending him to prophesy. Jeremiah receives at least six basic lessons. First, God says that Israel has broken their covenant with the Lord (2:1—3:5). This claim serves as the basis for all Yahweh's complaints against the people. Israel was once God's devoted "bride" (2:2) but has become a faithless spouse (2:3-4,33). Israel has "changed its gods" (2:11) by forsaking Yahweh to serve idols (2:11-13). These actions constitute spiritual adultery.

Second, the Lord informs Jeremiah that the people have time to repent (3:6—4:4). In fact, Yahweh promises to bless them if they will change (3:6-20). Indeed, the Lord will reunite the divided Northern and Southern kingdoms if the people's faithlessness ceases (3:18-20). Jeremiah himself begs the nation to admit their sins (3:22-25), and God explains that all idols must be removed from the land (4:1-14). Will the people repent?

Third, God warns that a "disaster from the north" will arise to punish Israel's sin (4:5-31). This phrase ultimately refers to Babylon, who will conquer Jerusalem later, though no specific aggressor is named now. The foe "from the north" will be fierce like a lion (4:7), strong like a "scorching wind" (4:11-12), and swift as an eagle (4:13). Israel will have no chance against such a foe. Unless change occurs, Israel will become as "formless" and void as the day the world was created (4:23-26).

Fourth, God states that practically no righteous people are left in the land (5:1-9). All the people, whether powerful or poor, have turned from the covenant (5:3-6). Therefore, Yahweh has every right to punish (5:7-9). Because of such widespread iniquity, God teaches Jeremiah a fifth lesson: the Lord will be avenged (5:10-31). Put another way, lies (5:12,31), blasphemy (5:12), and oppression (5:27-28) cannot go unchecked. God will not destroy Israel completely (5:18), but He must not let them continue to disobey forever.

Finally, Yahweh tells Jeremiah he must be a "tester of metals" (6:1-30). That is, the prophet must determine if the nation ought to be judged. The Lord challenges Jeremiah to "observe and test their ways" (6:27, NIV). According to Yahweh the people are "all hardened rebels" (6:28), and the prophet will soon know if God is correct or overly harsh.

With these lessons in mind, Jeremiah now begins his public ministry in the most public of places—the temple (chap. 7). God instructs Jeremiah to stand at the temple gate and preach repentance (7:1-3). Apparently the people believe God will never allow the temple to be destroyed (7:4). Perhaps they misunderstand Isaiah's earlier promises of hope for Jerusalem (Isa. 37:33-35). Clearly, they act as if God is obligated to protect them no matter what they do.

Jeremiah explodes this false notion. He tells the gathering worshipers that unless they champion the cause of the helpless their religious observances are worthless (7:4-8). Unless they stop their hypocritical ways the temple will be destroyed (7:9-15). God tells the prophet that the people are so far from change there is no need to pray for them (7:16). Judgment is inevitable (7:20). Israel has done these things despite all God has done for them (7:21-26). Therefore, their condemnation is just (7:27-29). The people's reaction to this message appears in chapter 26, but now no protest is recorded.

After the nation's idolatry and rejection of the law (7:30—8:17), God warns Jeremiah that he will soon face persecution. The prophet mourns for the people and their sin (8:18—9:2), but the people plot against him (9:3-6). Jeremiah must not even trust friends and family. Everyone will oppose him, just as 1:17-19 promised.

Undaunted, or perhaps unbelieving, Jeremiah continues his work. He claims that Israel's problems stem from their Baal worship and disregard of the Lord's law (9:7-16). Death will overtake the people, he says (9:17-24). Other wicked nations will perish as well (9:25—10:22). Strangely, Jeremiah seems to think Israel's neighbors are worse sinners than the Jews (10:23-25). He has yet to see, or experience, the depths of his own people's wickedness.

Finally, Jeremiah faces Israel's opposition. Once more he discusses the people's covenant breaking (11:1-17). This time, though, the people respond. His own hometown plots to take his life (11:18-20). His neighbors demand he stop preaching or they will kill him (11:21-23). Angered, Jeremiah predicts that Anathoth will be totally destroyed (11:23).

Because of this life-threatening episode, Jeremiah complains to God about his pain (12:1-4). This text is the first of five "confessions" Jeremiah offers about his ministry (compare 11:18—12:6; 15:10-21; 17:14-18; 18:18-23; 20:7-18).[6] Here he confesses his confusion about God's justice. How can Yahweh allow the wicked to harass him (12:1-2)? How long will they go unpunished (12:3-4)?

God answers rather roughly. If Jeremiah falters during such *easy* times, how can he survive the tougher days ahead (12:5)? Then, in a softer tone, God reminds Jeremiah of earlier warnings (compare 9:3-6 and 12:6). The prophet must expect hard times. Further, Yahweh asks him to get God's perspective on Israel. The Lord's family (Israel) has rebelled as well (12:7-13). Both characters have unfaithful families. God must punish Israel, then restore them in the distant future (12:14-17).

This first crisis past, Jeremiah continues to minister. God asks him to use symbolic acts and word pictures to explain Israel's situation. Yahweh instructs him to put a linen belt in a crevice in some rocks (13:1-5). Of course, the belt gets ruined, pointing out that God will ruin Israel (13:1-11). Following this episode, the Lord has Jeremiah speak of wineskins, which leads to a declaration that the people will soon act like drunkards (13:12-14). This means they will lose all common sense and leadership ability. They will thereby disintegrate as a nation. Military defeat will result (13:15-27).

A second crisis emerges when a drought devastates the land (14:1-6). Jeremiah prays for the people and even confesses their sins (14:7-9). Yahweh responds that the people are not repentant. Their sacrifices are empty gestures. Therefore, Jeremiah does not need to pray for them (14:10-12). Jeremiah protests. He blames lying prophets for Israel's woes (14:13). God agrees the prophets are part of the problem, yet He also notes the nation's transgressions (14:14-17).

Jeremiah simply cannot accept God's position. He prays again, hoping Yahweh will relent (14:19-22). God assures Jeremiah Israel's woes are not his fault. He is a good prophet, but not even Moses or Samuel could change the people now (15:1). Death, starvation, and deportation await Israel (15:2-9).

An even more serious exchange follows. Jeremiah laments the fact that he was ever born (15:10). He accuses Yahweh of not keeping some basic promises. God has not protected him, despite his own faithfulness (15:10-17). Indeed, he says his pain is continuous and his wounds incurable (15:18). God has become "like a deceptive brook, / like a spring that fails" (15:18, NIV). Certainly this second confession is more biting than the first.

God responds in a way calculated to correct and restore the prophet. First, he warns Jeremiah to repent of this rebellious and spiteful attitude (15:19). God never told him his life would be easy (note 1:17-19; 9:3-6). Second, Yahweh counsels him to be *Yahweh's* spokesman, which means he must not take the people's side against the Lord (15:19). Third, God promises to deliver him out of all his troubles (15:20). Fourth, God reassures him of His presence (15:20). Yahweh will never leave him unprotected (15:21).

More hard times lead to a third crisis and confession. God tells Jeremiah, "You must not marry and have sons or daughters in this place" (16:2, NIV). Further, he must not attend a funeral, nor may he attend a wedding (16:5-9). Why does Yahweh make such odd demands? Primarily because Israel's coming destruction will turn normal life upside down. Those who have no family will be happy, for they will not watch spouses and children die. Likewise, the dead will be more fortunate than the living, since they will not face destruction. Despite the accuracy of God's sentiments, carrying out the Lord's commands will leave Jeremiah a very lonely man.

As the book has stated repeatedly, punishment will come because of Israel's sustained sinfulness. Though they profess their innocence (16:10), the people have worshiped idols and neglected the law (16:11-14). Indeed the nation has grown more wicked with each new generation (16:12). Judah's sin has become engraved on their hearts (17:1) to the point that their hearts seem beyond cure (17:9). Someday, God will bless and redeem Israel (16:14-15), but now they will pay double for their sins (16:16-18).

Jeremiah's only hope is to trust God (17:5-8). He must stop defending the people and questioning God's justice. Despite his doubts (note 12:1-4 and 15:10-18), the prophet seeks a renewed relationship with God. Jeremiah asks the Lord to save and heal him (17:14). Next, he requests that Yahweh fulfill his predictions (17:15). Then he asks for protection from his enemies (17:17-18). Above all, Jeremiah wants to serve the Lord and to remain God's prophet (17:16). Apparently, the loneliness brought on by the commands in 16:1-9 forces Jeremiah to confess his faith in God.

The fourth confession occurs after another plot against the prophet. Once more God has Jeremiah preach in a public place. He stands "at the gate of the people, through which the kings of Judah go in and out" and condemns sabbath breaking (17:19-27, NIV). Neither king nor people pay any attention to him. Thus this sin is added to their guilt.

Another symbolic act pushes Jeremiah closer to confrontation with his enemies. He visits a potter's shop and notes how the craftsman shapes and reshapes a pot however he wishes (18:1-12). Similarly, God can shape a nation however *He* wishes. Yahweh can forgive repentant countries or punish rebellious peoples. Obviously, God will punish Israel (18:11-12), because they have traded Yahweh for other gods (18:13-17). They refuse to reverse their course of self-destruction.

Jeremiah's opponents react to these messages with defiance and slander (18:18). They deny that Israel's religion has any faults, and once more reject Jeremiah's claim that God will allow Israel to suffer defeat. Rather than threaten his life, as in 11:18-23, Jeremiah's foes try to discredit him. They speak against him, intending to ruin his reputation.

By this time Jeremiah has grown weary of constant opposition. In frustration he prays that God will destroy them all (18:19-23). He has told them the truth, yet they have lied about him (18:20). He has given up having a family (16:1-4) to save their children, but they have rejected his help (18:21). All he gets for his trouble is plots and threats (18:23). Clearly, this fourth confession marks a new crisis in Jeremiah's spiritual relationship. After seeking personal renewal in 17:14-18, he has slipped back into the complaining tendencies in 12:1-4 and 15:10-18.

One final crisis and confession makes Jeremiah ready to serve Yahweh for the rest of the book. Because of his constant problems, he wonders if he should be prophet at all (chaps. 19—20). Again Jeremiah speaks to Israel's elders. This time the Lord directs him to gather the nation's leaders and break a jar in their presence. The jar represents Israel, and its breaking, the coming judgment (19:1-13). The "breaking" will happen because of national sin (19:14-15).

When Jeremiah performs the act, he incurs the wrath of a priest named Pashhur, the chief officer in the temple (20:1). Pashhur has the prophet beaten and put in stocks (20:2). Upon release, Jeremiah renames Pashhur "terror on every side" (20:3, *Magor-Missabib* in Hebrew). The priest has terrorized Jeremiah, but he will soon be terrorized himself when he and his loved ones are exiled in Babylon (20:4-5). Too, he is a terror to the whole nation since his lies have led the people astray (20:6).

This confrontation with Pashhur depresses Jeremiah, who now launches his most extensive attack against Yahweh. He confesses his anger in three areas. First, he says God forced him to be a prophet (20:7). In language that very nearly accuses God of rape, he claims Yahweh "deceived," then "overpowered" him (20:7). Second, his message is always the same. He must always preach destruction (20:8). Third, this message brings him nothing but insult and reproach (20:8). Solitude and shame are his only companions.

Given these feelings, Jeremiah sought to stop preaching (20:9), but God has forced him to continue. The Lord's word felt like a "fire in his bones" (20:9) that he had to share. When he speaks, though, he has the pressure of addressing people who hope he will misspeak and therefore fail as a prophet (20:10).

How can he stand such pressure and frustration? Only by trusting and praising the Lord (20:11-13; note 17:5-13). Even then, Jeremiah feels like he should never have been born (20:14-18). Thus, what has he learned? First, he has accepted the difficulty of his call. He will continue as a prophet, but he will not expect acceptance or an easy life. Second, he knows the nation will be judged. Third, he understands that Yahweh is his only friend. Whatever strength he has comes from the Lord.

Jeremiah's confessions show that the prophets were real people with real hopes, dreams, and disappointments. They warn modern readers that serving God may not be easy. Finally, they illustrate the desperate times in which Jeremiah lived. If someone of Jeremiah's character dreaded the future, then the future was definitely something to fear.

His attachment to God now complete, the prophet denounces his, and God's, enemies in chapters 21—29. Each of these groups was introduced in chapter 1. Jeremiah first criticizes Israel's kings (21:1—23:8). Zedekiah, king from 597-587, asks for a sign that God will miraculously save Jerusalem from the Babylonians (21:2). Jeremiah says no sign will come, for the king perverts justice and oppresses his subjects (21:12). Before Zedekiah, King Jehoiakim (609-598) mistreated the alien, fatherless, and widow, and shed innocent blood (22:3). Jehoiakim thought building a luxurious palace was more important than ruling justly (22:15-17). Because of these sins, no one mourned Jehoiakim's passing (22:18-19), and Israel moved closer to destruction.

Only a righteous son of David can save the nation (23:1-8), a point Isaiah has already emphasized (Isa. 9:2-7; 11:1-9). This king will replace worthless leaders who abuse the people (23:1-4). He will rule wisely, restoring justice to the nation (23:5). This individual alone can make Israel secure and bring them back from exile (23:6-8).

Next, Jeremiah addresses Israel's prophets (23:9-40). The prophets are especially responsible for the people's downfall, since they have lied about Israel's spiritual condition. Not only do these prophets teach falsehood (23:13), they lead immoral lives (23:14). They fill the people with false hopes of surviving the Babylonian invasion (23:16), fabricate visions from God (23:16), and encourage religious rebellion (23:17). Obviously, Yahweh will punish such preachers (23:39-40). With so many lying prophets available, it is no surprise that the people reject Jeremiah's stern and uncompromising messages.

The people are also condemned, yet not as harshly (24:1—25:14). Though victims of poor leadership, they are accountable for their actions. Israel has become like a basket of spoiled figs (24:1-5). They will only get better by going to exile in Babylon (24:6-10). Israel must stay there seventy years (25:12), but then they will go home. Years of rejecting God's prophets have led to this result (25:4-7).

The nations, especially Babylon, act as Israel's punishers in the Book of Jeremiah. Still, they, too, have angered the Lord (25:15-38). The day of the Lord will affect all countries. Not even mighty Babylon's sins escape Yahweh's notice (25:12). Israel will experience Yahweh's wrath (25:34-38), but they will not suffer alone.

Jeremiah summarizes his complaints against the people, religious leaders, and politicians in chapter 26. This is the second time in the book that he preaches in the temple (note chap. 7). As before, Yahweh has Jeremiah tell the people that they must follow the Law (26:4) and obey the Prophets (26:5) or lose the land and the temple

(26:6). The priests, prophets, and people resent the message and demand Jeremiah be executed (26:7-9).

A hasty trial is convened. Government officials hear the people and religious leaders' charges against the prophet (26:10). Jeremiah's major "crime" is preaching Jerusalem's downfall (26:11). Jeremiah defends himself by saying that God has sent him (26:12-15). After hearing this explanation, the people and officials oppose the priests and prophets. They argue that Micah, Isaiah's contemporary, told Hezekiah to repent or suffer defeat (26:16-18). Hezekiah listened and thereby saved the nation from Assyria (26:19). Because of the officials' support, Jeremiah escapes (26:24). Not all prophets were so fortunate. One of Jeremiah's fellow prophets (Uriah) was killed for preaching a similar message (26:20-23).

In chapters 21—26 Jeremiah encourages the kings, priests, prophets, and people to repent. In chapters 27—29, though, he prepares them for exile. He tells the kings of Judah, Edom, Moab, Ammon, and Tyre that Babylon will conquer them all (27:1-6). Rebellion against Babylon is futile (27:7-11), so Jeremiah counsels his king to surrender (27:12-15). He warns the people and priests not to listen to the prophets who say the monarchy and temple will survive (27:16-22). The temple and all its furnishings will soon be in Babylonian hands.

Not surprisingly, the prophets attempt to contradict Jeremiah. A prophet named Hananiah predicts God will "break the yoke" of the king of Babylon in two years, will restore Jehoiachin to the throne, and will restore stolen temple articles to their place (28:1-4). In response, Jeremiah repeats his prediction that Babylon's power will grow (28:5-14). He also says Hananiah will die for misleading the people (28:15-16). Just as he predicts, Hananiah dies (28:17). God honors Jeremiah the true prophet, but He removes those who soothe the nation with false promises.

Even before 587 B.C., some Jews are taken into exile. In 605 B.C. and 597 B.C., two smaller groups of people are removed. Daniel leaves with the first exiles, and Ezekiel goes with the second. Jeremiah writes to the people already in Babylon and tells them they will be joined by others. What should these people do in exile? Jeremiah tells them to settle in the land. They should marry, build homes, and raise children (29:1-9). Why? Because they will remain in exile for seventy years (29:10). After that time Yahweh will return the people to Israel, where they will prosper (29:11). God has not given up on the people. When they seek the Lord, they will receive the Lord's blessings (29:12-14). Israel may have broken their covenant with God, but God will never break His covenant with them. Any prophet who disputes Jeremiah's advice simply does not know God's will (29:14-32).

Judah has run out of time. Their punishment is no longer tentative. Now it is inevitable. Jeremiah has done all he can to avert the disaster, but he has not succeeded. Judah's only hope lies in surrender to Babylon, an option the people particularly despise.

Jeremiah 30—33: Israel's Ultimate Restoration

Before he reports Jerusalem's actual defeat, Jeremiah presents the nation's future. Like all prophets, he believes God's judgment will lead to Israel's restoration. Thus, in chapters 30—33 the prophet announces God's plans to redeem, forgive, and renew the people. This emphasis on a glorious future helps soften the horrible destruction described in chapters 34—39.

Quite clearly, 30:1-3 announces the threefold plan of chapters 30-33. God will restore Israel's fortunes, bring them back to the land, and cause them to possess their lost homeland (30:3). The first issue takes precedence in 30:4-24, the second in 31:1-26, and the third in 31:27-40. These sections outline the futures of the people, kings, priests, and prophets. In chapters 32—33, the prophet illustrates the themes preached in chapters 30—31.

God first promises to restore the nation. Fear and despair will be replaced by hope (30:1-10), and Israel's enemies will be destroyed (30:11-17). Jerusalem will be rebuilt (30:18-20). A Jewish king will reign once more (30:21). Israel will be Yahweh's people again (30:22). In short, every segment of society will be redeemed. Yahweh will not rest until all these changes are accomplished (30:23-24). These promises come rapidly and are astounding in light of Jeremiah's previous comments on the nation's sin and well-earned punishment.

Before Israel's society can be reconstructed, the people must return to the land. This return will include all Jews, for Yahweh pledges to bring Northern Israel, who went into exile in 722 B.C., back to the land along with Judah (31:1-9). The Lord, who judged the people earlier, will become their shepherd and protector again (31:10-12). The joy this event brings (31:13-14) will remove the grief both halves of the nation have felt (31:15-20). Each succeeding verse leads to the reuniting of all twelve tribes in the land, which will begin to restore Israel's fortunes and will reverse more than a century of punishment.

Restored fortunes and a return to the land mean little if the new, united Israel cannot maintain its restored position. Therefore, Jeremiah now reveals how the people can keep the land. Chapter 31 ends with all aspects of restoration in place. The people, priests, and kings are rehabilitated, the nation united, and the land healed. Every problem the book raises has been solved.

Healing begins when Yahweh replants Israel in the land. In a clear reference to the themes announced in Jeremiah 1:10, God says the once-uprooted-and-torn-down nation will be built and planted (31:27). Earlier God "watched over" the people to destroy them, yet soon Yahweh "will watch over them to build and to plant" (31:28, NIV). When God acts in this manner, Israel will respond. They will no longer blame others for their sins (31:29-30). A new honesty and holiness will result.

Besides a renewed people, monarchy, and land Yahweh will also offer Israel "a new covenant" (31:31). The Mosaic covenant will be replaced. Why? Is Moses' covenant too harsh or unjust? Not at all, according to Jeremiah. The problem with the old covenant is that *the people break it* (31:32). The fault lies in the people, then, not in the covenant God revealed through Moses. To ensure its success, Yahweh will put the new law in the people's minds and write it on their hearts (31:33). Thus, everyone will know, understand, and keep this covenant (31:34); and God will forgive their sins (31:34).

This text has tremendous significance. From 31:31-34 comes the distinction between the Old and New Testaments (covenants). Further, Jesus states when sharing the Last Supper with His disciples that the wine represents "the new covenant in my blood" (Luke 22:20, NIV). Hebrews 8:8-12 indicates that early Christians believed Christ's death initiated the new covenant. Therefore, Jeremiah 31:31-34 is fulfilled in Jesus' death and in the life and work of the church. Ultimately, only Jesus can put the covenant in people's hearts and help them obey Yahweh. The new covenant, unlike its predecessor, will be permanent. As long as the earth endures the Lord will keep this new agreement (31:35-37).

One last promise completes the program of renewal. Jerusalem will be rebuilt. Every tower and gate will be put back in place (31:38-40). Once intact, the city will stand forever (31:40). God will never again turn the capital city over to destruction.

After the lofty speeches of chapters 30—31, Jeremiah 32 brings the story back to earth. It is wonderful to consider future glory, but the present reality for Jeremiah is that he and his contemporaries are in trouble. The Babylonians are coming. Sin and corruption are everywhere. Leadership is lacking. How can the prophet relate the present to the future?

With Babylon about to destroy Jerusalem, Jeremiah is confined in the king's courtyard (32:1-2). King Zedekiah does not appreciate Jeremiah's prediction that he will go into exile (32:3-5). In the midst of this difficult situation, Yahweh tells Jeremiah to buy a field in Anathoth, his hometown (32:6-8). The prophet obeys this strange command (32:9-15). Why buy land in a dying country? Because someday

God will restore the people to the land (32:26-44). Buying the land demonstrates the prophet's conviction that what seems worthless now will be valuable later.

During this same confinement, Yahweh reinforces the promises in chapters 30—32. Though Jerusalem will soon be conquered (33:1-5), it will one day "enjoy abundant peace and security" (33:6, NIV), have many inhabitants (33:7-9), and witness times of joy (33:10-11). Other fallen cities will rise again (33:12-13). The righteous son of David—the Messiah—will save Judah and fulfill God's promise to David (33:15-17). Good priests will serve the people (33:18). This covenant and these blessings will never cease (33:19-22), for Yahweh's compassion will overtake Israel's need for punishment (33:26).

Tragically, Israel had to lose everything before experiencing the new covenant. Even the righteous, such as Jeremiah, had to suffer the consequences of centuries of national rebellion against God. The Babylonian invasion would begin soon.

Jeremiah 34—51: Israel and the Nations' Fall

Jeremiah 34—35 introduce Judah's downfall by once again stating why the devastation approaches. As in earlier sections, direct prophetic preaching and symbolic action present the book's message. Three episodes illustrate why. Both king and people contribute to the nation's downfall.

In the first segment, Zedekiah, Judah's last ruler, learns he will be exiled to Babylon (34:1-3). Despite this horrible fate, Zedekiah will eventually die in peace (34:4-6). It is important to note that Jeremiah predicts these events before Jerusalem falls. He remains at all times an honest and accurate messenger of God.

Second, while the Jews battle the Babylonians, Zedekiah releases all slaves (34:8-10). Perhaps the slaves are expected to fight the enemy, or maybe the people try to gain God's favor. Regardless of the reason, Zedekiah changes his mind later and allows the people to enslave the servants again (34:11). Such oppression violates Moses' commands about mercy to slaves (34:12-22; note Ex. 21:2-11 and Deut. 15:12).

Third, Jeremiah compares the nation to the Rechabites, a clan committed to its heritage (chap. 35). God instructs the prophet to invite the Rechabites to drink some wine (35:1-5). The Rechabites refuse Jeremiah's hospitality, which normally would constitute a grave insult. They do not drink wine, they explain, because their ancestor Jonadab ordered them to abstain (35:6). They also live in tents instead of houses because of the same patriarch's command (35:7-11). Yahweh contrasts the Rechabites' obedience to their forefather and

Israel's rebellion against God. Surely, the Lord deserves the same respect an earthly father receives (35:12-16). Due to their disobedience, then, Israel will be punished (35:17-19).

The story now relates the decline and fall of the kings (chaps. 36—38). Like the people, the kings have ignored God's word for years. Perhaps Jehoiakim, king from 609-598, shows the least respect for Yahweh's warnings. Jeremiah dictates a message for the people (36:1-3). His friend and scribe, Baruch, writes the sermon on a scroll and reads it in the temple (36:4-10). The temple leaders decide the scroll must be taken to Jehoiakim (36:11-16). Because the sermon counsels repentance, the leaders advise Jeremiah and Baruch to hide (36:17-19).

Jehoiakim ignores Jeremiah's warnings. In fact, "Whenever Jehudi had read three or four columns of the scroll, the king cut them off with a scribe's knife and threw them into the [fire]" (36:23, NIV). Some of his attendants beg him not to destroy the text, but God's Word means nothing to him (36:24-25). Because of his attitude and actions, Jehoiakim's son will not rule Judah, and the monarchy itself will cease (36:27-31). Jeremiah makes another scroll that promises these disasters (36:32). Jehoiakim may burn a scroll, but he cannot silence Yahweh's word through the prophets.

Zedekiah does not act much better. He imprisons Jeremiah for saying Babylon will conquer Israel (chaps. 37—38). Jeremiah responds by asking what happened to all the prophets who said the Babylonians would vanish (37:18-20). Why should he be punished for telling the truth? Zedekiah relents and releases Jeremiah, only to allow him to be jailed again, this time in a muddy cistern (37:21—38:9). Once released, the prophet continues to speak the truth. Jerusalem will fall (38:14-28).

Finally, Babylon captures the city (chap. 39). Nebuchadnezzar, Babylon's king, has his army lay siege to Jerusalem (39:1). They break through the city walls (39:2), take control of city affairs (39:3), and chase Zedekiah and his officials into the desert (39:4). When the enemy captures Zedekiah, they kill his sons before him, then gouge out his eyes (39:5-7). Next, the Babylonians burn Zedekiah's palace and, presumably, the temple (39:8). Then they send most of the inhabitants to Babylon and place a governor in charge of what remains (39:9-14; 40:7). Allowed to go wherever he wishes, Jeremiah chooses to remain with the remnant left in the city (39:14).

Clearly, this destruction could have been avoided. Jeremiah spends four decades (627-587) trying to turn the nation back to Yahweh. Nothing he or the Lord says makes any difference. Still, even in the midst of this disaster, Yahweh promises to aid all who trust in the Lord (39:15-18). Mercy remains God's first and overriding impulse.

Chapters 40—45 focus on the aftermath of Jerusalem's fall. They also describe the punishment of the people. As usual, the people bring judgment on themselves. First, assassins kill Gedaliah, the Babylonian-appointed governor of the area (40:7—41:3). Second, the killers murder several Jews who may know about the governor's murder, then flee to Egypt (41:4-15). Third, expecting Babylonian reprisals for Gedaliah's murder, the people ask Jeremiah if they should also run to Egypt (42:1-6). Fourth, Jeremiah says God orders them to stay in the land (42:7-22), but they move to Egypt anyway (43:1-13). The people even force Jeremiah to go with them. Thus, in exile against his will, the prophet predicts disaster for all who have fled to Egypt (44:1-30). Even now the people reject his preaching (44:16-19). Indeed, the righteous are forced to suffer with the wicked (45:1-5).

Neither the kings nor the people exhibit any redeeming characteristics in these chapters. Jeremiah's earlier depictions of the nation as a group of committed sinners continues. Why does Jerusalem fall? Israel ignores God, practices idolatry, oppresses the defenseless, and makes poor political choices. Punishment, God's last resort, becomes inevitable.

Throughout the book, Jeremiah emphasizes God's universal rule. No nation, however great, decides its own destiny. For example, Egypt watches Israel suffer defeat and may feel superior to their smaller neighbor. Jeremiah says, though, that God will punish Egypt for *its* sins (chap. 46). Smaller nations who rejoice in the Jews' destruction, such as Philistia, Moab, Ammon, and Edom, will face Yahweh's wrath themselves (47:1—49:27). Even Babylon, the greatest power of the day, the conqueror of other lands, will pay for its sins (chaps. 50—51). Yahweh is not a national or regional deity. Yahweh determines history. Yahweh assesses and judges the proud oppressors of all nations.

Jeremiah 52: Summary of the Prophecy

Just as Jeremiah 1 introduces the book, so chapter 52 summarizes the prophecy's contents. The story's major characters, themes, and historical events are reviewed, except for Jeremiah, who remains conspicuously absent. The events are told very matter-of-factly, as if readers already know these details. Only one new piece of information arises, and that information is important since it helps the book finish on a cautiously optimistic note.

Six sections form this summary. First, 52:1-11 describes the fall of Jerusalem and Zedekiah's capture. Second, Jerusalem's destruction is depicted in 52:12-16. Third, 52:17-23 discusses Babylon's looting of the temple. Fourth, the nation's officials are executed in 52:24-27. Fifth, the text gives the number of people exiled (52:28-30). Finally, 52:31-34 describes Jehoiachin's latter years. Though he remains an exile for thirty-seven years, Jehoiachin receives honor in Babylon near the end of his life. His elevation proves God helps Israel in exile, a positive idea that should encourage the book's readers.

Various themes are reviewed in chapter 52. Punishment is highlighted through the discussion of the Babylonian invasion (52:1-30). Restoration is emphasized through the description of Jehoiachin's restored fortunes (52:31-34). Character groups are punished, including the king (52:8-11), officials (52:24-27), and people (52:28-30). Since the nations are denounced in chapters 46—51, all the prophet's enemies stand condemned. No real surprises emerge, then, but the chapter does tie together the prophecies' main emphases.

Conclusion

Few biblical characters exhibit Jeremiah's honesty, integrity, patience, and commitment. He ministered during extremely trying times, yet managed to retain his faith in God. Though he preached repentance to an unrepentant people, he never lost hope in God's future plans for Israel. No other prophet faced greater obstacles and disappointment, and no other prophet fulfilled his or her role better than Jeremiah.[7]

Questions for Reflection

1. How do Jeremiah's historical circumstances affect the content of his preaching?
2. Examine Jeremiah's conversations with God in 11:18—12:6; 15:10-21; 17:14-18; 18:18-23; 20:7-18. What do you learn about prayer from Jeremiah's experiences? What do you learn about the function of a prophet?
3. What does Jeremiah 31:31-34 mean when it speaks of a new covenant?

Notes

1. Compare J. A. Thompson, *The Book of Jeremiah*, New International Commentary on the Old Testament (Grand Rapids: Eerdmans, 1980), 10-27.

2. Michael Grant, *The History of Ancient Israel* (New York: Scribner's, 1984), 141-42.

3. James Leo Green, "Jeremiah," in *The Broadman Bible Commentary*, vol. 6 (Nashville: Broadman Press, 1971), 11.

4. Compare John Bright, *Jeremiah*, vol. 21 in *The Anchor Bible* (New York: Doubleday, 1965).

5. Compare C. F. Whitely, "The Date of Jeremiah's Call," *Vetus Testamentum* 14 (1964), 467-83.

6. Two of the best recent analyses of Jeremiah's confessions are A. R. Diamond, *The Confessions of Jeremiah in Context: Scenes of Prophetic Drama, JSOT* Supplement Series 45 (Sheffield: Sheffield Academic Press, 1987); and Kathleen M. O'Connor, *The Confessions of Jeremiah: Their Interpretation and Role in Chapters 1—25* (Atlanta: Scholars Press, 1988).

7. See also R. E. Clements, *Jeremiah,* Interpretation (Atlanta: John Knox, 1988); Peter C. Craigie, Page Kelley, and Joel F. Drinkard, Jr., *Jeremiah 1-25,* vol. 26 in *Word Biblical Commentary* (Dallas: Word Books, 1991); Elmer A. Martens, *Jeremiah,* Believers Church Bible Commentary (Scottdale, Penn.: Herald Press, 1986); William L. Holladay, *Jeremiah 1,* Hermeneia (Philadelphia: Fortress, 1986); William L. Holladay, *Jeremiah 2,* Hermeneia (Philadelphia: Fortress, 1989); R. K. Harrison, *Jeremiah and Lamentations,* Tyndale Old Testament Commentaries (Downers Grove, Ill.: Inter-Varsity Press, 1973).

10
Ezekiel: *Prophet of Restoration and Hope*

Plot: God explains to Ezekiel why Jerusalem falls, then promises to restore the people, the monarchy, and Jerusalem.
Major Characters: Ezekiel and Yahweh
Major Events: Ezekiel's call, Ezekiel's visions and symbolic acts, and Jerusalem's destruction
Major Themes: God's worldwide presence, Israel and the nations' sins, Israel's restoration, Jerusalem and the temple's restoration

Introduction

Ezekiel balances the messages of Isaiah and Jeremiah. Isaiah states the seriousness of Israel's sins and notes that only the coming of the Messiah and the day of Yahweh can change the people. Jeremiah discusses Israel's continuing rebellion, then details the fall of Jerusalem and its aftermath. Both books focus on hope at times, yet place that hope in the future. Ezekiel comments on sin as well. This prophet, though, encourages the people immediately before and after the nation's defeat. He offers hope that God still loves the exiles and will make the future brighter than the past.

As was mentioned in the introduction to Jeremiah, two smaller deportations of Jews precede the great exile of 587 B.C. Daniel and his friends go to Babylon in 605 B.C. Ezekiel is taken to Babylon in 597 B.C. along with several other exiles. Therefore, he does not experience Jerusalem's fall himself, but does mourn the event as a concerned Israelite. Like most of the exiles, Ezekiel seems to have a fairly good life in Babylon. He is a priest (1:3), has a wife he loves (24:16), and enjoys respect in the community (8:1).

Despite their good treatment, the exiles wrestle with some fundamental theological issues. First, they could easily lose their national and spiritual distinctiveness. They might easily adopt Babylon's life-style and religious beliefs. Second, the people wonder if God cares for them now that they are out of the promised land. Have their sins cut them off from Yahweh? Do they have a future? Third, they consider whether their God is more powerful than Babylon's many deities. After all, Yahweh did not keep the people out of exile. Is Yahweh all-powerful, then, or should the Jews seek another god to worship? Fourth, they question why they are in exile at all. They tend to blame their elders' sin and incompetence for their predicament.

God calls Ezekiel to address these issues. Because the book dates his messages, it is possible to note that he ministers from 593-571.[1] Ezekiel corrects, comforts, and informs the Jews in Babylon. Like the other prophets, he speaks of sin, punishment, and restoration. He both preaches sermons and performs symbolic acts. Unlike some of the other prophets, he has unusual visions. He sees angelic beings (chaps. 1—3), a valley of dry bones (chap. 37), and a new and beautiful Jerusalem (chaps. 40—48). He sees events in Jerusalem even though he no longer lives there (chap. 8). All these visions relate to Israel's questions about God and their future. What he sees, coupled with what he says and does, makes him a creative and powerful prophet.

Ezekiel 1—3: The Prophet's Call

Ezekiel's call experience is more unusual than Isaiah's or Jeremiah's. In 593 B.C. (1:2), when he is thirty years old (1:1), God shows Ezekiel a vision. While sitting by a river, Ezekiel observes a storm from the north (1:4). Four creatures, each with four faces and two wings, emerge from the storm (1:5-14). These angelic beings are followed by wheels moving in the directions the angels' four faces look (1:15-18). Together the angels and wheels cover each of the four directions (1:19-21).

Next, Ezekiel receives a vision of Yahweh. The Lord sits on a throne, high above the angels (1:25-26). God's appearance is firelike, brilliant, and colorful (1:27-28). This vision causes the prophet to fall on his face, overwhelmed at God's greatness (1:28). He hears a voice, which will presumably give him further instructions (1:28).

What do these visions mean? A number of interpretations have been offered, including the suggestion that Ezekiel saw a spaceship. Most likely, the vision of the angels and wheels indicates that God is present everywhere and sees everything. The wheels represent God's ability to move in all directions, and the eyes symbolize God's all-encompassing knowledge. Thus, Ezekiel learns Yahweh exists everywhere, even in exile. The Lord sees Israel, wherever they go. God had not forgotten Israel's exiles.

With this understanding of Yahweh in mind, Ezekiel now receives instructions about his work as a prophet. Douglas Stuart notes that five commissions define Ezekiel's task.[2] First, Yahweh informs Ezekiel that he is being sent to a rebellious people who will refuse to listen (2:1-7). His mission will be difficult, then, but he must never fear the people (2:6). He must preach, regardless of the people's response (2:7). Next, God gives him a sweet scroll to eat (2:8—3:3). This scroll is God's word, which determines the content of his preaching.

Second, the Lord tells the prophet Israel will be poor listeners. They will understand his messages, but they will reject them (3:4-9). Foreigners would listen to him (3:6). His own people, however, will not (3:7). Third, God's Spirit sends him back to the other exiles (3:10-15). This same Spirit will dictate his future activities.

Fourth, Yahweh states that Ezekiel will be "a watchman for the house of Israel" (3:16-21, NIV). As watchman, he must warn the wicked to change and challenge the righteous to remain faithful. God will hold Ezekiel responsible for his actions. If he warns the people to change and they refuse, then God will be pleased with his work (3:19). On the other hand, if he fails to warn the wicked, then God will hold him accountable for their rebellion (3:18). Clearly, the prophet has an awesome and dangerous mission.

Fifth, God strikes Ezekiel dumb (3:22-27). Why? So the prophet will remember to preach only God's word (3:27). No other opinions matter. No other word needs uttering. Once Yahweh speaks, it is the people's choice whether or not to respond (3:27).

Ezekiel serves the all-powerful, all-seeing Creator of the universe, Yahweh. He speaks only what God tells him and when God tells him. Therefore, his call resembles those of other prophets. The task will be difficult, as it was for his predecessors, but God will enable him to fulfill his ministry.

Ezekiel 4—24: Sermons about Judah

From his vantage point in Babylon, Ezekiel now begins to preach about his homeland. He first performs some symbolic acts that illustrate Jerusalem's future. He draws a picture of the city on a clay tablet, then lays siege against his model (4:1-3). Next, he lies on his left side for 390 days for Israel and on his right side for 40 days representing Judah (4:4-8). This time period represents the years between Solomon's sin and Israel's return to the land, the first part perhaps representing the period from the construction to the destruction of the temple. While on his side, he cooks his food over dung to emphasize the harsh conditions Jerusalem will experience during the Babylonian siege (4:9-17). Without question, Jerusalem will suffer greatly. Finally, Ezekiel shaves a third of his beard to show that only a portion of the people will survive the coming destruction (5:1-17).

Besides these symbolic deeds, Yahweh asks the prophet to preach to a symbolic audience. Ezekiel preaches to the mountains (6:1-14). Why? Because the mountains are home to the high places for idols. Thus the mountains will have a sword demolish its pagan altars (6:1-4). People will "lie slain among their idols around their altars" (6:13, NIV). When this devastation occurs, the end will have come (7:1-27). Then the people will seek help from God, but they will receive none (7:25). Their lying prophets, deceptive priests, and foolish elders will prove no help at that time (7:26-27).

Now the prophet has visions that explain why God will punish Jerusalem. A year after his call experience, or about 592 B.C., the Lord shows him a scene in Jerusalem (8:1-4). There he sees idols and pagan drawings in the temple itself (8:5-11). Worse still, men and women worship a variety of gods in God's house (8:5-17). God cannot allow such sin (8:18), so Ezekiel sees a group of six avengers kill Jerusalem's wicked (9:1-11).

As if these visions were not sad enough, Ezekiel sees an even more regrettable sight. Once more Ezekiel views God's glory, the angels, and the wheels (10:1-17). While he watches, God's glory leaves the temple (10:18-22). Yahweh no longer favors the people's worship. God has deserted the nation that has deserted its Lord.

Following this staggering event, Ezekiel hears Yahweh say Jerusalem's leaders will be punished (11:1-15). These individuals have killed the innocent (11:6). For this brutality they will suffer painful deaths themselves (11:7-12). Ezekiel even watches the first of these leaders die (11:13-15). Despite such corruption, though, God will eventually gather Israel from exile (11:16-17), give the people a desire to obey Yahweh (11:18-21), and restore God's glory to Jerusalem (11:22-25). Ezekiel preaches hope even in the midst of his bleakest comments.

Symbols and sermons alternate in chapters 12—17. The prophet acts out Jerusalem's exile by packing for a trip and digging through the city wall (12:1-9). When his friends ask why he does these things, he explains that Jerusalem's inhabitants will soon leave their homes for Babylon (12:10-28). Because they have failed to warn Israel to repent, Ezekiel denounces the nation's false prophets (13:1-23). They have depended on false visions and sorcery for their messages instead of Yahweh (13:23).

What about the people? Do they bear any guilt? God tells the prophet that idolatry has ruined Israel (14:1-5). All who repent may be forgiven, even the false prophets (14:6-11). No such change appears imminent, however, so judgment will come (14:12-23). They have become like a useless vine, which is only fit for burning (15:1-8). They may have had poor leadership, but the nation has chosen to sin on their own.

Yahweh further illustrates Israel's sin by comparing the nation to an unfaithful wife (16:1-63). Israel was once an abandoned child, but God cared for her (16:1-8). Yahweh raised, clothed, and fed her (16:9-14). Israel grew beautiful, yet used her beauty to become a prostitute (16:15-19). She even pays lovers to sleep with her (16:32). This whole story represents Israel's idolatry, which Yahweh considers spiritual adultery. Both Northern and Southern Israel treat the Lord spitefully like a wife wronging her husband (16:44-58). Due to this unfaithfulness, God will send a great eagle (Babylon) to destroy Israel (17:1-21). Later, though, Yahweh will once again plant the Jews in their land (17:22-24).

Those already in exile blame their ancestors for their difficulties. They claim their fathers ate sour fruit, but it is their teeth that have been set on edge (18:1-2). In other words, they say they are suffering for their parents' mistakes. God rejects such notions. Righteous people please God (18:3-9), even if their children sin (18:10-13). Sinful children receive the penalty for their actions. Each person, then, gets fair and equal treatment from God (18:30-32).

Unfortunately for most Jews, though, fair treatment means punishment. Israel's once-powerful leaders are caged by Babylon (19:1-14). The people have rebelled against God since Moses' time (20:1-29), especially through idolatry (20:30-44). Babylon has thus become Yahweh's punishing sword for Judah, just as Assyria played that role for Northern Israel (20:45—21:32).

Jerusalem's sins have grown as distasteful as her "sister's," Samaria. Like Samaria, Jerusalem has shed innocent blood in her streets and has made idols to worship (22:1-4). Political corruption occurs repeatedly (22:6). Parents, widows, aliens, and orphans have no advocate in Jerusalem, nor does Yahweh (22:7-8). Priests "do violence" to God's law (22:26). Officials brutalize their people (22:27), and prophets cover over these acts by false visions (22:28). God has looked for a spiritual leader in the capital, but He has found no one willing to help avoid punishment (22:30-31).

Indeed, Jerusalem and Samaria have acted like sisters engaged in prostitution (23:1-4). They lusted after Egypt and Assyria and, therefore, made alliances with these nations (23:5-8). Assyria raped both sisters (23:9-10), yet they still desire their rapist (23:11-13). Both women become insatiable, constantly looking for new lovers (23:11-22). When the Assyrians and Egyptians are finished with them, the sisters chase minor nations (23:22-45). No lewd behavior is beneath these women.

God must put an end to their embarrassing conduct (23:46-49), so He decrees that Babylon will destroy the sisters. Babylon will cook Judah like a massive stew (24:1-12). Then neither sister—Israel or Judah—will practice her prostitution any longer (24:13-14).

A sad symbolic act closes this portion of the book. Yahweh informs Ezekiel that his wife, "the delight of [his] eyes" (24:16), will die. Despite this personal loss, the prophet may not "lament or weep or shed tears" (24:16, NIV). The people ask Ezekiel why he acts this way (24:18-19). Ezekiel tells them that just as he has lost his "delight," so Judah will lose Jerusalem, its delight (24:20-27). Jerusalem's loss will be like a death in one's family.

Ezekiel's voice from exile sounds like his preexilic friends'. He joins Isaiah and Jeremiah in offering Israel the opportunity to repent. Unfortunately, he, like Jeremiah, is forced to spend time in a foreign land. He will live well past 587 B.C., however, so he must find new ways to minister to his people.

Ezekiel 25—32: Doom for Israel's Enemies

Israel will not face punishment alone. As Isaiah 13—27 and Jeremiah 46—51 have already stated, Yahweh, the Creator of all nations, will judge all nations. Like Isaiah, Ezekiel condemns Egypt strenuously (Ezek. 29—32), possibly because Israel trusted Egypt to save them from the Babylonians. He also denounces traditionally hostile neighbors like Ammon (25:1-7), Moab (25:8-11), Edom (25:12-14), and Philistia (25:15-17). Each of these are judged for malice towards and hatred for the Jews (note 25:6,12,15).

Tyre receives the longest condemnation (chaps. 26—28). Isaiah 23 and Jeremiah 25:22 criticize Tyre, but no prophet makes harsher comments about this island kingdom than Ezekiel. Why he detests Tyre so much is unclear since, historically, Israel had good relations with Tyre. Perhaps God isolates Tyre because of its pride in its scenic beauty (27:3), military security (28:2), political status (28:3-5), and international trading reputation (28:18). This pride will cease when Babylon lays siege to Tyre's cities (chap. 26). Small nations with large reputations may think they are gods (note 28:2), but they, too, must bow to Yahweh.

This section on the nations reinforces Ezekiel's earlier comments about God's universal presence (note Ezek. 1—3). Yahweh moves everywhere and sees everything. Thus, God knows what countries are filled with hatred for Israel, with overwhelming pride, or with false promises for smaller, dependent nations. Israel's exiles can be sure that their God rules the earth. Not even Jerusalem's defeat can erase this fact.

Ezekiel 33—48: Future Glory for Israel

Other prophets may describe sin more powerfully then Ezekiel. Some may make punishment sound more fearful or repentance more attractive. Ezekiel's vision for Israel's restoration, though, is arguably the greatest of all the prophets. In the early years of the exile, he sees a future people, temple, and capital that exceeds in greatness any period in Israel's history. This vision intends to comfort and challenge an understandably dispirited people.

Chapters 33—36 pave the way for restoration by reversing the problems announced in Ezekiel 1—24. First, God reestablishes Ezekiel as Israel's "watchman." He still must warn the people to repent and will be held responsible if he does not do so (33:1-11). In turn, the people who ignore his message will die in their sins (33:12-20). Yahweh promises to make all the prophet's words come true (33:21-33). Regardless of the people's response, then, God will honor Ezekiel.

Second, the Lord pledges to give Israel new leadership. The old "shepherds" have abused the nation (34:1-19). Therefore, God will restore David's family to the throne (34:20-24). This messiah will rule justly, and Yahweh will "make a covenant of peace" with the people (34:25, NIV). Then the land will have rest and security (34:26-31). Third, Israel's old enemies, such as Edom, will harm them no more (35:1-15).

Fourth, whereas chapter 6 prophesies doom to Israel's mountains, now Ezekiel offers hope to these mountains. The hills will no longer serve as places for idols or as plunder for foreign armies (36:1-7). Instead, they will produce fruit for Israel and once more be home for the Jews (36:8-15). Soon the Lord will bring the people back from exile (36:16-23). Then the nation will receive a new heart, spirit, and attitude (36:24-32). Then they will honor God and keep their land (36:33-38).

With these obstacles removed, Ezekiel envisions ever-greater signs of Israel's renewal. The prophet sees a valley filled with dry bones (37:1-2). God asks a seemingly ridiculous question: "Son of man, can these bones live?" (37:3, NIV). Ezekiel responds that only God would know (37:3). Next Yahweh tells Ezekiel to command the bones to reassemble, take on flesh, and receive breath (37:4-6). When he obeys, Ezekiel sees the bones transformed into a great army (37:7-10). God says these bones are Israel, which has been cut off, apparently without hope (37:11). Despite their current condition, Yahweh will reassemble the nation (37:12-14). The people will return to the land. The Northern and Southern Kingdoms will reunite, build the temple, and live under Davidic rule (37:15-28). This vision clearly teaches God's determination to help Israel no matter what the people have done.

What if enemies attack the new nation? God says all foes will be routed (chaps. 38—39). Both 38:2 and 39:1 state an enemy named Gog, from a place called Magog, will fail to conquer the Jews. Various theories about Gog's identity have been offered. Some popular writers have described Gog as Russia and have predicted that the Soviet Union will invade Israel someday.[3] Biblical scholars suggest that Gog symbolizes all Israel's enemies,[4] an unspecified future invader,[5] or the descendants of a king named Gyges of Lydia.[6]

Gog's identity is impossible to determine with absolute accuracy. It is possible, though, to draw conclusions from chapters 38—39. First, God will secure the resurrected nation in the land. Second, whoever invades the protected people will suffer defeat (38:1-16). Third, this defeat will teach non-Jews and Jews alike God's greatness and holiness (38:16-23; 39:25-29). All nations will discover Yahweh's identity. Then all the world, not just Israel, will experience restoration.

Ezekiel not only envisions a restored people in a secure land, he also dreams of a glorious new Jerusalem (chaps. 40—48). Once more God shows the prophet an astounding sight. A new, larger temple, complete with gates, courts, and rooms for priests, will be built (chaps. 40—42). God's glory, which departed the temple in chapter 10, will return (43:1-12). The altar will be used again, this time for proper sacrifices (43:13-27).

The priests in this new temple will be pure and will teach the law correctly (chap. 44). Land will be given for holy places (45:1-12), and holy days will be observed (45:13—46:24). Israel will draw its life from the temple. Ezekiel illustrates this point by envisioning a life-giving river flowing from the altar (47:1-12). The land around the temple will be divided equitably among the tribes (47:13—48:35). Indeed, when all these things happen, "the name of the city from that day shall be 'Yahweh is there' " (48:35). Nothing less than God's presence in Jerusalem can make these miracles occur.

Scholars debate whether Ezekiel's vision of the city is symbolic or literal. Was the temple of Jesus' day the temple Ezekiel describes? Will the temple be rebuilt again? Or do these chapters speak of heaven? Certainly a case could be made for each of these viewpoints. It is safe to say, though, that God will provide such a place for all who trust the Lord. Ultimately, those who obey Yahweh will dwell in a New Jerusalem, a place where God lives with His people.

Conclusion

Ezekiel's messages informed and encouraged the exiles of his day. They answered many *why* questions. Why did Jerusalem fall? Because the nation committed religious, sexual, and societal sin. Why should the exiles retain faith in Yahweh? Because God still loves them and plans a bright future for them. Ezekiel teaches that God holds Israel responsible for their sins, yet He is also present with them wherever they go. Ezekiel stresses the future to people with a dismal present. In short, he prophesies to a nation of dry bones that they can live again as a restored people.[7]

Questions for Reflection

1. How would Ezekiel's messages encourage the people of his day?
2. What does Ezekiel 18 say to modern parents?
3. What hope does Ezekiel give you?

Notes

1. Note the discussion of Ezekiel's historical context in Walter Zimmerli, *Ezekiel One*, Hermenia Series (Philadelphia: Fortress, 1979), 9-21.

2. Douglas Stuart, *Ezekiel*, Communicator's Commentary (Waco: Word, 1989), 37-52.

3. E. G. Thomas S. McCall and Zola Levitt, *The Coming Russian Invasion of Israel* (Chicago: Moody Press, 1987).

4. Walter Eichrodt, *Ezekiel: A Commentary*, Old Testament Library (Philadelphia: Westminster, 1970), 522.

5. Stuart, 355.

6. G. A. Cooke, *The Book of Ezekiel*, International Critical Commentary (Edinburgh: T. and T. Clark, 1985), 408.

7. See also William H. Brownlee, *Ezekiel 1—19,* vol. 28 in *Word Biblical Commentary* (Waco, Tex.: Word Books, 1986); Leslie C. Allen, *Ezekiel 20—48,* vol. 29 in *Word Biblical Commentary* (Dallas: Word Books, 1990); Moshe Greenberg, *Ezekiel 1—20,* vol. 22 in *The Anchor Bible* (Garden City, N.Y.: Doubleday, 1983); F. B. Huey, Jr., *Ezekiel, Daniel,* vol. 12 in *Layman's Bible Book Commentary* (Nashville: Broadman Press, 1983).

11
The Book of the Twelve: *Partners in Prophecy*

Plot: Israel and the nations have sinned against God and one another. They must therefore face the day of Yahweh. God restores Israel in the land and offers salvation to the nations.
Major Characters: Yahweh, the prophets, the nations, Israel's sinful majority, and Israel's righteous remnant
Major Events: The defeats of Northern and Southern Israel, Assyria's destruction, and the rebuilding of the temple
Major Themes: God's anger at Israel and the nation's sin, the coming day of the Lord, the restoration of Israel and the conversion of the Gentiles, and the coming of the Messiah

Introduction

One of the most noticeable differences between the English and Hebrew Bibles is how each counts the twelve smaller prophetic books. The English Bible considers them twelve separate books. The Hebrew Bible, however, counts them as a single prophecy. How can twelve prophecies, written at different times, operate as a unified whole? What do they discuss that Isaiah, Jeremiah, and Ezekiel have not already covered?

The Twelve emphasizes sin, punishment, and restoration in some unique and creative ways. First, it has an interesting structure. The first six prophecies describe Israel and the nation's sin, the next three stress the punishment of sin on the day of the Lord, and the last three emphasize the restoration of Israel and their neighbors. Second, the Twelve portrays some fascinating characters. Yahweh appears as father, husband, king, and judge. The prophets are obedient (Hosea), rebellious (Jonah), and intellectual (Habakkuk). Israel emerges both as a God-fearing minority and a callous, perverse majority. The nations can be either wicked or repentant. Thus, reading these prophecies as a unified whole provides some new insights on prophecy itself.

The Twelve also contains historical details and theological themes not found in Isaiah, Jeremiah, and Ezekiel. For instance, Hosea and Amos describe Israel just before Isaiah's time. Haggai, Zechariah, and Malachi address the people returned from exile. Jonah shows that God's love extends to even the Assyrians. Habakkuk questions how God can allow the wicked to prosper. Clearly, the Twelve possesses a literary and theological richness as a group it could never have as separate books.

Because the twelve prophecies do not appear in chronological order, it is best to read them with their thematic emphases in mind. Thus the following outline will be followed:

Sin

Hosea: Israel's general spiritual adultery;
Joel: Israel's sin, plus the nations' general wickedness;
Amos: The specific sins of Israel and the nations;
Obadiah: Edom's hatred of Israel;
Jonah: Israel's hatred of Assyria;
Micah: The solution for sin.

Punishment

Nahum: Assyria's punishment;
Habakkuk: Israel and Babylon's punishment;
Zephaniah: Punishment of all nations.

Restoration

Haggai: Restoration of the temple;
Zechariah: Restoration of Jerusalem and the nations;
Malachi: Restoration of the Jewish people.

Hosea: Israel's Adultery

Hosea's ministry lasts from about 752 to 724 B.C.[1] In general, these were good years for the Northern and Southern Kingdoms. Both nations enjoyed political security due to the long reigns of Jeroboam II (North) and Uzziah (South).[2] Economic growth resulted from this leadership as well.[3] Traditionally powerful countries like Egypt, Assyria, and Babylon were temporarily weak, allowing both Jewish nations to extend their borders. Assyria would soon rise again, though, a fact Hosea uses to threaten the people. Not since Solomon's time had the Jews enjoyed such wealth and prestige.

Unfortunately, good times do not always produce good worship. Yahweh claims the people have become spiritual prostitutes. They chase after idols of all kinds and thereby break the covenant. When Hosea informs the people of God's displeasure, they are amazed. After all, if Yahweh is so angry, why is the nation so blessed? Hosea's preaching sounds like nonsense to them. How will the prophet get their attention?

Hosea preaches almost exclusively in Northern Israel. Most of the places he condemns, such as Samaria, Bethel, and Gilgal, are Northern cities. He never mentions Jerusalem or any Southern town, yet he does care about all twelve tribes.[4] His messages need to be read, then, as warnings to both parts of the divided kingdom. Spiritual adultery was committed by all the people. Therefore, God allowed Assyria and Babylon to devastate the land.

Hosea 1—3: Israel's Adultery Dramatized

God uses Hosea's marriage to illustrate Israel's sin. Of course, Isaiah and Ezekiel have already used their families as prophetic symbols, so readers may expect this strategy. What readers do not expect, though, is the shocking way Hosea's marriage explains Israel's actions. Yahweh commands the prophet to marry an adulterous wife and have "children of adultery" (1:2). Why? Because Israel has committed open adultery with other gods.

Scholars have offered several opinions about this command. Gomer may have been a prostitute when Hosea married her, or, she may have become unfaithful later. Hosea may also marry two different women, Gomer in chapter 1 and a second woman in chapter 3.[5] The clearest meaning of 1:2 is that Hosea knows his wife's character when he marries her. Thus, like Isaiah, who walks naked for three years, or Jeremiah, who refuses to attend vital social ceremonies, Hosea must act in a questionable way. Yahweh asks him to do a seemingly unthinkable deed.

To fulfill God's command, Hosea marries Gomer (1:3). She bears him a son (1:3). Like Isaiah's sons (Isa. 7:3; 8:1-4), this child has a symbolic name. He is called Jezreel, because God intends to judge Jehu's massacre at Jezreel (1:4-5; compare 2 Kings 9). Gomer then has a daughter called Not Pitied, whose name indicates Yahweh will no longer pity Israel (1:6-7). Judgment will fall soon. Finally, Gomer has a son named Not My People, or Illegitimate. Israel has acted like they are not Yahweh's people. Someday God will restore the people, but only after they are punished (1:10-11).

A close reading of chapters 1 and 2 indicates Gomer is unfaithful to Hosea. She "bore him a son" in 1:3, a phrase not used to describe the other births. Worse still, the last son is even named Illegitimate. Chapter 2 consists of comments made by two spurned husbands: Hosea and Yahweh. Hosea complains to Gomer's children that their "mother has been a harlot, and she has conceived them in shame" (2:5). Yahweh claims Israel has loved other gods, despite the blessings they have received (2:8-13). Therefore, God must punish the nation in order to make them His people again (2:21-23). Gomer and Israel have been the same type of wife.

Chapter 3 explains how Yahweh and Hosea reclaim their wives. Apparently Gomer has sold herself into prostitution, for God tells Hosea to buy her back (3:1-3). He pays for her, then takes her home. She must reject all other men and be faithful to Hosea (3:3). Likewise, God will restore Israel after their time of punishment. The people will cling to the Lord and renounce all idols (3:4-5).

Without question, Hosea suffers more personal humiliation than any other prophet. Twice he has to love an adulterous woman. His obedience to God costs him dearly. Still, he does not suffer alone. Israel sins like Gomer. Yahweh experiences the humiliation of the covenant people worshiping idols. Both God and prophet, then, pay a huge price to redeem their straying spouses. Few other biblical texts combine divine and human pain so keenly.

Hosea 4—14: Israel's Adultery Detailed

Hosea 4—14 demonstrates Israel's spiritual adultery through a series of alternating speeches. First God or the prophet speaks, then the other responds. For instance, Hosea says God has a charge to bring against Israel in 4:1-3. He mentions five sins, with adultery concluding the list. Yahweh responds by denouncing priest (4:6-9), prophet (4:5), and people (4:9-14) as lovers of adultery and prostitution. Hosea warns Judah to avoid Samaria's adultery, for he has no hope that Samaria will repent (4:15-19).

Israel's descent into sin continues to be described as adultery through chapter 10. Yahweh (5:3) and Hosea (5:4) agree that a "spirit of prostitution" will lead Israel to destruction. Further, God charges that Israel has given birth to illegitimate children, which refers to the pagan rituals the nation has instituted (5:7). The Lord must punish such sins (5:14-15), so Hosea warns the people to repent (6:1-3). God doubts the harlot will change (6:4-10), since she delights in her wickedness (6:11—7:7). Northern Israel is determined to sell herself to new lovers (8:9).

The nation's fate is summarized in 8:7 (NIV): "They sow the wind / and reap the whirlwind." Israel's prosperity will cease, for she will go into exile in Egypt and Assyria (9:1-3). In marriage terms, the nation will no longer receive her husband's support. She will have no home (9:15), children (9:16), food (10:8), or protection (10:13-15). Israel and their king will be totally destroyed (10:15).

Despite Israel's covenant breaking (11:1-7), however, God continues to love the people. Yahweh decides to restore the fallen spouse (11:8-11). Sin will be punished first (11:12—13:16). Then Israel will confess her sins (14:1-3). God will respond by healing and loving Israel (14:4). Israel will once more flourish in the land (14:4-8). Wisdom will prevail (14:9).

God does not order Hosea to do something God will not do. Like Hosea, Yahweh will buy back Israel from her owners. Hosea predicts this love before Assyria conquers the Northern Kingdom. Sadly, this whole sequence of events could have been avoided if Israel had kept the covenant. Spiritual adultery has ruined Israel's marriage to Yahweh.

Joel: Prophet of Apathy and Cruelty

It is difficult, if not impossible, to fix Joel's exact date. Scholars have suggested dates as early as the 800s and as late as the 300s. References to Israel's scattering (3:1-3) and Greece's role as slave trader (3:6) point to a post-587 B.C. setting. Still, these verses are not conclusive. Joel's role in the Twelve does not depend on its date. Rather, its twin emphases on Israel's religious apathy and the nations' cruelty to Israel make it an excellent successor to Hosea.

Joel prophesies after a locust plague devastates the land (1:2-12). He warns that Israel needs to repent (1:13-20), lest something worse happen to the nation. The people's sin is left unstated, but hints emerge in the text. Priests are asked to mourn (1:13), and the people are told to fast (2:15). All Israel is admonished to "Rend your heart / and not your garments" (2:13, NIV). Each of these commands relates more to the nation's inward state than to any outward disobedience. Perhaps the people have simply ceased to care about such things. If so, the day of Yahweh will come upon them (2:1-2). A great army will swarm the land like a locust plague (2:3-11).

If the nation repents, though, God will forgive them (2:12-17). Yahweh will feed them (2:19), deliver them (2:20), and restore the land (2:25). "Afterward," God says, "I will pour out my Spirit on all people" (2:28, NIV). Men, women, young, and old will prophesy (2:28). At that time whoever turns to God will be saved (2:29-32). Of course, Peter says Pentecost fulfills this prediction (Acts 2:14-21). When the Holy Spirit came upon the early church, every person became a prophet of God, and thousands trusted in Jesus.

After the day of judgment, God will punish Israel's neighbors (3:1-3). Why? Because they sold Jews into slavery (3:3,6-8). They robbed Israel's treasury (3:4-5). Therefore, God will arm Israel for war (3:9-

11), lure the nations into battle (3:12-13), and destroy them all (3:14-16). The Jews, on the other hand, will once again be God's special people (3:17-21). Like a roaring lion, Yahweh will devour His prey (3:16).

Like Hosea, Joel portrays Israel's sin in fairly broad terms. Hosea says Israel is a covenant-breaking prostitute. Joel claims the people do not care about their sin. Apathy and unfaithfulness are a dangerous combination. Joel adds the nations to the Twelve's list of sinners. He and Hosea both despise Israel's sins, but he notes that Israel does not sin alone. God will judge all the wicked—whatever their national origin.

Amos: Prophet of Justice

Amos preaches about 760 to 750. Scholars establish this date because of the earthquake mentioned in 1:1 and the political situation reflected in the book.[6] Like Hosea, Amos ministers during the reigns of Jeroboam II and Uzziah. Israel enjoys peace, prosperity, and prestige. Assyria will march again under the leadership of Tiglath-Pileser III (745-727) but has yet to move.[7] Thus, Amos' audience lives seemingly blessed, contented lives (4:1-5; 6:1-6).

Amos shatters Israel's peace and disturbs the people's pride. He preaches mostly against Northern Israel's pagan worship sites (7:10-17), yet he also declares Judah's wickedness. Thus, he shares Hosea's convictions about his fellow Jews. He also agrees with Joel's assessment of the nations. They, too, have broken God's laws. Both Jew and Gentile alike, then, will face the day of the Lord. Unlike Hosea and Joel, though, Amos condemns a number of specific sins. Each sin relates to the practice of justice and love for neighbor.

Amos 1—2: The Worldwide Lack of Justice and Love

According to Amos, all Israel's neighbors have sinned against God. How? By sinning against one another. For example, Damascus has mistreated Gilead (1:3-5). Gaza has sold whole communities into slavery (1:6-8), as has Tyre (1:9-10). Edom has bought Gaza and Tyre's victims (1:11-12). Ammon and Moab are even worse. Ammon has ripped open pregnant women when capturing cities, and Moab has desecrated graves (1:13—2:3). All these sins break "the covenant of brotherhood" (1:9). These nations know they mistreat one another, yet they perpetuate international hatred.

If Amos preached 1:1—2:3 to a Jewish audience, they probably enjoyed his message. They agree. Their enemies *are* horrible people. Amos does not stop, however, after denouncing Israel's enemies. Instead, he claims Judah has broken the Sinai covenant (2:4-5). Then he says that injustice occurs daily in Northern Israel. The righteous and needy are sold into slavery for small debts (2:6). The poor are trampled, and immorality and idolatry are common (2:7-8). This behavior has arisen despite God's work on their behalf and the prophets' warnings (2:9-12). Therefore, punishment looms on the horizon (2:13-16). Oppression of the weak cannot continue.

Amos 3—6: Injustice in Israel

With his main themes of injustice and punishment introduced, Amos lists specific ways Israel sins. Yahweh has chosen Israel (3:1-2), but the nation has rejected the Lord's standards. Horrible, comprehensive judgment will overtake this people that does "not know how to do right" (3:10, NIV). Only pieces of the nation will survive (3:12).

Samaria's women "oppress the poor and crush the needy" (4:1, NIV) so they can have enough wine. They are sleek and well-fed "cows," while the poor lack food and shelter (4:1). The women also brag about what they give to God (4:4-5). Amos predicts they "will be taken away with hooks, / the last of you with fishhooks" (4:2, NIV). Whoever defeats Samaria will apparently use hooks to drag these fine women into exile. This oppression has continued despite Yahweh's repeated warnings (4:6-11), so the people must "prepare to meet [their] God" (4:12, NIV).

Israel's men are no better. They visit pagan worship centers (5:4-6), corrupt the judicial system (5:7-10), and trample the poor (5:11). Their bribes keep the poor from receiving justice (5:12). They are rich and complacent (6:1), lie on luxurious beds (6:4), eat choice meats (6:4), enjoy playing and improvising harp music (6:5), and "drink wine by the bowlful" (6:6, NIV). Despite their ease, or perhaps because of it, they do not care about their nation's spiritual condition (6:7). Yahweh despises their prideful disregard of others (6:8-14).

The day of the Lord will punish these oppressors. Judgment day will be a time of darkness for the wicked (5:18). No speck of light will penetrate the gloom (5:20). Wailing will sound in the streets (5:16-17), and the people will be exiled to a distant land (5:27). The people may bring sacrifices to pacify Yahweh, but punishment will still fall (5:18-23). What does the Lord want? "Let justice roll like a river, / and righteousness like an ever-flowing stream!" (5:24). Only justice and kindness can stop God's wrath now.

Amos 7:1—9:10: Visions of Coming Destruction

A series of visions demonstrates the severity of the future judgment. First, Amos sees locusts coming to eat all the crops (7:1-2). He intercedes, though, so God relents (7:3). Second, Amos envisions a consuming fire (7:4). Again he prays, and again Yahweh relents (7:5-6). Third, the prophet observes the Lord measuring the nation for destruction (7:7). This time God refuses to spare Israel any longer (7:8-9). Clearly, judgment will devastate the land, leaving it barren and wasted.

Amos shares his message throughout Northern Israel. Not surprisingly, the priests and king do not appreciate his condemnations (7:10-11). The high priest warns him to go back to Judah (7:12-13). Amos refuses to flee, however, since God has called him to prophesy (7:14-15). Instead, he tells the priest that Israel will go into exile and that the priest's own family will be killed or forced into prostitution (7:16).

Amos' final comments on the day of Yahweh begin with another vision. He sees a basket of ripe fruit, which means Israel is ripe for punishment (8:1-3). God will wait no longer, for injustice increases daily (8:4-6). Religious festivals and prophetic messages will cease (8:9-12). Even the young will faint (8:13-14), for the Lord will pursue sinners into exile and kill them there (9:1-4). Israel has become as sinful as other countries, so God will punish them as if no covenant ever existed between them (9:5-10).

Amos 9:11-15: Future Hope

Amos has left no doubt about Israel and their neighbors' immediate future. Injustice will cause them all to fall. After punishment, though, Yahweh will return Israel to their homeland (9:11-12). The barren land will be fruitful again (9:13), and the exiled people will come home (9:14-15). Despite his pointed messages on sin and judgment, Amos still envisions renewal and restoration for the covenant people.

So far the Twelve has chronicled Israel and the nations' sins. Neither group will escape destruction. Is there any hope? Could Israel be reconciled to God and her neighbors?

Obadiah: Prophet of International Hatred

Obadiah is the shortest book in the Bible. Written near 587 B.C., Obadiah highlights Edom's hatred for Israel. When Jerusalem is destroyed, the Edomites delight in the disaster (v. 12). They kill refugees from the city and take plunder (vv. 9-14). For their pride (vv. 2-4), hatred of brother and neighbor (vv. 9-10), and viciousness (vv. 15-18), Edom will be punished (vv. 5-8,18). Edom, Babylon, and others look for opportunities to harm Israel. Does Israel return this hatred? Or do they love their neighbor as they love themselves?

Jonah: Prophet of Israel's Hatred of Neighbor

Jonah has always generated a great deal of discussion. Scholars have debated whether Jonah was really swallowed by a fish, and thus whether the book is a literal account or a parable. These arguments have tended to obscure the book's message, or at least push it into the background. Jonah's main theme is Israel's hatred of neighbor. It, therefore, logically follows Obadiah's treatment of Edom's hatred towards Israel.

The setting for Jonah is probably the first half of the eighth century B.C. (800 to 750). This date is correct if Jonah is the same character mentioned in 2 Kings 14:25. That Jonah lived during Jeroboam II's reign (about 786-746)[8] and had a good reputation as a prophet of God. Since Jonah preaches to Assyria, it is important to note that country's situation in the late eighth century B.C. Assyria had grown weaker over time but would rise again under Tiglath-Pileser III (745-727). Tiglath leads Assyria to new heights as a conquering, terror-inducing world power. God sends Jonah to Nineveh, Assyria's capital city, then, to turn the nation towards righteousness before it gets more wicked.

Jonah feels no compassion for Nineveh's spiritual problems. God calls him to preach to Nineveh (1:1-2), but the prophet takes a ship heading in the opposite direction (1:3). Yahweh interrupts Jonah's cruise by creating a great storm (1:4). Jonah confesses his sin to the sailors, who throw him overboard (1:5-16). Only after a night in the belly of a "great fish" (1:17) does Jonah decide to obey the Lord (2:1-10).

Once in Nineveh, he preaches half-heartedly. In Hebrew his message uses only five words (3:1-4). He mentions punishment, yet he says nothing about repentance or restoration. Despite his preaching style, the Assyrians repent (3:6). They proclaim a fast and humble themselves (3:6-9). Seeing their change of heart, Yahweh forgives them (3:10).

Finally, and worst of all, Jonah becomes angry and depressed over the Lord's mercy (4:1). He wants God to destroy Nineveh. In fact, he feels more distress over the withering of a shade-giving plant than over the city's death (4:9). Yahweh rebukes him, then asks, "Should I not be concerned about Nineveh, that great city?" (4:11).

Because of Jonahlike attitudes, Israel demonstrates as much hatred for Assyria as Edom has for Jerusalem. Indeed, Nineveh seems more inclined toward righteousness than Israel. After all, Nineveh obeys God's commands. Jonah's story parallels the message of Hosea and Obadiah. Like Jonah, Israel ran from God (Hosea), failed to obey God's word (Amos), and hated their neighbor (Obadiah). No solution to injustice and hatred has emerged.

Micah: Prophet of Hope Beyond Judgment

Micah preaches about the same time as Isaiah. Both men minister during the reigns of Jotham, Ahaz, and Hezekiah (1:1; Isa. 1:1). Thus, Micah works sometime between 750 and 686 B.C. He addresses Southern Israel after Northern Israel falls in 722 B.C. He also warns Judah of its sins during the Sennacherib crisis of 701 B.C. (Note 2 Kings 18—19; Isa. 36—37.) This prophecy summarizes the Twelve's emphasis on sin, yet also hints at a better future for Israel.

Chapter 1 begins with what, at this point in the Twelve, seems a logical conclusion. God will punish Jerusalem and Samaria for their sins (1:1-6). Idolatry and spiritual adultery will cause the destruction of Israel's cities (1:7-16). The people are guilty of defrauding and coveting (2:1-2), false prophecy (2:6-11), accepting bribes (3:11), and fortune telling (3:11). Both halves of Israel have taken God for granted, believing God will bless them no matter what they do (3:11-12). They are wrong, for God promises to level Jerusalem (3:12).

Before continuing his comments on sin and punishment, Micah offers a glimpse of restoration. This strategy resembles Jeremiah's placing of chapters 30—33 before chapters 34—51. Micah states that "in the last days" (4:1) the temple will be rebuilt (4:1). People from many nations will come to Jerusalem to worship Yahweh (4:2). Peace and love will result (4:3-5). Hatred and injustice will cease, and the oppressed will return home (4:6-7). Israel's sorrow will turn to joy at that time (4:9-13).

How will this restoration begin? A son of David will be born in Bethlehem (5:2). He will "shepherd his flock / in the strength of the Lord, / in the majesty of the name of the Lord his God" (5:4, NIV). "He will be their peace" (5:5, NIV), for he will defeat enemies like the Assyrians (5:5-6). Israel will be established among the nations (5:7-9) and will cast off its idols (5:10-15). These wonderful events, though, lie in the future. Judgment awaits now.

One more time the Lord voices a complaint against Israel. Chapter 6 mentions God's past actions on their behalf (6:1-5) and describes the fate of the dishonest, violent, and materialistic (6:9-16). God requires mercy, humility, and fellowship with Him (6:6-8). These are not impossible standards. No wonder Micah mourns in 7:1-6 and prays for hope in 7:7. Yahweh will keep all promises made to Israel (7:7-17), but sin currently blocks future blessings (7:18-20). Only the day of Yahweh can remove Israel's sin and start the restoration process.

By now readers should sense the depth of worldwide sin. Israel and the nations hate one another. Both parties spread hatred and injustice. Judgment has become inevitable. All nations will suffer. Individuals who are righteous, such as Jeremiah and Ezekiel, will suffer with the wicked. Still, punishment will eventually redeem Israel by separating the righteous remnant from the wicked majority.

Nahum: Prophet of Assyria's Punishment

God's patience with the Gentile nations will not last forever. Their punishment must take place. Nahum announces that Assyria, the fierce conqueror of Northern Israel, will be destroyed. This prediction begins the punishment emphasis in the Twelve. Nahum mentions the fall of Thebes (663 B.C.) and Nineveh (612 B.C.). Therefore, he preaches sometime between 663 and 612 B.C. Assyria has already defeated Samaria and other countries and now begins to decline. Babylon manages to overrun Nineveh in 612 B.C. Assyria maintains a presence in the region for a time but ceases to be the major force.

Nahum stresses that the Lord does not punish Assyria because of personal vindictiveness. Yahweh is patient (1:3), good (1:7), and "a refuge in times of trouble" (1:7, NIV). Punishment comes because Assyria "plots against Yahweh" (1:11) by worshiping idols and oppressing other countries (1:14-15). Since Assyria opposes God, God stands against Assyria (2:13). Their army will collapse, and the city will be looted (2:5-12). This fate fits a nation that has raped and terrorized others (3:1-7).

The whole earth will rejoice in Assyria's demise (3:18-19). Why? Because the whole earth has experienced Assyria's cruelty (3:19). Some commentators think Nahum's attitude is wrong since the Old Testament, and especially the New Testament, teaches love of enemies.[9] Such criticisms fail to recognize God's victory over sin here.[10] They also fail to accept normal human emotions. Is it proper to mourn the death of a Hitler or Stalin? Ancient peoples put Assyria in a similar category.

Punishment has begun. If Assyria's power is no match for Yahweh, then smaller nations are in trouble too. Because judgment begins with a major power, the totality of Yahweh's "day" becomes evident. What about Israel? How long can the covenant people escape unless they repent?

Habakkuk: Prophet of Faith Amidst Chaos

Habakkuk prophesies about the same time as Jeremiah. Before one of the Babylonian invasions (or before 605, 597, or 587 B.C.), he questions God about world events. Yahweh's answers reveal that judgment will soon fall on Israel and Babylon. Both covenant and noncovenant nations must face the day of Yahweh. Habakkuk's probing questions mark him as one of the brightest of the prophets.

Like other Old Testament characters, Habakkuk wonders why the evil in his nation escape punishment (1:2-4). The wicked are violent, unjust, destructive, and divisive, yet God lets them live (1:3). Their actions "paralyze" the courts and pervert justice (1:4). "How long" (1:2) will such activities continue?

Yahweh responds by informing the prophet that Babylon will punish Israel's wicked (1:5-11). Exile will cleanse the land of unjust and violent persons. Not yet satisfied, Habakkuk observes that Babylon defeating Israel leaves the wicked still prospering. Who will punish Babylon, evil conqueror of wicked Israel (1:12—2:1)?

The Lord's answer has two parts. First, Yahweh reminds Habakkuk that in the devastating days ahead, "The just shall live by faith" (2:4). Only faith will sustain the faithful in tough times. The apostle Paul builds his theology around this concept. Martin Luther, John Calvin, and John Wesley formed Christian movements partly based on this verse. Second, Yahweh assures Habakkuk that Babylon will pay for its sins (2:2-20). Thus, the wicked never escape. All nations who build empires by bloodshed (2:12) and idolatry (2:19) will perish. God remains in control of the whole earth (2:20).

These answers satisfy Habakkuk. In a concluding hymn he says, "I stand in awe of your deeds, O Lord" (3:2, NIV). He pledges to live by faith. Regardless of how difficult times become (3:16-18), the prophet knows God will be his strength and direct his steps (3:19).

Though Yahweh's day has not come yet, Habakkuk knows punishment is inevitable. It will affect foreign sinners, as Nahum suggests. Assyria and Babylon are powerful, yet under God's control. Habakkuk adds Israel to the list of the wicked. If the covenant people can expect devastation, then what must the other nations expect?

Zephaniah: Prophet of Universal Punishment

Writing sometime during Josiah's reign (640-609 B.C.), Zephaniah leaves no doubt about the universal scope of the day of Yahweh. Individuals will be punished. Officials (1:4), royalty (1:8), and common citizens (1:12-13) will be swept "away" (1:2-3). Nations will be judged. Smaller countries like Judah (2:1), Philistia (2:4-7), and Moab and

Ammon (2:8-10) will not survive. Influential nations such as Ethiopia (2:12) and Assyria (2:13-15) will fall too. Clearly, Zephaniah summarizes judgment in the Twelve, much like Micah summarizes sin.

Will anyone survive judgment? Zephaniah offers some hope. The day of Yahweh will rid the earth of evil people (3:6-13). A remnant of righteous persons will emerge from this purging (3:8-9). This group will come from all nations and will serve Yahweh together. God promises to bless, heal, and favor this faithful group (3:14-17). By emphasizing the remnant, Zephaniah shows that punishment can lead to hope.

Judgment overtakes Jerusalem in 587 B.C. Babylon punishes Israel's wicked, as Habakkuk said they would. Before then, Babylon defeats Assyria in 612 B.C., which confirms Nahum's ideas. In turn, Persia crushes Babylon in 539 B.C. All these events represent *days* of Yahweh. Still, the prophets look forward to a still greater "day." On that day, evil will be eradicated. Then God will rule through the remnant (Mic. 4; Zeph. 3:8-9). For those who experience Jerusalem's destruction, though, that defeat defines all future punishments.

Haggai: Prophet of Temple Restoration

Much time passes between Zephaniah and Haggai. Babylon crushes Jerusalem in 587 B.C. Most Jews are deported to Babylon. Because of the Assyrian-enforced exile of 722 B.C., few Jews remain anywhere in the promised land. In 539 B.C., however, Persia defeats Babylon. Cyrus, Persia's leader, issues a decree that allows Jews to return to Jerusalem. He thinks defeated peoples will gladly serve Persia if they are allowed to live and worship in their own land. Isaiah 44:28 and 45:1 present this event as Yahweh's direct intervention in history. Punishment has ended. Restoration can now begin.

Guided by a religious leader (Joshua) and a civic leader (Zerubbabel), many Jews return to Jerusalem between 538 and 535 B.C. What they find discourages them. The city lies in ruins without protective walls. The temple remains a heap of rubble. Is this the glorious homecoming the earlier prophets promised? How will Yahweh restore Israel?

Between this initial return to the land and Haggai's ministry (about 520 to 516 B.C.), Israel struggles. These fifteen to twenty years bring famine, economic depression, and keen disappointment (1:5-11). Haggai says these disasters occur because the people have not rebuilt the temple (1:9). They have built themselves homes (1:2-4), yet they leave God's house a ruin. The remnant must learn to put God first. A new temple will demonstrate their desire to serve Yahweh faithfully.

PALESTINE UNDER PERSIAN RULE
Scale of Miles
0 10 20 30
Scale of Kilometers
0 10 20 30 40
Mediterranean Sea
Mt. Lebanon
SIDON
Mt. Hermon
Tyre
DAMASCUS
TYRE
Kedesh
Achzib
Hazor
ACHZIB
Acco
KARNAIM
ACCO
Karnaim
GALILEE
Sea of Kinnereth
Yarmuk River
HAURAN
Mt. Carmel
Beth-yerah
Dor
Strato's Tower
DOR
Plain of Sharon
Narbatah
Pella
GILEAD
Samaria
Mt.Ebal
Shechem
Apollonia
Mt.Gerizim
Jabbok River
Jordan River
SAMARIA
Aphek
Accrabbah
Joppa
Ono
Shiloh
Neballat
Lower Beth Horon
Rabbah
Lod
Hadid
AMMON
Gittaim
Beeroth
Bethel
Gilgal
Tyre of Tobiah
Jamnia
Gezer
Mizpah
Ai
Ramah
Jericho
Kiriath Jearim
Gibeon
Geba
Heshbon
Azekah
Anathoth
Kephirah
Jerusalem
Ashdod
ASHDOD
Beth Hakkerem
YAHUD
Zanoah
Bethlehem
Medeba
Adullam
Ashkelon
Keilah
Netophah
Beth Zur
Tekoa
Mareshah
Nebo
Lachish
Gaza
Hebron
En Gedi
Dead Sea
Arnon River
Gerar
Ziklag
En-rimmon
IDUMEA
MOAB
Beersheba
(EDOMITES)
NABATEAN

Therefore, Haggai advises the people's leaders to build immediately (1:12). Unlike earlier generations, this group obeys the prophet. Joshua and Zerubbabel organize workers and begin construction at once (1:13-15). Apparently the people fear another day of punishment (1:12) and believe Yahweh will bless the work (1:13-14).

After only a month of labor (compare 1:14-15 and 2:1), the people dedicate the temple.[11] It is much smaller than Solomon's temple, so it may seem "like nothing" to the people (2:3). So God encourages the people by promising that "The glory of this present house will be greater than the former, says the Lord of hosts, and in this place I will give peace, declares the Lord of hosts" (2:9). Yahweh also pledges to bless the people (2:19), their land (2:15-19), and their leaders (2:4; 2:20-23). In other words, temple renewal will lead to national restoration. God will help the people when they make worshiping Yahweh their top priority.

Zechariah: Prophet of Jerusalem's Restoration

Temple construction alone cannot restore Israel. Zechariah, who prophesies at virtually the same time as Haggai,[12] thinks Jerusalem must also be rebuilt for Israel to rise again. This opinion agrees with statements made by Micah (4:1-5), Isaiah (54:11-17), and Jeremiah (31:38-40).

Zechariah is somewhat difficult to understand for several reasons. First, the book describes eight unusual visions without always divulging their meaning. Second, scholars disagree about its date and authorship. Many writers believe chapters 1—8 and 9—14 are so different that the sections must come from different authors. Other commentators, however, think the book is a unified whole and argue that Zechariah wrote it all.[13] Third, it is not always easy to tell whether Zechariah's predictions have occurred, or are yet to happen.

Despite these difficulties, most authors recognize the importance of Jerusalem's renewal in Zechariah. This theme appears throughout the prophecy, linking its various parts.

Zechariah 1—8: Visions of a Restored Jerusalem

Before any renewal develops, the prophet explains Israel's history (1:1-6). In the past, Israel constantly broke Yahweh's commands (1:4). Therefore, punishment overwhelmed the nation (1:5). Now, however, the remnant repents and admits their sins (1:6). Because of this humility, Yahweh can bless Israel again.

Eight visions show how the Lord responds to repentance (1:7—6:8). The first vision asks how long God will judge Zion (1:12). God answers that He is still "very jealous for Jerusalem" (1:14, NIV). Yahweh will therefore "return to Jerusalem with mercy" and rebuild the temple (1:16, NIV). He will once "again comfort Zion and choose Jerusalem" (1:17, NIV). The third vision portrays "a man" measuring Jerusalem (2:1-3). God promises this man that Jerusalem will be an unwalled city protected by the Lord (2:4-5). Vision four predicts the priesthood's cleansing and bases the cleansing on Yahweh's love for Jerusalem (3:2). No other vision mentions Jerusalem by name, but temple construction is discussed (4:9; 6:12). Zechariah says people from many countries will come to rebuild the sanctuary (6:15). Thus, the resettling of Jerusalem will lead to the cleansing of the priesthood, the return of the exiles, and the rebuilding of the temple.

Chapters 7—8 summarize Zechariah's messages from the Lord. The prophet states again God's claim that Israel's sins led to exile (7:14). How will God reunite the people? Zechariah claims God will "return to Zion and dwell in Jerusalem. Then Jerusalem will be called the city of truth, and the mountain of the Lord of hosts will be called the holy mountain" (8:3). God's presence will guarantee peace in the city (8:4-5). Exiles will gladly return home (8:7-8). The temple will be rebuilt (8:9), the land will become fruitful (8:12), and the people will be righteous (8:14-19). Then Israel will bless all nations (8:20-23). Jerusalem's restoration triggers all these wonders.

Zechariah 9—14: Security for the Restored Jerusalem

Of course, Israel's enemies will attempt to stop the restoration process. Too, Israel may be tempted to turn away from the Lord again. How will Yahweh address these potential problems?

Zechariah declares that God will fight for Israel (9:8). Old regional foes will oppose Israel, but they will be defeated (9:1-7). Indeed, any survivors will convert to Yahweh worship (9:7). These victories will occur because a savior will come to Jerusalem, "gentle and riding on a donkey" (9:9-13, NIV). At that time God will protect the people from harm (9:14-17). New Testament writers quote 9:9 when describing Jesus' entry into Jerusalem at the start of passion week (Matt. 21:5; John 12:14-15). They believe only Jesus can save and protect God's people.

More promises follow in chapters 10—13. Yahweh pledges to restore the whole land (10:1-12) and vows to give the people good shepherds, or leaders (11:1-17). A "worthless shepherd" will never again guide them to destruction. Jerusalem's citizens will repel all invaders, for the Lord will "destroy all the nations that attack Jerusalem" (12:9, NIV). Then Israel will mourn for their sins (12:10-14), and God will cleanse them all (13:1-6). Clearly, Yahweh will use punishment to create a new, faithful nation (13:7-9).

Finally, on an ultimate day of Yahweh, the Lord will defeat all Israel's enemies (14:1-8). Then, God will rule the earth (14:9). All nations will worship Yahweh in Jerusalem (14:16-19). Every person and item in Jerusalem will be "holy to the Lord" (14:20, NIV), for every wicked individual will be banished (14:21). At this time, then, all peoples, Jew and Gentile alike, will worship the Lord together. Again, it is the restoration of Jerusalem that initiates this process. Yahweh will eliminate all obstacles to this glorious conclusion.

Malachi: Prophet of Restoration of Israel's People

A restored temple and city mean little if the people themselves fail to serve the Lord. During Haggai and Zechariah's ministries the people are receptive to the Lord's commands. They repent, rebuild the temple, and plan to restore Jerusalem. As the decades pass, though, the people sin again. By the time Malachi preaches, temple worship has grown corrupt (1:6-10), the priests have lost respect for God (2:1-9), and divorce has become common (2:10-16). Most scholars date Malachi about 430 B.C. since the events in the prophecy are similar to those described in Ezra and Nehemiah. Thus, Israel has gone backwards spiritually in the ninety years between Zechariah and Malachi.

Israel's attitude leads to much of this decline. First, they doubt God's love, perhaps because they have not been very prosperous (1:1-2). Yahweh reminds the people that He chose Jacob, their father, over Esau (1:3-5). Their problems do not stem from a lack of divine support. Second, the priests and people disdain proper worship (1:6-14). They bring crippled, worthless animal sacrifices to the temple and expect God to be pleased (1:6-11). They consider the whole worship process a waste of time (1:12-13). God warns that this mind-set is unacceptable (1:14). Third, the priests have no reverence for God's law (2:1-9). They have lied about Yahweh's standards, so the Lord has humiliated them (2:9).

Certain actions have also hurt the nation. The men have divorced their wives without cause and have broken their marriage vows (2:10-16). They have also "robbed God" by withholding their tithes and offerings (3:6-9). Yahweh, therefore, withholds blessings from the land (3:10-12). Finally, they speak against God. How? By claiming that God blesses the wicked. After all, the wicked seem to always get rich (3:14-15).

By now readers should know God's response. The day of the Lord will purge evil from the land. God will send a "messenger of the covenant" to purify the priests and the temple (3:1-5). This messenger will be Elijah, who will help the people repent (4:5-6). Jesus says John the Baptist was this Elijah who prepares the way of the Lord (3:1; Matt. 11:14). John prepared many Israelites to believe in Jesus. Malachi knows, then, that only the Messiah can truly change Israel permanently.

Thus, a restored Jerusalem and temple are not God's ultimate goal. Yahweh still desires friendship with a holy people. Israel will receive God's blessings if they will keep their covenant with Yahweh. So Malachi stresses restoration in a very practical way. He believes Zechariah's lofty predictions can only come true if Israel's attitudes and actions demonstrate their commitment to the Lord.

Conclusion

The prophets answer three ultimate *why* questions. Why did the nation perish? Because of idolatry, of course, but also because of greed, oppression, injustice, pride, political miscalculation, and a host of other sins and results of sins. Israel broke every command, in every century, at every opportunity. Yahweh sent the prophets to warn the people. The prophets tell the truth and often receive only ridicule and persecution for their efforts. A just God cannot tolerate such wickedness.

Why have hope for the future? Because God's promises to Abraham are never ending. Yahweh uses even punishment to redeem and renew the people. A faithful people will receive the blessings of an always-faithful Lord. The most important of these blessings is the appearance of the special Son of God, the King who will bring the nation back to God. Since the Messiah's reign will never end, hope should never die. Isaiah, Jonah, Micah, Zephaniah, and other prophets claim that all nations will be served by the Messiah.

Why believe in God? Because God is just, merciful, and loving. Yahweh stands ready to forgive all sins and right all wrongs. The prophets are confident that God defends them and will defend all who follow Yahweh's commands.

Yahweh, Israel, the prophets, and the nations are interesting characters. They interact in unique and creative ways. While doing so, they interpret Israel's history. They set an agenda for the future by explaining the past. They teach readers to think, to imagine, and to believe in God.[14]

Questions for Reflection

1. How do the ethical teachings found in Amos and Hosea apply to today?
2. What does Hosea's marriage experience teach about God's nature, the prophet's job description, and marriage?
3. How does Joel characterize God? How do you respond to a God like this?
4. Describe Obadiah's vision of the day of the Lord and of the kingdom of God.
5. Does it matter if Jonah is a fictional book?
6. Compare Isaiah 2:1-4 with Micah 4:1-5. What does this teach you about the nature of prophecy?
7. Is Nahum's attitude about Assyria's defeat improper?
8. What does Habakkuk's experience on the watchtower teach about the nature of prophecy and faith?
9. In what way may Zephaniah have surprised Israel with his words about the foreign nations?
10. Why do Haggai and Zechariah emphasize rebuilding the temple so strongly? Do you think they have misplaced priorities?
11. Explain the differences between Malachi's view of God's covenant and the view of the people he addressed.

Notes

1. Hans W. Wolff, *Hosea*, Hermenia Series, trans. Gary Stansell (Philadelphia: Fortress, 1974), xxi.

2. Uzziah ruled about 783-742, and Jeroboam II reigned about 786-746. Compare John Bright, *A History of Israel,* 2d ed. (Philadelphia: Westminster, 1972), 254-55.

3. Wolff, xxi.

4. Wolff, xxii.

5. Note Douglas Stuart's excellent survey of relevant opinions in *Hosea-Jonah*, vol. 31 in *Word Biblical Commentary* (Waco, Tex.: Word Books, 1987), 11-12.

6. James Luther Mays, *Amos: A Commentary*, Old Testament Library (Philadelphia: Westminster, 1969), 2.

7. Thomas J. Finley, *Joel, Amos, Obadiah*, Wycliffe Exegetical Commentary (Chicago: Moody Press, 1990), 107-09.

8. Bright, 254.

9. J. M. P. Smith, W. H. Ward, and J. A. Bewer, *A Critical and Exegetical Commentary on Micah, Zephaniah, Nahum, Habakkuk, Obadiah, and Joel*, International Critical Commentary (New York: Scribner's, 1911), 281.

10. John D. W. Watts, *The Books of Joel, Obadiah, Jonah, Nahum, Ha*

bakkuk, and Zephaniah, Cambridge Bible Commentary (London: Cambridge, 1975), 120.

11. Three temples are mentioned in Scripture. Solomon finished his temple about 966 B.C. Zerubbabel and Joshua's temple was built about 520-516. Herod the Great, who ruled Jerusalem 37-4 B.C., built the magnificent temple that was standing in Jesus' time.

12. Carol L. Meyers and Eric M. Meyers, *Haggai, Zechariah, Malachi,* vol. 25B in *The Anchor Bible* (Garden City, N.Y.: Doubleday, 1987), xli.

13. Meyers and Meyers represent the former viewpoint and Joyce Baldwin, *Haggai, Zechariah, Malachi*, Tyndale Old Testament Commentaries (Downers Grove, Ill.: Inter-Varsity Press, 1972), the latter position.

14. See also Roy L. Honeycutt, Jr., and others, "Hosea—Malachi" in *The Broadman Bible Commentary,* vol. 7 (Nashville: Broadman Press, 1972); Peter C. Craigie, *Twelve Prophets,* vol. 1 in *The Daily Study Bible Series* (Philadelphia: Westminster, 1984); David Alan Hubbard, *Hosea, Joel, and Amos,* vols. 22A and 22B in *Tyndale Old Testament Commentaries* (Downers Grove, Ill.: Inter-Varsity Press, 1989); Billy K. Smith, *Hosea, Joel, Amos, Obadiah, Jonah,* vol. 13 in *Layman's Bible Book Commentary* (Nashville: Broadman Press, 1982); Francis I. Anderson and David Noel Freedman, *Hosea,* vol. 24 in *Old Testament Library* (Philadelphia: Westminster, 1969); Gary V. Smith, *Amos,* Library of Biblical Interpretation (Grand Rapids: Regency Reference Library, 1989); Thomas J. Finley, *Joel, Amos, Obadiah,* The Wycliffe Exegetical Commentary (Chicago: Moody Press, 1990); Page H. Kelley, *Micah, Nahum, Habakkuk, Zephaniah, Haggai, Zechariah, Malachi,* vol. 14 in *Layman's Bible Book Commentary* (Nashville: Broadman Press, 1984); Ralph L. Smith, *Micah—Malachi,* vol. 32 in *Word Biblical Commentary* (Waco, Tex.: Word Books, 1984); Elizabeth Achtemeier, *Nahum—Malachi,* Interpretation (Atlanta: John Knox, 1986).

THE MEDO-BABYLONIAN KINGDOM
SCYTHIANS
Aral Sea
SCYTHIANS
Black Sea
Caucasus Mountains
Caspian Sea
SCYTHIANS
THRACIANS
CAPPADOCIA
URARTU
GREEKS
Aegean Sea
PARTHIA
ASSYRIA
Athens
Sardis
KUE
Haran
LYDIA
Tarsus
Carchemish
Nineveh
Calah
Sparta
Aleppo
Euphrates
Tigris
MEDIAN EMPIRE
Ecbatana
Lycia
Riblah
Tadmor
Sippar
CYPRUS
SYRIA
Susa
Damascus
NEW
Babylon
Nippur
ELAM
Tyre
BABYLON
Larsa
Mediterranean Sea
Erech
Megiddo
BABYONIAN
Ur
AMMON
Jerusalem
LIBYANS
MOAB
EMPIRE
PERSIA
Sais
EDOM
Memphis
Dumah
Elath
Persian Gulf
ARABS
EGYPT
Tema
Nile
Dedan
Thebes
Red Sea
Elephantine
ETHIOPIA
SCALE OF MILES
0
100
200
300
SCALE OF K ILOMETERS
0
100
200
300
400
500

Part IV
The Writings

Introduction

Despite all we have learned about Israel's story and why it happened, several questions remain unanswered. Most of these questions relate to how Israel applied their faith. For example, how did people of faith worship? How did they wrestle with doubts, increase their knowledge of God, or survive harsh circumstances? How did they comfort the hurting? How did they celebrate love and encourage one another? In short, how did following Yahweh affect their daily lives?

The Writings—Psalms, Job, Proverbs, Ruth, The Song of Songs, Ecclesiastes, Lamentations, Esther, Daniel, Ezra-Nehemiah, and Chronicles—address these, and other, questions. These books guide readers through a broad range of human emotions, experiences, and thoughts. The Psalms introduce us to the richness of Israel's individual and group worship. Job's doubts about God's justice challenge us to think about our faith. Proverbs quotes Solomon and other sage men and women to teach us how to attain wisdom. Ruth, Esther, and Daniel illustrate how to survive life's harsh realities. Ezra, Nehemiah, and Chronicles encourage all who face seemingly insurmountable problems. Lamentations and Ecclesiastes help us release grief and cynicism, while the Song of Songs reminds us of the joy of love.

Thus, the Writings complete the Old Testament by teaching us how to live. Readers should not, however, expect easy answers to life's problems. The characters in these books struggle to know how to make their faith work. They often think and act without the certainty that they are correct. As we join their struggles, we can learn from their mistakes and their victories. If we accept life's challenges with the courage they demonstrate, then we too can possess meaningful, consistent faith.

12
Psalms: *How to Worship*

Major Characters: David, Yahweh, Israel, and unnamed individual worshipers
Major Events: David's personal struggles, the Assyrian and Babylonian invasions, the fall of Jerusalem, and exile
Major Themes: God's power, love, and forgiveness; God's covenants with Abraham and David; the need for individual and national deliverance; praise of Yahweh; mourning personal sins; and lamenting national sin

Introduction

The Psalms represent the best prayers, hymns, and calls to worship that Israel produced. They were collected over a long period of time, as the different historical events they describe indicate. All are poetic in form and, therefore, utilize the three types of parallelism mentioned on pages 23-24 and 139-140. Their broad subject matter and poetic genius have long made the Psalms popular with readers.

There are basically three ways to interpret the Psalms. First, many people read them as general individual expressions of spirituality. These readers expect Psalms to speak to their personal lives, regardless of the text's original setting or purpose. This type of interpretation too often misuses Scripture. Texts can be made to mean whatever a reader wishes. Too, this kind of interpretation misses the opportunity to apply the Psalms to national and community issues.

Second, the Psalms can be analyzed by their literary type, or form, and their use in Israel's worship. They can then be applied appropriately to today. Hermann Gunkel pioneered the study of psalm forms. He groups psalms that have similar content, tone, and settings. Gunkel notes five basic types of psalms: hymns of praise, royal psalms, individual thanksgiving songs, individual laments, and community laments.[1] Claus Westermann thinks these categories come from either praises or laments, while other scholars prefer to expand the number of forms.[2] Though his list is not perfect, Gunkel's five types provide an adequate introduction to psalm types.

Hymns of praise usually consist of a call to praise, reasons for praising God, and a concluding praise. Psalm 113:1-3 commands God's servants in all lands to praise the Lord. Next, 113:4-9a says Yahweh deserves praise for being powerful and helping the poor and barren. Finally, 113:9b concludes the psalm with a second call to praise. Hymns of praise exalt God for various reasons. For example, worshipers praise the Lord as Creator (Pss. 8; 29; 104), Savior (Pss. 100; 103), and King of Israel (Pss. 46; 48).

Royal psalms comment on the lives and actions of Israel's kings. While doing so, they often refer to the messiah, the coming king. Royal psalms follow no set pattern. They also cover a variety of situations, such as coronation (Ps. 2), marriage (Ps. 45), or battle (Ps. 144). The clearest messianic royal psalm is 110, which speaks of a king who is also "a priest after the order of Melchizedek" (v. 4). Hebrews refers to this text five times to describe the person and work of Jesus Christ (5:6,10; 6:20; 7:17,21).

Thanksgiving psalms mention particular times and ways God has blessed an individual or the nation. They are therefore more specific in nature than hymns of praise. These psalms open with a statement of praise, describe some past trouble, note how God helped in that situation, and conclude with a statement of gratitude. For instance, Psalm 30 thanks Yahweh for His help (v. 1), calls the problem life threatening (vv. 2-5), claims God heard the cry for help (vv. 6-9), and promises to thank God forever (vv. 10-12). Other thanksgiving psalms include 18; 32; 107; 116; and 138.

Individual laments appear more often than any other psalm type. They mourn personal sin (Pss. 6; 32; 51), the presence of enemies (Pss. 3; 7; 13), or even sickness and disease (Pss. 31; 102). Typically, individual laments unfold in four segments, as Psalm 51 illustrates. The worshiper offers a general prayer for deliverance (vv. 1-2), describes the problem (vv. 3-6), asks for help (vv. 7-12), and pledges to serve God when forgiveness is granted (vv. 13-19).

Community laments are, of course, similar to individual laments. They differ in that they help the whole nation mourn together when war, famine, drought, or some other disaster afflicts Israel. Psalms 44; 74; 79; and 80 are all community laments. Psalm 80 shows that community laments call on God (vv. 1-3), complain about a situation (vv. 4-7), review Yahweh's past help (vv. 8-11), petition for new help (vv. 12-17), and vow to serve God when trouble passes (vv. 18-19). Modern readers are often offended at the way community and individual laments complain to God. We must remember, though, that these psalmists believe Yahweh will solve the problem. They therefore base the complaint on faith in God.

Not all psalms fit neatly into these categories, as Gunkel admits. Still, readers can understand most psalms by following these patterns. The main problem with this approach is that it does not make sense of the canonical order of the psalms. Readers must read each individual psalm, classify it, then move to the next text. Little continuity emerges.

A third way to interpret the psalms is to find meaning in the book's present order. Obviously, Psalms' diversity of material makes this a difficult task. Recently, however, Gerald Wilson and John Walton have suggested some ways to read Psalms as a book.[3]

Wilson notes that the Hebrew Bible divides Psalms into five parts: 1—41; 42—72; 73—89; 90—106; and 107—150. This division reflects some purposeful arranging of the book. He also analyzes the titles attached to the psalms. Seventy-three psalms are traced to David, twelve to Asaph, eleven to the "sons of Korah," two to Solomon, and one each to Moses and Ethan. Asaph and the sons of Korah were probably groups of singers, but nothing is known about Ethan. Other titles describe a psalm's composition or note its use on special occasions.[4] Some of the oldest psalm manuscripts, such as the Dead Sea Scrolls, leave out the titles. Thus, most scholars conclude that the titles were probably added after the psalms were written. Since they were added by students of Israel's history, though, they may still provide accurate information about the psalms.

Based on his analysis of the book, Wilson thinks the Book of Psalms discusses how Israel has kept or broken their covenant with Yahweh. Chapters 1—41 proclaim the covenant. Chapters 42—72 discuss the passing on of the covenant to the next generation, but chapters 73—89 reveal that the covenant has not been kept. Therefore, chapters 90—106 may state how an exiled Israel should repent. Chapters 107—150 then conclude the book by offering hope to those who ask the Lord to forgive them.[5] This format parallels the prophets' emphases on election, sin, punishment, and restoration.

Walton agrees that Psalms charts Israel's relationship to the covenant. He takes the psalm titles seriously and uses them to date the five sections of the book. Walton says Psalms 1—2 introduce God's love for the righteousness and special covenant with David. Then, chapters 3—41 deal with David's conflict with Saul, and chapters 42—72 with David's reign. Next, chapters 73—89 discuss the Assyrian crisis. Finally, chapters 90—106 reflect on the temple's destruction, while chapters 107—145 contemplate the return of worship in Jerusalem. Psalms 146—150 complete the book by commanding the nation to praise Yahweh.[6] Walton's scheme helps readers see how

Psalms parallels the historical events discussed in Samuel and Kings.

This book will try to combine the last two ways of interpreting Psalms. It is important to observe the book's many distinct literary types. It is also important to note how the book unfolds. The former and latter prophets indicate that Israel sins against God, loses the promised land, and will someday rise again. Likewise, Psalms moves from lament, to praise, and back again, thus showing how the worship of Israel's faithful kept pace with the nation's good and bad times.

Psalms 1—41: Worshiping God in Times of Trouble

Worship must be durable to be authentic. Psalms 1—41 stress maintaining faithfulness to God under extreme pressure. Most of these psalms are personal laments, and most of the titles connect them to David. Of course, David had many problems, including Saul's jealousy and Absalom's rebellion. Israel also experienced many national problems, even when they tried to follow Yahweh. Troubles helped strengthen and purify Israel and David's faith. Their problems were real, but they were not the most important reality in their lives. God occupied that position.

Psalms 1—2 introduce the book's main emphases—the human struggle to honor God and Yahweh's greatness. Psalm 1 contrasts the fate of the righteous and that of the wicked. The righteous refuse the counsel of the wicked (v. 1). They spurn the life-style of sinners and obey God's law (v. 2). Thus, they are secure in life and will be secure after death (v. 3). On the other hand, the wicked will blow away like chaff from the threshing floor on judgment day (vv. 4-5). Yahweh knows, and will not tolerate, their breaking of the law (v. 6).

The wicked, though, never accept God's sovereignty. They oppose the Lord and His people (2:1-3). Such rebellion is foolish. God laughs at the wicked (2:4). Yahweh rules the earth and has established David's throne forever (2:5-7). The nations will belong to David's (and God's) son (2:8-9), so they should stop their ridiculous behavior. They should bow to David's authority, as God commands (2:10-12).

Unfortunately, Israel's enemies ignore these warnings. As a result, troubles abound. Psalms 3—7 ask God for deliverance from harm, as do Psalms 9—14 and 16—17. Psalms 8; 15; and 18 break the chain by praising Yahweh's majesty, by describing the person who pleases God, and by thanking the Lord for saving the righteous in the past, respectively. Psalms 19—21 praise Yahweh as Creator (19:1-6), Author of Scripture (19:7-14), Helper of the righteous (20:1-9), and Defender of the king (21:1-13). Still, at times God's people feel deserted (22:1), humiliated (22:6), exhausted (22:14), and near defeat (22:19-21). They promise to praise God when deliverance comes (22:22-31).

Again the book returns to its two great themes. The great God shepherds the righteous (23:1-6). Those who trust in Yahweh have all they need (23:1-3) and should not even fear death (23:4-6). Psalm 24 exalts God as king and promises that Yahweh shares His kingdom with the righteous. Still, the great king does not release the righteous from all troubles. The godly have enemies (25:1-3). They long for vindication from foes (26:1), from evildoers (27:2-3) who "do not regard the works of the Lord" (28:5). Such difficulties teach worshipers to believe that their Creator (Ps. 29) will heal (30:2) and hide them (Ps. 31) in all circumstances.

How can the faithful maintain their relationship with God? By confessing their sins (Ps. 32). By fearing God and counting on Yahweh's goodness (33:18-22). By realizing that the righteous suffer many afflictions, but that God delivers them from all troubles (34:19). With these attitudes in place, Yahweh's followers can learn not to worry about the success of the wicked (Ps. 37). They can let God "contend" with the wicked (35:1) and expect the Lord to deal with those who refuse to fear Him (36:1).

Even faithful worshipers, though, can fall. What can they do then? They can expect that God will not forsake or destroy those who repent (Ps. 38). God knows humans live only a short time (39:1-6) and will not withhold compassion for long (40:11). Yahweh "considers the poor" (41:1), and protects those who are unjustly attacked (41:9-10). Because of such confidence, the worshiper concludes this section of Psalms by blessing Yahweh, the everlasting God of Israel (41:13).

Psalms 42—72: Teaching Worship to the Next Generation

Worship will not happen by accident; it must be taught to each new generation. Laments, praises, and thanksgiving psalms, like those in Psalms 1—41, can aid any person who knows them. It is important, then, for such poems to be handed down, or faith may die in Israel. The titles in part 2 of Psalms continue to highlight David's life but also feature psalms of Korah, Asaph, and Solomon. The psalms attributed to David model proper worship. The other psalms focus on God's continuous relationship with Israel.

Psalms 42—49 are linked to Korah, and Psalm 50 to Asaph. This break with the David psalms helps readers recognize the section's transition theme. Regardless of their generation, all who worship God must seek the Lord like a "deer pants for the water brooks"

(42:1). They must earnestly seek the living God (42:2) and God's light and truth (43:3). The faith their parents taught them (44:1-3) must become their faith, if they are to receive help from Yahweh (44:4-26). When faith becomes personal to new worshipers, major national events like royal weddings (Ps. 45), natural disasters (46:1-3), and wars (47:1-4) will not shake them. Instead, they will live simply in Jerusalem (Pss. 48—49) and will offer proper sacrifices as they worship in the temple (Ps. 50).

What role does the older generation play in the development of their descendants? The next seventeen chapters, most of which are David psalms, help answer this question. Psalm 51 echoes the preceding psalm's emphasis on the proper motivation for worship. God does not want sacrifices unless they are given by a person with "a broken and contrite heart" (51:17, NIV). Sins must be confessed before Yahweh will consider a sacrifice valid. Not even David can sin and come to worship as if nothing has happened. Psalm 51 may be David's prayer after his sin with Bathsheba. If so, the poem's honesty and depth of repentance teaches future generations the seriousness of sin and the greatness of God's forgiveness.

The wicked also teach their beliefs to their children. Therefore, the righteous will always have enemies. The righteous must oppose the boastful sinner (52:1), who claims God does not exist (53:1). This position will not be popular, however, so Psalms 54—64 teach new worshipers to share their problems with God and wait for the Lord's help. Their patience will be rewarded, for the God of Zion (65:1), Creator of the earth (65:5-13), hears their prayers (66:16-20). God will indeed "cause his face to shine" (67:1, KJV) on the righteous. The Lord's power will thereby become known throughout the earth (67:2-7).

The new generation learns that God overcomes all enemies (68:1-2) and cares for the widows and prisoners (68:5-6). Yahweh bears the people's burdens (68:19). Yahweh rescues those who call on Him (Pss. 69—70), whether they are old or young (71:14-24). Generations come and go, but Yahweh's faithfulness never falters.

Psalm 72 describes the changing of kings in Israel. The psalm is attributed to Solomon, but 72:20 (KJV) says, "The prayers of David the son of Jesse are ended." Apparently, David prays for his son here (v. 1). He asks God to make his son judge correctly (v. 2), aid the afflicted (vv. 4,12-15), and thus enjoy a long and prosperous reign (vv. 8-11,16-17). God alone can make the new king successful (vv. 18-19). David ends his prayer knowing his own life has not been flawless, but he is certain that he has tried to teach Solomon how to serve Yahweh.

Psalms 73—89: The Consequences of Rejecting a Godly Heritage

Godly parents do not always produce godly children. David himself fathers both Solomon and Absalom. The Book of Judges shows what happens when later generations do not follow the good example of their parents (Judg. 2:10). Of course, 1 and 2 Kings chronicle Israel's descent into idolatry and national defeat. Similarly, Psalms 73—89 describes a nation that loses the faith that had sustained David. As a result, the people experience devastation and exile. Even during these bleak times, the righteous continue to seek God and pray for their country's restoration.

This section seems to open with just another thanksgiving psalm. The author thanks Yahweh for deliverance from the wicked (73:15-24) and notes that the Lord destroys all who are unfaithful (73:27). The psalm has ominous overtones, however, since Israel becomes unfaithful over time. Because of this slide, God allows Israel's foes to destroy all of Jerusalem, even the temple. Yahweh's followers still worship the Lord (Pss. 75—76), yet they wonder "how long" God will punish Israel (74:1; 77:7-10).

How did Israel fall into this terrible position? Psalm 78 addresses this question by surveying the nation's history. Yahweh made a covenant with the people and expected them to teach it to their children (vv. 5-8). But these children "refused to walk in his law" (v. 10, KJV). They rebelled against God after the parting of the sea (vv. 11-20), in the wilderness (v. 40), and after they were given the land (vv. 54-57). Yahweh chose David's house, but eventually it, too, strayed from God. Thus, Israel constantly rebels against Yahweh throughout its history. Judgment is the natural result, then, of their actions.

What can the righteous do when their worship center has been destroyed? They can pray that God will save the people and show the nations Yahweh's power (79:10). They can pray for those who have become prisoners (79:11). They can pray that God will choose Israel again and lead others to serve Yahweh when the miracle occurs (Pss. 80—81). Until God restores Israel, though, the godly can only pray for justice (Pss. 82—83), praise God (Pss. 84—85), and continue to seek Yahweh's salvation (Pss. 86—88).

Psalm 89 summarizes the conflicting emotions that are so evident in this section. The worshiper exalts God's greatness (vv. 1-18), yet he recognizes that Israel is under judgment (vv. 38-45). Therefore, the author reminds the Lord of the promises to David (vv. 19-37). If David will always have a son on the throne, then how can God forsake Israel? "How long" can the punishment last (vv. 46-48)? Despite these questions, however, the psalmist waits on God, hoping for some future mercy (vv. 52). Perhaps what has been lost can be regained.

Psalms 90—106: Worship and Patience

The righteous are forced to wait for some time before they see Yahweh redeem Israel. While waiting, they attempt to strengthen their commitment to the Lord. To achieve this goal, they must continue to believe in God's goodness and power. They must strive to teach others to accept their faith, which will avert further disaster. Most importantly, they must build a theology that will sustain them through this time.

Psalms 90—99 stress God's sovereignty. First, Psalm 90, which is attributed to Moses, notes that Israel's "secret sins," or spiritual transgressions, have brought them public shame (v. 8, NIV). Still, Israel can trust that Yahweh's covenant love will redeem them (vv. 14-17). Second, Psalms 91—92 state that the Lord is the Protector of the righteous (91:11-13) and the Possessor of absolute integrity (92:15). Third, 93:1; 97:1; and 99:1 declare that God reigns over the whole earth. Therefore, God's enemies will perish (Ps. 94), even if those enemies are Israelites (Ps. 95). Fourth, Psalms 96 and 98 proclaim Yahweh as judge (96:13; 98:9). The Ruler of the earth certainly has the right to assess its inhabitants. Surely the righteous can wait in hope for this kind of God to redeem Israel.

Psalms 100—106 praise the sovereign God. Worshipers are encouraged to come before God with joy and thanksgiving (100:4). They are told to put aside their sins (101:1-5), for the Lord rejects deceitful worshipers (101:6-8). When they repent, the faithful can enjoy God's unchanging grace (Ps. 102), pardon (103:3), healing (103:3), acceptance (103:6-14), and sovereignty (103:19). The great Creator delivered the Israelites from Egypt and will not forget them now (Ps. 105). Psalm 106 surveys Israel's history much like Psalm 78. This passage analyzes the nation's sinful past (106:1-43), yet the psalmist does not lose hope. The author believes Yahweh will someday remember the people (106:44-46). Surely the Lord will gather the people from the nations where they have been scattered (106:47).

Psalms 107—150: Worship and Restoration

Eventually, the righteous have their patience rewarded. God hears their prayers and ends the exile. This redemption calls for celebration. It also calls for a faith that will eliminate future disaster. The last section of the book focuses on these two emphases. Here the faithful no longer merely wait and watch for deliverance. Now they try to secure Israel's future.

Psalms 107—110 announce Israel's return to the land and reaffirm God's covenant with David. Because of Yahweh's covenant kindness (107:1), Israel has been "gathered from the lands" (107:3, NIV). The people were once "in misery and chains" (107:10) but are now free. Renewal has begun. Yahweh blesses the needy with a fruitful land (107:33-40); thus, they can praise the Lord's "loving kindness" (108:4) and know their enemies will flee (Ps. 109). Most importantly, the Israelites can expect a future son of David to be both a king and priest (110:1-4) who will "shatter kings" and "judge the nations" (110:5-6). God's covenant with David will be kept.

Because of these assurances, the righteous can praise Yahweh's unfailing goodness (Ps. 111). They can fear the Lord (Ps. 112), knowing that God makes the poor "sit with princes" (113:7-8). As the exiles return, they realize they are experiencing a new exodus (Ps. 114), one that reminds them to dismiss all idols (Ps. 115) in favor of the Lord of salvation and truth (Pss. 116—118).

How can Israel secure the future? How can the people avoid the sins of the past? Psalm 119, the longest chapter in the book, stresses that obedience to God's word is Israel's first priority. This psalm is an acrostic poem composed in twenty-one stanzas of eight verses each. The first word in each block of eight verses begins with the same letter of the Hebrew alphabet. Verses 1-8 begin the alphabet, and verses 169-176 end it. The poet notes the blessings that accompany keeping the law. God's word keeps worshipers pure (v. 9), revives the weary (v. 25), comforts the afflicted (v. 50), and guides the believer (vv. 105-112). Delighting in God's word will allow all true worshipers to live and flourish (vv. 174-176).

Newly restored to the land and committed to the covenant, the people can once more journey to Jerusalem to worship. Psalms 120—134 are designated *songs of ascent.* These songs were perhaps sung while pilgrims traveled the steep roads to Jerusalem. The texts speak of God's house and God's worship with great joy. Truly Israel has reason to bless Yahweh in Zion again (135:21).

Israel's restored condition contrasts greatly with their experience in exile. Now the nation can recite responsive praises like Psalm 136 fervently. In captivity, however, their songs seemed flat and useless. There they wept instead of sang (137:1-3). There they longed for Jerusalem (137:4-6) and hoped for their enemies' destruction (137:7-9). Their bitterness was real and not to be copied. God has exalted the lowly now, however, so such attitudes can be put aside (138:6-8).

The people must guard their restored relationship with Yahweh. They must ask the ever-present God to find and remove any wickedness they may treasure (Ps. 139). They must bring their fears to the Lord (Pss. 140—143), knowing Yahweh will fight for them (Ps. 144).

Most of all, they must "bless [God's] name for ever and ever" (145:1, NIV). Why? Because the Lord is "gracious and merciful" (145:8), "good to all" (145:9, NIV), and "righteous in all his ways" (145:17, NIV). It is fitting, then, that Psalms 146—150 all command worshipers to "Praise the Lord!" Indeed it is right to demand that "everything that has breath praise the Lord" (150:6, NIV). If Israel worships this way consistently, they will not be so prone to rebellion.

Conclusion

Psalms is a beautiful and potent book. It contains soaring praise and horrible confessions. It spurs individuals and the whole nation to purer worship, yet it also condemns the behavior of God's people. Psalms provides instruction, rebuke, and encouragement. In other words, it defines, inspires, and safeguards worship. All who accept its principles nurture their relationship with God. All who ignore its truth seek God on their own terms, an attitude that will lead to destruction.

How should we worship? By confessing our sin and enjoying God's forgiveness. By lamenting our pain, but expecting Yahweh to help us. By thanking God properly, and by sharing our faith with the next generation. By keeping God's Word and waiting for our final redemption. All these actions honor God. They demonstrate our commitment and love for the Lord. In short, they give God the glory He deserves.[7]

Questions for Reflection

1. Does understanding the various types of psalms help you use them today? yes
2. How does understanding the structure of the Book of Psalms help you know more about its teachings?
3. In what way does the entire Book of Psalms help you become a person of blessing rather than one who is wicked?
4. Summarize lessons you learn from Psalms about worship.

Notes

1. Hermann Gunkel, *The Psalms: A Form-Critical Introduction,* trans. Thomas M. Horner (1930; reprint, Philadelphia: Fortress, 1982).

2. Note Claus Westermann, *Praise and Lament in the Psalms,* trans. Keith R. Crim and Richard N. Soulen (Edinburgh: T. T. Clark, 1981); Arthur

Weiser, *The Psalms,* trans. Herbert Hartwell (Philadelphia: Fortress, 1962).

3. Gerald Wilson, *The Editing of the Hebrew Psalter* (Chicago: Scholars Press, 1985); John H. Walton, "Psalms: A Cantata about the Davidic Covenant," *Journal of the Evangelical Theological Society* 34 (March 1991): 21-31.

4. Note Psalms 7; 30; 38; 56-60; 70; and 92.

5. Wilson, 209-27

6. Walton, 24.

7. For further study see Christoph Barth, *Introduction to the Psalms* (New York: Charles Scribner's Sons, 1966); Bernhard W. Anderson, *Out of the Depths,* rev. ed. (Philadelphia: Westminster, 1983); Helmer Ringgren, *Faith of the Psalmists,* (Philadelphia: Fortress, 1963); Peter C. Craigie, *Psalms 1—50,* vol. 19 in *Word Biblical Commentary* (Waco, Tex.: Word Books, 1983); Marvin E. Tate, *Psalms 51-100,* vol. 20 in *Word Biblical Commentary* (Dallas: Word Books, 1990); Leslie C. Allen, *Psalms 101-150,* vol. 21 in *Word Biblical Commentary* (Waco, Tex.: Word Books, 1983); Sigmund Mowinckel, *The Psalms in Israel's Worship,* 2 vols. (Nashville: Abingdon Press, 1962); Leslie Allen, *Psalms,* Word Biblical Themes (Waco, Tex.: Word Books, 1987).

13
Job: *How to Struggle with Doubt*

Major Characters: Job, God, Eliphaz, Bildad, Zophar, Elihu, Satan, Job's wife and children
Plot: Though Job is a righteous man, God allows Satan to test him through personal loss and physical pain. Puzzled, then angered, by his predicament, Job lashes out at God. Shocked at his attitude, Job's friends rebuke him and demand his repentance. Undaunted, Job seeks an audience with God, which he receives.
Major Themes: Job's righteousness, Satan's vindictiveness, the relationship between sin and suffering, God's hiddenness, and the search for wisdom

Introduction

Job has long been considered a literary masterpiece. Its stimulating discussion of the human-divine relationship, portrayal of fascinating characters, and use of rich imagery and irony place it among the best works in world literature. Written mostly as a drama, the book's alternating speeches gradually force readers to consider God's character, especially as it relates to human suffering. Properly understood, the book teaches us the value of struggling with our faith.

Job, Proverbs, and Ecclesiastes are part of a great ancient tradition called Wisdom Literature. Wisdom Literature was written in many countries, including Babylon, Egypt, Edom, and Israel. Its authors sought to teach people how to live wisely. To achieve this goal, they explored life's mysteries, such as why the righteous suffer and how God will judge people. Wisdom writers also cataloged common, everyday advice, such as how to relate to neighbors, how to serve the king, and how to avoid seductive men or women. Most Wisdom Literature is very conservative. It gives us rules to follow that will make our lives go well. It claims that those who keep the rules prosper;

those who do not, suffer. Some Wisdom Literature, however, is rather radical. It discusses what happens when the rules do not work. Job fits into this category.[1]

It is impossible to know when Job was written. The text has both very old and relatively late Hebrew words, which probably means the book was copied and recopied over a long period of time. Its setting is perhaps during Abraham's era. There is no Mosaic law, and Job acts as priest for his family. The story takes place in Uz, an unknown location in the East. Simply put, Job takes place "long ago in a faraway land." This hero's story has kept him famous for centuries. What he suffers and what he learns justify this fame.

Job 1—2: The Testing of Job

The book begins with the narrator's description of Job and his wealth. Job's character is flawless. He is blameless and upright, fears God, and shuns evil (1:1). What more could anyone ask? Job has seven sons and three daughters (1:2). He has large numbers of animals and servants and is, in fact, "the greatest of men in the east" (1:3). Job is also pious. He offers sacrifices for his children while they feast together, just in case they have "cursed God in their hearts" (1:5, NIV). Clearly, Job is one of the greatest individuals in Scripture.

Next, the text shifts from the narrator to a scene in heaven. God is receiving reports from messengers when Satan, whose Hebrew name literally means "the Adversary," comes before the Lord. Yahweh asks Satan if he has considered Job, the man of flawless character (1:8). Satan takes this question as a challenge, for he charges that God is overly protective of Job (1:9-10). Satan asserts that Job will curse God if he loses his many possessions (1:11). Certainly, Satan has seen other people reject Yahweh this way. God allows Satan to proceed against Job, but He commands him not to afflict Job's body (1:12).

Satan carries out his plan with a vengeance. One-by-one, messengers bring Job bad news. His animals and servants have been captured and killed (1:13-15,17). Fire "from heaven" has burned up his crops (1:16). Worse still, a great storm has flattened the house where his children were feasting together. All were killed (1:18-19). Job now owns nothing, and his children are dead. Will he curse God? He does not, because he realizes that he can take nothing with him to the grave. The narrator notes, "Through all this Job did not sin nor did he blame God." (1:22).

A second scene occurs in heaven. Once more Satan presents himself to God, and once more Yahweh asks Satan about Job (2:1-3). God observes that Job remains blameless and upright, maintaining his integrity. All this, God says, "although you incited me against him to swallow him up without cause" (2:3). Satan accepts the renewed challenge. Now he claims Job will curse God if he loses his health (2:4-5). Again, many people act this way. The Lord agrees but commands Satan to spare Job's life (2:6).

Satan strikes Job with a horrible disease. Job develops boils from head to toe (2:7). Itching, he scrapes his sores with a bit of broken pottery (2:8). His wife tells him to cast off his integrity. She counsels him to "curse God and die" (2:9, NIV). He rebukes her, on the grounds that he must accept both good and bad from God (2:10). Job's wife leaves the scene, but three friends, Eliphaz, Bildad; and Zophar, take her place (2:11). They have come to comfort their friend whose disease has left him disfigured (2:12). They weep with him and fall silent for seven days (2:13). Who will break the silence? What can be said about these terrible tragedies?

Job 3—31: Job's Dialogues with Eliphaz, Bildad, and Zophar

The book now begins its dramatic format. Job speaks; his friends reply; then Job speaks again. Three cycles of such speeches appear though Zophar does not use his last turn. The discussion gets very heated. Strong men exchange strong words. Two very distinct viewpoints on life appear; readers are left to decide which is correct.

Job opens the discussion with a lament that mourns the day he was born (3:1-10). He says he wishes he had died in infancy, if he had to be born at all (3:11-19). Because of his pain and loss, he prefers death to life (3:20-26). This lament differs from those in Psalms. Those texts also state the worshiper's faith in God at some point in the poem. Job offers no such statement. His friends are shocked at this omission.

Eliphaz, who is probably the oldest in the group, answers. He begins slowly, perhaps in recognition of Job's suffering (4:2). At first Eliphaz praises Job's past life, especially his teaching of the hurting (4:3-6). Soon he comes to the point. He asks Job. "Remember, who ever perished being innocent?" (4:7). He adds, "Those who sow trouble harvest it" (4:8). Clearly, Eliphaz says that Job has sinned, which explains his problems. Eliphaz supports his belief by recounting a rather vague vision he experienced one night (4:12-21) and by quoting wisdom sayings he has learned (5:1-7). He counsels Job to place his cause before God (5:8). God must be disciplining Job for his sins, so Job should repent (5:17-27) and accept God's forgiveness (5:9-16). Eliphaz apparently holds the conservative Wisdom Literature position that people get what they deserve in life.

Job rejects Eliphaz's solution. He has not sinned, so why should he repent? God has afflicted him for no reason (6:4-7), and now his friend Eliphaz has become his attacker (6:14-23). Job challenges Eliphaz to prove he has sinned (6:24-30), and he asks God to do the same (7:20). He accuses God of bullying him (7:11-21), a charge that provokes Bildad's anger.

Of the three friends, Bildad seems the harshest. He lashes out at Job, calling him a windbag (8:1-2). Pointedly, Bildad asks Job, "Does God pervert justice?" (8:3, NIV). Then, almost cruelly, he states that Job's children must have died because of "their transgression" (8:4). He urges Job to repent, for God will still forgive (8:5-7). Bildad also tells Job to go search the teachings of past Wisdom writers (8:8-10). These texts will agree with Job's friends (8:11-22).

Again Job does not budge. He asks a new question, "Can a man be righteous before God?" (9:2). In other words, can human beings ever please Yahweh? After all, God is powerful, and people are weak (9:1-11). Too, people can hardly bring God into court (9:12-20). God would win every time, for God is the world's ultimate Judge and can decide cases however He wishes. Further, God seems to mock the plight of the innocent, for the wicked prosper (9:23-25). If the righteous please God, why does Yahweh allow the wicked to defeat them? These conclusions again drive Job to challenge the Lord to reveal the reason for his suffering (10:2). Once more Job laments (10:18-22).

Zophar's comments are quite simple. He calls Job a talkative and boastful man (11:2-4). Then he informs Job that God has not punished him sufficiently (11:5-6). Zophar claims that God's ways are too difficult to understand (11:7-12). Job should take life at face value. Job should repent and let God heal him (11:13-20). Life is simple. If we sin, we suffer. If we repent, the suffering stops.

Job scoffs at such simplistic ideas. Quite sarcastically, he replies, "Doubtless you are the people, / and wisdom will die with you!" (12:2, NIV). Job claims to know what they know (12:3), but he has the nerve to say what they are afraid to say—the wicked *do* prosper (12:6). He also cites a list of proverbs to demonstrate his own familiarity with Wisdom writings (12:4—13:2). Because of the friends' inability to help him, Job turns to God again. Simply put, he wants an audience with God (13:3-12). He offers his first statement of faith as well, saying that he will trust in the Lord even if God kills him (13:15). Still, he wants to know God's complaints against him (13:20-28). Until this answer comes, he will continue to lament (14:1-22).

The friends try again. They attack Job on two fronts. They continue to argue that sin causes suffering. They also begin to tell Job God will not answer his questions personally. Eliphaz starts this process in his second speech. He, too, calls Job's comments worthless (15:1-3);

he adds that Job is irreverent (15:4), guilty (15:5-6), and too arrogant to accept the teachings of the past (15:7-16). He reproaches Job for wanting to know God's secret ways (15:8), soberly warning his friend to repent and accept Yahweh's consoling forgiveness (15:11,17-35).

At this point Job has become weary. He says the friends tire him by repeating themselves. They are "sorry comforters" (16:2). They attack him because they have never suffered. If he were in their place, he would be kinder (16:3-5). God also exhausts him by punishing without saying why (16:6-17). Yet he clings to God since the Lord is his only advocate (16:19-20). Job somehow hopes for the chance to "plead with God as a man with his neighbor" (16:21). His spirit seems broken (17:1-9), but he gathers himself and challenges the friends to further debate (17:10).

Without hesitation, Bildad speaks again. This time he calls Job a prima donna. Job acts like the whole world should stop just because he has suffered (18:1-4). If Job is so wise, he should know that the wicked always meet a horrible end (18:5-21). Bildad refuses to shift his arguments to answer why the wicked prosper or why God will not answer Job. Apparently, he and the other friends believe they and their tradition represent God to Job.

This position hardly satisfies Job. He claims both the friends and God have wronged him (19:3-5). Faced with placing his hope for answers in God or the friends, however, Job chooses God. Though Yahweh has humiliated him (19:7-22), still he seeks God. Why? Because he knows his "redeemer lives, and at the last will take his stand on earth" (19:25). This Redeemer will eventually vindicate him, even if after death (19:26). God remains Job's only hope since the friends reject him (19:21-22).

Zophar launches what will be his final assault on Job. This time he speaks with more depth. He retraces many of the friends' arguments, yet adds a new point. Zophar admits the wicked prosper for a short time but will *eventually* suffer judgment (20:5-29). Thus, he answers Job's question about the wicked in a way that may incriminate Job. Perhaps Job himself prospered for a while only to suffer justly in due time!

Job replies in a bitter tone. He wants to speak a bit, then they can mock some more (21:1-3). In response to Zophar, Job notes the length of the wicked's prosperity. Not only do the wicked live and die in comfort, their children are established as well (21:8-16). They live as they wish, and die fat and rich (21:17-26). How, then, can Zophar think the wicked prosper only briefly? All three friends speak nonsense (21:34).

One last time, Eliphaz attempts to break down Job's defenses. Forsaking his earlier friendly approach, he now accuses Job of irreverence towards God (22:4) and callous indifference to the weak (22:5-11). Apparently, he hopes Job will admit at least one of these transgressions. Again he asks his friend to confess and receive Yahweh's pardon (22:21-30). To Eliphaz's credit, he maintains his concern for Job's spiritual condition.

In response, Job revives his request for a direct conversation with the Lord. Perhaps he could enter God's courtroom, present his complaint, and plead his innocence (23:3-4). Surely God would judge his case on its merits rather than simply throwing him out of court (23:6-7). For now, though, Job seeks, but cannot find, the Lord (23:8-9). Thus, he is left to question why the wicked have what they want, while the poor and needy are left without help (24:1-12). Who can dispute that the world is an unjust place (24:25)?

Bildad's last speech is very short, and Zophar has no third speech. Scholars have suggested that these speeches have somehow gotten lost or dislocated as the text was copied over time.[2] Perhaps they are correct, but the friends may simply run out of arguments. They have not convinced Job and are, therefore, reduced to repeating their earlier statements. Here Bildad claims that Job wants to know the unknowable. God is all-powerful (25:1-3), so how can people prove Him wrong? How can Job be justified when even the moon and stars pale in comparison to God's glory (25:4-6)?

Job's final comments cover chapters 26—31. He blasts the friends one last time by saying. "What a help you are to the weak!" (26:2). He already knows God's power first-hand through what he has suffered (26:5-14). Further, he refuses to accept his friends arguments. Instead, he will cling to his integrity (27:1-6). To do otherwise *would* make him wicked and, thus, deserving of punishment (27:7-23). He will seek wisdom, however difficult it may be to discover (28:1-28). No matter what happens, he will continue to fear the Lord as his means of gaining understanding (28:28). Still, this commitment does not keep him from longing for the past. Then he was respected (29:1-25), but now even worthless men taunt him (30:1-17). God has been cruel to him (30:18-31) despite his obvious piety (31:1-40). With his case presented fully, Job stops speaking (31:40).

The dialogue has ceased with the combatants deadlocked. Job refuses to renounce his integrity by admitting to sin. He knows standard Wisdom traditions but finds them lacking. He will not rest until God tells him why he has suffered. The friends, on the other hand, believe Job is a wicked, self-serving, unrepentant sinner. They have tried to help him, but he has rejected their wisdom.

Job 32—37: Elihu's Monologue

Eliphaz, Bildad, and Zophar have nothing else to say to Job, since he is "righteous in his own eyes" (32:1, NIV). A new character enters, though, who has more arguments. Elihu, a young man who has been listening to the speeches (32:2-11), now addresses Job. Since Elihu is not introduced elsewhere, some scholars believe these chapters are a late addition to the story.[3] Other writers think Elihu acts as a human intercessor between Job and God.[4] At the very least, Elihu summarizes the friends' position. He also adds a few interesting theories of his own.

Elihu may be young, but he is confident of his abilities. He has allowed his elders to speak first, yet knows they have failed to refute Job. Therefore, he feels compelled to speak his mind (32:11-14). After a lengthy introduction, in which he announces his own brilliance (32:15—33:7), Elihu tells Job he is wrong (33:8-12). He offers four reasons for this conclusion.

First, Elihu notes that Job wants a revelation from God. Job believes God has been unnecessarily silent (33:13). Elihu says that Yahweh does speak, both through visions (33:14-18) and through pain (33:19-22). Pain, in particular, serves to warn people. Before something worse happens, the sufferer ought to repent (33:19-33). Elihu seems to say that Job's pain may be a warning, not a punishment.[5] All who accept such warnings are "redeemed . . . from going to the pit" (33:28).

Second, Elihu repeats Job's charge that the Lord is unjust. He responds that it is unthinkable for God to act wickedly (34:12). God watches the earth to make sure justice prevails (34:16-20). God always punishes the wicked (34:21-30). Therefore, Job's charges against Yahweh are very serious. He "ought to be tried to the limit" (v. 36) for saying such things. Elihu obviously agrees with Eliphaz's assessment of Job.

Third, Elihu recalls Job's longing for the past. He informs Job that he wants forgiveness and restoration without repenting (35:1-8). Job desires blessings without seeking God (35:9-13). This attitude marks Job as a wicked man and makes all his words "without knowledge" (35:16). Here Elihu parallels Bildad's comments.

Fourth, Elihu has heard Job's statement about how God lets the wicked prosper. This claim implies that God mismanages the world. Elihu defends Yahweh's conduct (36:2). God's work should be exalted for its beauty and complexity. God makes the rain (36:27-33), snow (37:6), and winds (37:17). Yahweh inspires awe in storms (37:21); but God remains hidden, so Job should accept the knowledge he has and get on with his life (37:21-24). These ideas sound much like Zophar's.

Job 38:1—42:6: Yahweh Confronts Job

Before Elihu can continue, Yahweh abruptly answers Job out of the kind of storm Elihu was just mentioning (38:1). This appearance alone proves the friends were wrong in asserting that the Lord would not answer Job personally. Will Yahweh also reject their notion that sin always causes suffering?

God makes two speeches: one in 38:2—40:2 and one in 40:6—41:34. In the first speech God uses illustrations from nature to rebuke Job. Yahweh begins by saying that Job "darkens my counsel with words without knowledge" (38:2, NIV). Therefore, God tells Job to stand up and answer some questions (38:3). Yahweh asks Job if he knows how to build the earth (38:4-7) or govern the seas (38:11). Does Job know how to direct light and darkness (39:12-15)? Can he explain great secrets such as death (38:16-24)? Can Job water the earth, make the stars shine, or care for the animals (38:25—39:30)? If not, how can he find fault with God? How can he reprove the Lord (40:2)?

Overwhelmed, Job answers humbly. He confesses his lack of knowledge and pledges to speak no more (40:3-5). Job does *not* say sin caused his suffering, but God never asks him to do so.

Yahweh's second speech is similar to the first. Again God challenges Job to answer (40:6-7). Does Job want to condemn God to justify himself (40:8)? In other words, does Job want to take God's place? If so, can Job adequately judge the wicked (40:9-14)? Can Job tame the fiercest animals on earth (40:15—41:34)? If not, the world would be a much worse place if Job were in control! This conclusion leaves Job with the option of trusting God or running his own life.

Job's reply to God's second speech is vital for the book's interpretation. He makes two very important points. First, God's comments help him know that God's purposes are not evil (42:2-3). They are often beyond human understanding (42:3), but they are not wicked. Second, God's appearance shows Job that the Lord cares about people on a personal level. Yahweh's presence satisfies Job's—and the friends'—concern about the Lord's hiddenness. Job was right. God has seen fit to answer his questions in person. God's character and works have been vindicated.

Job 42:7-17: Healing and Restoration

Now God vindicates Job. The Lord expresses anger at Job's friends for not speaking "of me what is right, as my servant Job has" (42:7, NIV). To atone for their sins, they must offer sacrifices to God, and Job must pray for them (42:8-9). God also restores Job's fortunes. In fact, he receives twice as many possessions as before (42:12). He also has ten more children, including three very beautiful daughters (42:15). Job enjoys a long life, long enough to see grandchildren born into the family (42:16). This man who held fast his integrity, questioned God, and accepted Yahweh's explanations has emerged victorious from his struggles.

Conclusion

Many Christians believe doubting and questioning God constitutes a lack of faith. Job shows doubts come even to the blameless. They are a part of life. Thus, doubts, however severe, should be taken to God. Yahweh is not intimidated by human questions. In fact, the Lord is willing to reveal answers to those who ask. God is present with even the doubter, as long as the doubter truly seeks God.

Unfortunately, many Christians also agree with Job's friends. They believe suffering always results from sin or from a lack of faith in God's restorative power. Job demonstrates suffering may result from sin but does not necessarily do so. Therefore, we ought to show compassion, or God may treat us like Eliphaz, Bildad, or Zophar.[6]

Questions for Reflection

1. Using Job as a basis, explain why you think God allows people to suffer. Does all suffering have purpose and meaning?
2. Are Job's friends correct in any of their statements?

Notes

1. Note R. B. Y. Scott, *The Way of Wisdom in the Old Testament* (New York: Macmillan Publishing Co., 1971), 32-33.

2. Norman Habel, *The Book of Job,* Old Testament Library (Philadelphia: Westminster, 1985), 366-68.

3. S. R. Driver and G. B. Gray, *A Critical and Exegetical Commentary on the Book of Job,* International Critical Commentary (Edinburgh: T. and T. Clark, 1986), xl-xli.

4. Habel, 443-44.

5. John Hartley, *The Book of Job,* New International Commentary on the Old Testament (Grand Rapids: Wm. B. Eerdmans, 1988), 485-86.

6. For further study see Gerhard von Rad, *Wisdom in Israel* (Nashville: Abingdon Press, 1972); C. Hassell Bullock, *An Introduction to the Old Testament Wisdom Books,* rev. ed. (Chicago: Moody Press, 1988); David J. A. Clines, *Job 1—20,* vol. 17 in *Word Biblical Commentary* (Dallas: Word Books, 1989); J. Gerald Jantzen, *Job,* Interpretation (Atlanta: John Knox, 1985).

14
Proverbs: *How to Develop Wisdom*

Major Characters: The wisdom teacher, the learner, the fool, wisdom, and foolishness
Plot: The learner slowly gains the knowledge and experience necessary to become a wise person.
Themes: The value of wisdom and the danger of foolishness; gaining wisdom by fearing the Lord, which leads to hard work, kindness, discretion, respect, and honesty

Introduction

Job discusses life gone bad. It teaches how to absorb life's blows, think about them, and come to an understanding of our relationship with God; but what about "normal life"? How should we live in everyday circumstances? How do we develop character that pleases the Lord? How can we relate well to others? Proverbs deals with such practical questions. It examines the art of living well, so it addresses issues that affect everyone. Proverbs admits that wisdom is difficult to attain but available to all who will learn from life.

Because of their special nature, it is particularly important to learn how to interpret Proverbs correctly. The Hebrew word for "proverb" is *mashal,* which probably means "to rule" or "to be like." A proverb, then, is a comparison about life, drawn from life.[1] A proverb attempts to teach by showing what life is "like." Proverbs state the *normal results* of correct or incorrect behavior. Thus, they are not absolute promises. To treat them as such leads to some very difficult interpretational problems.

For example, Proverbs 10:3 says, "The Lord will not allow the righteous to hunger, but He will thrust aside the craving of the wicked." Certainly Yahweh usually feeds the righteous. Still, some righteous people have starved. The writer may speak of eternity, probably using this comparison to warn the wicked. Similarly, Proverbs

10:4 says, "The hand of the diligent" makes its owner rich. Some people work hard, yet are poor. Normally, however, those who are industrious have what they need. Lazy people are often destitute. Again, Proverbs comments on how life unfolds in common, everyday circumstances. Job discusses abnormal circumstances. By including both Job and Proverbs, the Old Testament offers a balanced view of life.

By its very nature, then, Proverbs belongs to the conservative side of Wisdom Literature. It sets patterns that lead to success. Where did this type of Wisdom Literature originate? Of course, authors in other nations wrote proverbs. Egyptian proverbs particularly seem to influence Israelite proverbs at times.[2] Still, Israel's proverbs have their own unique style. They do not just imitate other traditions.

Originally, proverbs may have been recited in families. Often in Proverbs, a teacher calls the learner "my son" (1:8; 2:1; 3:1; 4:1; and 5:1). Chapter 31 contains a mother's advice to her son.[3] Later, the royal court produced proverbs. Solomon spoke many proverbs (1 Kings 4:29-34), and Hezekiah collected some of Solomon's material (Prov. 25:1). Advice to an unknown king concludes Proverbs (31:1). During the time of the kings, wisdom teachers shared proverbs and other types of Wisdom Literature with the people (note Jer. 18:18). They, too, probably called their students "my son." They may even have set up schools in which they taught wisdom to civil servants and other interested persons. Due to their wide background, the lessons in Proverbs speak to numerous life situations. They instruct leaders and followers, rich and poor, young and old.

The material in Proverbs was composed and gathered over a long period of time. Three texts link Solomon to the book (1:1; 10:1; and 25:1). Thus, some of the proverbs date at least from after 950 B.C. Solomon could also have recited proverbs older than himself. One text mentions Hezekiah (25:1), who lived about 715 B.C. Other proverbs follow that are probably even later. Therefore, most scholars date the book's contents approximately 1000-400 B.C. Like Psalms, Proverbs contains the best literature of its type from many periods in Israel's history.

It is extremely difficult to divide Proverbs into large sections. Chapters 1—9 clearly stress pursuing wisdom and avoiding foolishness. On the other hand, chapters 10—31 change subjects rapidly, seemingly at random. Despite this problem, some unifying factors do exist. Six headings appear in the book (1:1; 10:1; 22:17; 25:1; 30:1; and 31:1). After each heading, a proverb or exhortation follows that announces at least the section's main purpose. The different segments parallel and intersect one another, but the major emphases remain evident. Each section moves the learner closer to the goal of wisdom.

Like all Wisdom Literature, Proverbs teaches us how to live. It seeks to convey a mind-set, a worldview, that will guide readers. Knowledge is important, since it begins the process. Wisdom only results, though, when a learner applies wisdom teachings to life. The knowledgeable persons must become disciplined and skilled enough to act consistently. When this goal has been reached, the person will be wise. This individual will have learned how to live.

Proverbs 1—9: Choosing Wisdom—Avoiding Foolishness

The first stages of a new venture are often the most important. Choices and plans made then can determine the project's success or failure. This tendency holds true for learning how to live wisely. Learners must make some decisions in Proverbs 1—9. These decisions include how to view themselves, whom to follow, and how to sustain interest in the quest for wisdom.

Proverbs 1:1-7 introduces the entire book. Solomon's (1:1) proverbs have been preserved for a purpose. Proverbs intends to make readers discerning, righteous, and just (1:2-3). It wants to help inexperienced youths gain knowledge and discretion (1:4). It also hopes older, wiser persons will "increase in learning" (1:5). How will these goals be achieved? By learning proverbs, word pictures, traditions, and riddles (1:6).

What attitude should learners bring to this process? They must fear the Lord, for this "is the beginning of wisdom" (1:7). *Fearing* God means admitting that God alone possesses total wisdom. It therefore means respecting Yahweh and asking the Lord for help in learning. Thus, learners must choose to be humble, to be dependent on God. Any other attitude springs from pride and will doom the quest for wisdom before it even begins.

More choices await individuals who fear the Lord. First, they must choose between traditional values and those of brash sinners. Proverbs 1:8 implores, "Listen, my son, to your father's instruction / and do not forsake your mother's teaching" (NIV). Why? Because sinners entice youths to become violent and lawless (1:10-19). Second, and similarly, they must choose between wisdom and foolishness. Both are personified in Proverbs. Wisdom calls out in the streets, inviting all naive ones to learn from her. She promises great blessings, including protection in troubled times (1:20-23). All who reject her choose foolishness and doom themselves (1:24-28). They hate knowledge and fear of the Lord (1:29), so they will perish. Clearly, new learners choose between life and death.

Many benefits come to those who choose Wisdom and her traditional values. God will gladly grant them wisdom (2:6). They will understand justice, discretion, and the necessity of avoiding wicked company (2:9-15). Young men will not love wicked women (2:16-22), a theme that recurs repeatedly. The children who embrace their parents' teachings trust God, who in return makes their paths smooth and straight (3:5-6). They treat their neighbors well (3:27-30) and refuse to envy the wicked—no matter how successful they are (3:31-34). Wisdom will teach them to watch their step and choose their words carefully (4:23-27).

How can Wisdom dispense such blessings? Because she was with God from the beginning of time (8:22-23). God used Wisdom to create and sustain the world (8:24-31). Thus, Wisdom knows how to instruct kings and peasants alike (8:15-17). She is quite humble herself, for she is willing to accept the simplest person as a pupil (8:1-11). Only the self-destructive spurn her help (8:35-36).

What happens to people who choose Foolishness? They risk becoming thieves (1:10-19) and adulterers (5:1-23). They make poor business decisions (6:1-5). They become lazy (6:6-11), liars (6:12-15), proud (6:17), and divisive (6:19). In short, they tear down the community. No vital institution is safe from these fools.

Above all else, foolish young men are likely to desire wicked women. Several texts in this section warn against sexual sins (note 2:16-22; 5:1-23; 6:24-35; and 9:13-18), but chapter 7 offers the most creative caution. Here the teacher tells his "son" a story. One day he looked out his window and saw "a youth who lacked judgment" (7:7, NIV). How does he know the youth's character? Because the fool walks towards "her house" (7:8) as night falls (7:9). Who is this "her"? A loud, roving, predatory woman dressed like a prostitute (7:10-12). Brazenly, she kisses him, which no respectable Middle-Eastern woman would do, and invites him to bed (7:13-18). She says her husband is gone (7:19-20) and seduces him with other sensual comments (7:21). Like an animal unaware of a trap, the foolish young man lies in her bed, not realizing "it will cost him his life" (7:22-23). Indeed, her ways are "chambers of death" (7:27, NIV).

This scene could have been avoided (7:24). A wise man would not have desired this kind of woman. In fact, he would not go near her (7:25). Once in her presence, the foolish man feels her sensuality. He hears her pleas, considers her offer, and discards his principles. He is lost from the start. Wisdom keeps her followers from such compromising situations.

Given Wisdom's blessings and Foolishness's pitfalls, the young and inexperienced should choose Wisdom. They should accept Wisdom's invitation to enter her house, eat her food, and drink her wine (9:1-2). Wisdom, coupled with fear of the Lord (9:10), will teach the simple (9:4) "the way of understanding" (9:6, NIV). These choices made, beginners can take the next step in learning how to live.

Proverbs 10:1—22:16: Becoming a Righteous Child

Proverbs 10:1 announces the next stage of the quest for wisdom. Already, learners have chosen the path of humility before God and have rejected Foolishness in favor of Wisdom. Now, a new set of Solomon's proverbs explain how learners can truly please their parents. The parents' traditions introduced in chapters 1—9 are now described in detail. Each proverb intends to build the young seeker's character and reinforce proper behavior in older persons.

Several traits appear repeatedly in this section. They are described in antithetical poetry, which contrasts two opposites. This strategy allows readers to choose between dissimilar patterns of behavior.

The section first encourages learners to work hard (10:1-5). Lazy people will go hungry, but the diligent will have plenty. Next, learners should guard their mouths lest they become like babbling fools whose words cause violence and strife (10:6-12). The wise store up knowledge (10:14), then dispense acceptable words at the proper time (10:32). The foolish, however, teach no one (10:21) and always speak perverted words (10:32).

Further, learners should strive for righteousness in every area of their lives. Greedy persons will use dishonest scales to make extra money; God hates such behavior (11:1). The righteous are guided by humility (11:2), integrity (11:3), and the knowledge that riches will not matter on judgment day (11:4). Wicked people lie about their neighbors (11:9-13). They withhold help from the community (11:26) and trust in wealth (11:28). Wise persons aid neighbors (11:26). They protect their friends, which wins them community-wide respect (11:10). Because of their consistent goodness, "the righteous will flourish" (11:28, NASB).

Righteous persons accept advice about life's crucial decisions (12:1). Why? Because they want to choose fitting spouses (12:4). They desire to learn their trade well (12:10-12) and want peace, not anxiety (12:25). Wise children desire parental instruction (13:1) so they can gain wealth by honest means (13:1-12) and then leave an inheritance to *their* children (13:22). Children who accept discipline will also learn how to instruct their own families (13:24).

If the righteous achieve success, how can they remain humble and fear God? How can they secure their home life (14:1), avoid trusting their own wisdom (14:12), and elude arrogance and carelessness (14:16)? One way to combat pride is to care for the poor (14:19-20). It is easy to love the wealthy, but it is difficult to be kind to those who cannot repay a kindness. Those who help the poor will be happy (14:21) while those who oppose the poor really oppress God, who made them (14:31).

Homes will survive when fear of God and quiet, nonabusive words abound (14:26-30). Soft answers will turn away anger (15:1). Words of wisdom will instruct family members (15:2). Joyful hearts will guard against shattered spirits and their resulting turmoil (15:13-17). Hot-tempered parents make poor guides for children, but those who are peacemakers teach their children the best paths of life (15:18-24). God will tear down the homes of the proud and corrupt, but He will establish those who follow righteousness and fear of Yahweh (15:25-33).

Pride can be overcome through absolute commitment to Yahweh. The righteous must allow God to weigh their motives (16:2). They must submit their plans to God for approval (16:3). After all, God is sovereign (16:4). Fearing God in these ways will bring peace even with enemies (16:7). Humility will save the righteous from destruction (16:18) that arises from wicked acquaintances and poor planning (16:19-25). It will preserve domestic and community unity (16:32—17:28). Those who reject pride and divisiveness honor and delight their parents (17:21,25); these take significant strides towards wisdom.

What should developing learners shun? They must not cut themselves off from their community, thereby rejecting their heritage (18:1). Those who spurn counsel so they can speak their uninformed minds are fools (18:2). Such people offend their brothers (18:19), refuse responsibility for the community's poor (18:23), and do not recognize true friends (18:24). Fools rage against God and neighbor (19:3). Therefore, they become false witnesses (19:5,9) and shame their parents (19:13). They stop listening to either God or their parents (19:21-27). Punishment can be their only reward (19:29).

Other sins will tempt the righteous. Wine tastes good, yet it mocks the drinker (20:1). Quarrels are stimulating, but they produce enemies (20:3). Leisure always seems more fun than work; however, too much recreation can ruin a business (20:4). Unjust gain delights the wicked until it ruins them (20:17). Gossip and revenge satisfy for a moment, then come back to haunt their perpetrators (20:19,22). Violence serves various ends—none of them good (21:7). Pleasure is enjoyable but very expensive (21:17).

The wise must resist such temporary benefits for those that last. Righteous children seek permanent victories, which can only come from God (21:30-31). They realize a good name is better than undeserved riches (22:1), so they seek humility and fear of the Lord (22:4). The perverse fall into all kinds of traps (22:5), but the righteous cling to their parents' teachings (22:6). They help the poor (22:9). They work hard, unlike the lazy (22:13). Without question, those who accept wise instruction make progress in righteousness.

Proverbs 22:17—24:34: Sustaining Righteousness

Many people serve God for a time, only to fall back into foolishness later. Proverbs anticipates this possibility. It therefore addresses individuals who have become established in life (note 22:23,26; and 23:1). They are still addressed as "sons" by their teachers, not because they have not progressed in wisdom but because they have not reached full maturity. Several dangers still threaten their quest for wisdom. All emerge from the frustrations involved in achieving worldly success. All help advanced learners "know the certainty of the words of truth" (22:21, KJV).

The section begins with four warnings and an encouraging comment. First, the righteous must not oppress the poor or deny them justice simply because such sins are seemingly without penalty (22:22). Making money at the poor's expense brings God's wrath (22:23). Second, hot-tempered companions must be shunned (22:24). Otherwise, the learner may adopt their habits (22:25). Third, the righteous ought to practice economic common sense (22:26). Guaranteeing others' debts could lead to poverty (22:27) or to tactics like abusing the poor. Fourth, traditional land boundaries should be maintained (22:28). Finally, those who stay consistent and become skilled in their work will be honored. Vicious and wicked schemes are therefore unnecessary. God *will* reward the faithful.

The wise parent warns that many lusts and jealousies will tempt the learner. Those who dine with the king may desire power and luxury, both of which make "deceptive food" (23:3). Acquiring wealth seemingly requires nonstop labor (23:4), yet it is not worth the effort (23:5). The wicked rich (23:6-8) and the fool (23:9) only appear to be worth one's friendship. At times, disciplining a child seems to exhaust both parent and child. The effort must be made, though, to save the child from hell (23:13-14). Besides these things, envy (23:17), hedonism (23:20-21), sensuality (23:26-28), and strong drink (23:29-35) all conspire to sidetrack the learner from the path of wisdom. Wine seems to be especially tempting (23:31), but in the end it leads to stupidity and bondage (23:35).

Wisdom's path seems long and hard. Those who build their lives on it, however, find food for their souls (24:3-4,13-14). They do not rejoice at their enemy's defeat because they do not worry about evildoers (24:17-20). Instead, they focus on justice (24:23-26), honesty (24:28-29), and working hard rather than avoiding honest toil (24:30-

34). Such behavior marks them as people who sustain their righteousness in the difficult middle years of the quest for wisdom.

Proverbs 25—29: Becoming a Righteous Leader

Many of the proverbs in these chapters instruct leaders and those who deal with leaders. The opening verses say that kings enjoy searching for truth (25:2), and kings, therefore, quickly tire of wicked and egocentric persons (25:3-7). These two principles help shape what follows. It seems, then, that Proverbs now addresses those who have achieved some success. Early tests of wisdom have been passed. What remains to be seen is whether the successful will choose to secure their gains.

Community leaders must have a proper attitude. As the book has stated repeatedly, humility must characterize all learners. For leaders, humility means allowing the king to praise them, rather than praising themselves (25:6-7). It means settling disputes with neighbors quietly, instead of spreading gossip (25:8-10). Humble people speak words that comfort (25:11-14), and they even help their enemies (25:21-22). A humble person possesses security and confidence.

Choosing good companions and promoting worthy people is also important for leaders. Fools deserve no honor (26:1), for they are hopelessly addicted to their own opinions (26:4-5) and their foolish ways (26:11). Lazy persons should not be trusted. Their only goals are to sleep and eat (26:13-16). Gossipers also make poor companions. They offer opinions, but only those that cause contention (26:20-27). Even their flattery cannot be taken seriously (26:28). Wise leaders choose friends who can offer valid and valuable counsel (27:6,9). Good friends can be better than close relatives (27:10), especially if those relatives are unfaithful and contentious (27:13-16). Indeed, close, honest friends sharpen one another's character like iron sharpens iron (27:17).

Leaders have specific duties to fulfill. They must take good care of their own business interests (27:23-27). More importantly, they must also work towards their entire community's well-being. Thus, able leaders boldly stand against oppression, lawlessness, injustice, and lack of integrity (28:1-10). Righteous leaders admit their faults (28:11-15), refuse crooked gain (28:16-20), and show no partiality (28:21-28). Such individuals ignore bribes and flatterers, since they lead to oppression of the poor (29:4-7). Instead, they protect the poor, knowing that God has made all people (29:13-14). Wise leaders raise children that obey parents (29:15). In short, they keep the law, oppose sinners, and believe that the person "who trusts in the Lord will be exalted" (29:25, NASB).

Like all the steps towards wisdom, this advanced stage is not easy. Few people can accept responsibility for their community's welfare and maintain their own integrity. Proverbs insists, though, that some must become leaders. The principles shared in earlier chapters still apply and must be taught to a wider audience. As before, Wisdom and fear of God lead to success.

Proverbs 30: Dealing with Pride

Throughout Proverbs 1—29 pride has been declared the deadly enemy of wisdom. Despite such comments, even the wise sometimes trust their own intellect. In this chapter, Agur, an unknown teacher, declares the agony of his own stupidity as a warning against pride. He admits not knowing enough wisdom teachings and regrets his lack of knowledge about God (30:1-4). Agur states very clearly, however, that God's Word conveys all the wisdom anyone needs (30:5-6). Therefore, he asks that Yahweh give him a balanced life (30:7-9), one that will lead to peace instead of turmoil. Anyone prone to self-confidence ought to adopt this attitude.

Agur offers several numerical sayings that prove his need for more learning. He lists two, three, even four things he does not understand. This strategy invites readers to make their own lists and, thereby, learn humility. Many of the items in his lists are striking for their apparent dissimilarity. For example, he notes four things that are never satisfied: death, barren wombs, parched earth, and consuming fire (30:16). He links eagles, serpents, ships, and men loving women (30:19) as sights he cannot explain.

Of course, Agur has been very crafty here. He claims to know little, yet he demonstrates tremendous insight. Thus, he seems to caution lesser, but more prideful, individuals to check their egos. All who have been haughty should close their mouths before they get into trouble (30:32-33). Nothing good comes from pride. It is one attitude that can halt the march toward wisdom at any time.

Proverbs 31: Choosing a Life Partner

Proverbs also consistently cautions learners to avoid sexual sins. Here Lemuel, an unknown king, receives advice from his mother. Among other things, she tells him not to give his strength to women (31:3). She then proceeds to tell him what sort of wife to marry. Her comments set high standards for women, obviously, yet also prod men to become suitable husbands for worthy wives.

An excellent wife is very difficult to find and, thus, extremely valuable to her husband (31:10-12). She works cheerfully and diligently in the home and the community (31:13-15). She purchases property (31:16). Still, she finds time to show compassion to the poor (31:20). Her efforts help her husband become a respected leader (31:23), and she herself teaches others (31:26). Of course, she works hard (31:27). Fittingly, her family praises her efforts (31:28-31). No one doubts her value to her community or to her home.

This woman contrasts totally with the wicked, adulterous woman in 7:6-27. The first woman ruins several households while the latter benefits all. One deserves praise, but the other should be feared like death itself. The wise man chooses a virtuous woman for a life partner. This decision seems simple enough, yet Proverbs states that many choose incorrectly. By taking wicked women to wife, many learners all but abandon the quest for advanced wisdom.

Conclusion

Proverbs carefully leads readers in a seminar on how to live. It guides seekers through the various stages of acquiring wisdom, always identifying dangers yet never making the process seem impossible. However difficult the task may be, wise persons will determine to learn to fear God, embrace humility, accept discipline, and, thus, develop character. Other paths are easier to travel, the Proverbs writer admits, but no other path yields true and lasting benefits.[4]

Questions for Reflection

1. Define wisdom.
2. How does knowing the definition of *proverb* help you interpret the book?
3. Compare the teachings about wealth in Job and Proverbs. Briefly describe your own view of the value of wealth.

Notes

1. Marvin E. Tate, Jr., "Proverbs," in *The Broadman Bible Commentary,* vol. 5 (Nashville: Broadman Press, 1971), 5.

2. For example, the Egyptian "Instruction of Amen-Em-Opet sounds similar to Proverbs 22:17—24:22. Note James B. Pritchard, ed., *Ancient Near Eastern Texts Relating to the Old Testament*, 2d ed. (Princeton: Princeton University Press, 1955), 421-25.

3. Though the text refers to "sons," the ethical principles in Proverbs certainly apply to men and women alike. Unfortunately, in ancient times

only men received formal education.

4. More information on Proverbs is available in Derek Kidner, *Proverbs,* vol. 15 in Tyndale Old Testament Commentaries (Downers Grove, Ill.: Inter-Varsity Press, 1964); William McKane, *Proverbs,* The Old Testament Library (Philadelphia: Westminster, 1970); R. B. Y. Scott, *Proverbs, Ecclesiastes,* vol. 18 in *The Anchor Bible* (Garden City, N.Y.: Doubleday, 1965); L. D. Johnson, *Proverbs, Ecclesiastes, Song of Solomon,* vol. 9 in *Layman's Bible Book Commentary* (Nashville: Broadman Press, 1982).

15
Ruth: *How to Survive Personal Difficulties*

Major Characters: Naomi, Ruth, and Boaz
Minor Characters: Naomi's husband and sons, an unnamed relative of Boaz's, and Orpah, Naomi's other daughter-in-law
Plot: Naomi loses her husband and sons, which places her in a seemingly impossible financial situation. She is rescued by her own cunning, the beauty and industriousness of her Moabite daughter-in-law, and Boaz's kindness.
Themes: God's protection of the weak, Ruth's faithfulness to Naomi, and Boaz's generosity

Introduction

Several Old Testament stories point out life's difficulties. Some individuals cause problems for themselves. Other characters, though, such as Abel and Job, suffer despite their innocence. Ruth presents a story of two women who encounter personal setbacks through no fault of their own. Because they are widows, they appear helpless and frail. Through a series of events that conveys tragedy, courage, comedy, and intrigue, these women prove they are hardly weak or without resources. This story follows very naturally after Proverbs in the canon, since Proverbs concludes with a discussion of a virtuous woman.

To really appreciate this short story, it is important to know a few ancient customs. First, widows were to be provided for by their sons. Thus, it was important for women to bear sons to support them in their old age. Second, if a widow had no son but could still bear children, the deceased husband's brother was supposed to produce a son with her (Deut. 25:5-10). Individuals who performed this duty were called "kinsmen redeemers." The child would be the *dead man's* son and would care for his mother. Third, land owned by the dead man could be purchased by his family. This practice kept property from passing from the family's possession. Fourth, it was rare for foreigners to adopt the religion of another nation. Understanding these details will help readers grasp the tension in Ruth.

Ruth occurs during the time of the judges. In other words, it takes place when Israel does whatever is "right in [their] own eyes" (Judg. 17:6; 21:25, KJV). Chaos reigns. Many people groups are moving through the region. No one knows when the book was actually written. David is mentioned, though, so it must be dated after his time. The era in which they lived makes Naomi and Ruth's story even more remarkable. They survive during one of Israel's most difficult periods.

Ruth 1: Naomi's Grief

The book's first five verses announce the problem the book must solve. As if living in chaotic times were not bad enough, a famine arises during the time of the judges. An Israelite family is therefore forced to go live in Moab (1:1). This must have been a hard decision given Moab and Israel's hatred of one another. There are four persons in the family: Elimelech the husband, Naomi the wife, and two sons named Mahlon and Chilion. Naomi seems well-set for the future. After all, she has three men to support her.

Sadly, her husband dies (1:3). Still, she has her two sons. The sons marry Moabite women named Orpah and Ruth, and they settle in the land for ten years. Then, Mahlon and Chilion die. This leaves three widows and no men to father more sons (1:5). Orpah and Ruth can remarry, but Naomi has no hope. She decides to return to her old home, Bethlehem, and live among her people.

Naomi advises Orpah and Ruth to go back to Moab and search for new husbands (1:8-9). Both younger women weep and profess their loyalty to Naomi. They say they will go with *her* people (1:10). Naomi tells them she can bear no more sons for them, so they should leave (1:11-13). Orpah departs, but Ruth clings to Naomi (1:14). Ruth begs Naomi not to make her go. She even promises to accept Naomi's people and Naomi's God and says only death will separate them (1:16-17). In effect, then, Ruth converts to Israelite culture and to the worship of Yahweh.

The women travel to Bethlehem (1:19). There Naomi declares her bitterness at what God has done to her (1:20-21). She once had a husband and sons. Now she is left with only Ruth. Barley harvest is beginning (1:22), which seems to contrast Naomi's sense that her time of fertility is past. The harvest for the women, however, is about to begin.

Ruth 2: Glimpses of Hope

Ruth decides to provide food for herself and Naomi. She gathers grain in the field of a man named Boaz, a relative of Naomi's dead husband (2:1-3). After Ruth has labored for some time, Boaz himself arrives. He notices Ruth almost immediately and asks his servants about her (2:4-7). Boaz has heard how Ruth has cared for Naomi, so he tells his servants to protect her and leave extra grain for her to collect (2:8-16). His actions show that Boaz is a kind man and may also show that he finds Ruth attractive.

At day's end Ruth reports to Naomi. She explains where she worked and how Boaz "took notice" of her (2:17-19). When she hears Boaz's name, Naomi seems to come out of her depression. Why? Because Boaz is a "kinsman redeemer" (2:20). Perhaps he can do more for the women than just be kind to Ruth! Naomi praises God for linking them with Boaz (2:20). She also counsels Ruth to continue working in Boaz's fields (2:21-23). Ruth and Naomi's situation no longer looks as desperate, but they still need long-term protection. What can they do?

Ruth 3:1—4:17: Solution to the Problem

Naomi now attempts to repay Ruth's loyalty to her by helping Ruth find a new husband. She says, "My daughter, shall I not seek security for you, that it may be well for you?" (3:1). Of course, security for Ruth will mean security for Naomi as well. Naomi notes that Boaz is their close relative (3:2). He also likes Ruth, so he is a likely candidate for kinsman redeemer.

Apparently, Naomi thinks Boaz needs some encouragement, for she tells Ruth to bathe, put on perfume, and dress in her best clothes (3:3). Ruth must sneak down to the threshing floor, where Boaz will spend the night. Once he has eaten, had plenty of wine, and fallen asleep, Ruth must act. She must "uncover his feet" and lie next to him (3:4). Naomi feels confident Boaz will respond to this less-than-subtle hint (3:4).

Ruth does as Naomi suggests. Boaz has had enough wine to make "his heart glad" (3:7), and he sinks into a contented sleep. Stealthily, Ruth lies next to him (3:7). During the night, something rouses Boaz. He wakes, "and, behold, a woman lying at his feet!" (3:8). Obviously, this does not happen to him every night. Understandably, he asks the woman her name. Ruth's response amounts to a proposal of marriage. She invites him to spread his covering over her since he is a kinsman redeemer (3:9).

Boaz is delighted. He thanks Ruth for wanting him, rather than some younger man (3:10), and he promises to marry her (3:11). There is only one small problem. Another man is a closer relative than Boaz (3:12). Still, Boaz will deal with this man the next day. He asks Ruth to stay with him until morning (3:13). She leaves just before daylight and reports to her mother-in-law (3:14-17). Naomi understands Boaz well. She tells Ruth that Boaz will settle the matter quickly. Indeed, "the man will not rest until he has finished the matter today" (3:18).

Business was conducted at the city gates in this era. Therefore, Boaz gathers the other potential kinsman redeemer along with ten witnesses and begins to negotiate for Ruth (4:1-2). First, he notes that Naomi must sell her husband's land, so it will not leave his family's possession (4:3). He asks the man if he wants the land, and the man says he does (4:4). Second, he informs the man that whoever buys the land must also shelter Ruth and father a child by her (4:5). The man cannot afford the land *and* the woman, so he allows Boaz to redeem them both (4:6). Third, Boaz announces he will purchase the land and, more important to him, Ruth (4:7-12). He has kept his promise to settle the issue quickly.

With all obstacles removed, Boaz and Ruth marry (4:13). Soon, they have a son (4:13). Naomi and Ruth now have the security they lost in chapter 1. Boaz rejoices to have a young and faithful wife. Ruth has found love again, and Naomi can age in peace. A happier ending is hard to imagine.

Ruth 4:18-22: Appendix

Boaz and Ruth's marriage has great long-term impact in Israel. Their son (Obed) will become David's grandfather. God not only blesses Ruth with present security, He also gives Ruth permanent prominence in Israel's history. Not only has Naomi arranged security for Ruth, she has also helped secure, through David's eternal kingdom, all who trust in Christ.

Conclusion

How did these women survive their personal tragedies? They remained faithful to one another. They trusted in God, who provided Boaz to care for them. Too, they used their own wits and ingenuity to achieve their desired results. Far from being helpless, with God's help and their own daring, they are a very capable duo. Their success encourages others in distress. That God used Ruth to help produce David shows that even seemingly obscure persons can be used for eternal glory.[1]

Questions for Reflection

1. Does Ruth compromise her integrity when she visits Boaz at the threshing floor?
2. What does Ruth teach us about God's covenant with David?

Note

1. For further study see Robert L. Hubbard, *The Book of Ruth* (Grand Rapids: Wm. B. Eerdmans, 1988); Jack Sasson, *Ruth* (Baltimore: Johns Hopkins Press, 1979); A. Graeme Auld, *Joshua, Judges, and Ruth,* The Daily Study Bible Series (Philadelphia: Westminster, 1984).

16
Song of Songs: *How to Enjoy Love*

Major Characters: Bride and Bridegroom (Solomon)
Minor Characters: Chorus of Bride's friends and city watchman
Plot: The lovers praise one another, seek time together, and regret all time apart.
Themes: The excitement of physical attraction and the joy of human sexuality

Introduction

Proverbs 31 began a series of texts on love and marriage. Comments there on the virtuous woman are followed by the life of a virtuous, loyal, hardworking woman named Ruth. That story ends with a marriage. The Song of Songs continues this trend by rejoicing in the beauty and joy of love. This book is a series of love poems set in a dramatic framework. The two lovers exult in one another, and their doing so instructs readers how to enjoy and express their appreciation for their own beloveds. Because of its celebration of love, I will call the book Song of Songs. Many scholars prefer its other traditional title, Song of Solomon.

The Song of Songs has stirred much controversy over the centuries. Scholars have seldom agreed on its interpretation because of its theme and contents. For one thing, the book never mentions God's name. Too, at times its love poetry becomes very explicit. Neither of these facts seem very spiritual or edifying, so many commentators have treated the book as an allegory or symbolic story. In this scheme Solomon represents God, and his beloved represents Israel or the church. Their love, then, demonstrates God's love for His people.

Such interpretations may ease embarrassment over the book's nonreligious nature but are really unnecessary. After all, the Writings section of the canon explains how to live. It has already discussed a wide range of life situations, so it is appropriate that it also talk about human sexuality. This issue has certainly always been of interest to people of all ages. Besides, attributing some of the poetic images to Christ and the church may prove more embarrassing than admitting they address love itself. It is best, then, to read these poems as what they appear to be—ecstatic statements about the excitement of romantic love.

It is impossible to determine when, or by whom, the book was written. This Song of Songs, or "best of all songs," is attributed to Solomon. Perhaps Solomon wrote the text, or maybe someone else wrote it for one of his many marriages. Though the exact setting cannot be recovered, the general life situation is clear. Two people in love long to be together. They are probably a bride and bridegroom, though this idea rests mostly on 3:11. The book has been divided several ways, usually by its themes or speeches. Since expressions of love and longing to be together are the two main emotions, it is appropriate to divide the story by the three times these feelings overlap.

Song of Songs 1:1—2:2: First Expressions of Love

Both lovers announce the other's attractiveness. She desires his kisses because of the taste of his lips and the smell of his body (1:2-4). She wonders, though, if her own skin makes her unattractive to him (1:5-7). Hardly, for he called her the "most beautiful of women" (1:8, NIV) and compliments her face and neck (1:8-11). She responds by noting how much she enjoys his head lying between her breasts (1:12-14). He adores her eyes (1:15) and says their relationship will endure (1:16-17).

Song of Songs 2:3—3:11: The Desire to Be Together

People in love want to see each other. The woman reflects on her lover's strength and love and feels faint (2:3-5). She longs for the moment when he will fulfill her sexual desires (2:6). Other times together were sweet (2:7-17). Thus, when he was gone, she sought him, found him, and would not let him go (3:1-5). Now she waits again. She sees Solomon coming, carried on a chair by his servants, ready to marry her (3:6-11). Patience will soon be rewarded.

Song of Songs 4:1—5:1: More Statements of Affection

At this point, the man describes his lover's beauty. Earlier, he spoke about her eyes and face (1:10,15). He begins with these again but slowly moves down her body. Her eyes, hair, teeth, and lips are lovely (4:1-3). Further, her neck is attractive (4:4). Finally, her breasts are perfectly shaped (4:5). Such thoughts make his heart beat faster (4:7-9). To him, her love is better than wine (4:10). It has its own special tastes (4:11-15), so he wants to enjoy its fruit (4:16—5:1).

Song of Songs 5:2—6:3: Further Longing for Love

The woman awakes. She hears her lover knocking at the door (5:2), but she has undressed (5:3). Should she rise? Thoughts of him overwhelm her, so she goes to the door, only to find him gone (5:4-6). Was it a dream? She looks for him in the streets, but a watchman strikes her (5:7). Desperate, she asks the city's women (the chorus) to help her find him (5:8).

Naturally, the women need a description of her lover (5:9). She describes him from head to toe (5:10-16). He has no faults. The women ask where to look (6:1). She replies that he must be working (6:2-3). If so, she wants to be with him.

Song of Songs 6:4—7:9: Final Praises for Her Beauty

He desires her presence too. Thus, he details her beauty again, once more focusing on his lover's eyes and face (6:4-7). He decides that though there are many pretty queens and maidens, his beloved is special among them (6:8-9). Even these other women praise her beauty and purity (6:10-12). All who meet her want another look at her (6:13).

At last the man speaks of her whole body. Her feet are beautiful "in sandals" (7:1). Her hips curve like jewels, and her belly is plump, which was considered attractive then (7:2). Moving higher, he compliments her breasts, neck, eyes, and hair (7:3-5). To him, she has no physical faults, and her personality is pleasing (7:6). In a last burst of desire, he compares her height to a tree, her breasts to its fruits, and says he wants to climb the tree and taste its fruits (7:7-8).

Song of Songs 7:10—8:14: The Desire to Be Together Permanently

Both lovers now express their need for lasting companionship and love. Responding to his praises, she tells him she will give him her love in the countryside (7:10-12). He has spoken of love as fruit. She promises to give him new and choice fruits (7:12-13). The woman wishes they were considered family; then she could be with him always (8:1). She could feed him the fruits of love at any time (8:2). He, in turn, could satisfy her sexual desires whenever she wished (8:3).

The man pledges that they will always be together. She must not become jealous of other women or doubt his love for her (8:5-6). He reminds his lover, "Many waters cannot quench love, / Nor will rivers overflow it" (8:7, NASB). Her love means more to him than riches (8:7), an extraordinary statement for Solomon to make. As for his lover, she simply asks him to hurry to her side (8:14). She wants his promises to become reality.

Conclusion

The Song of Songs may not teach great theological truths, but it does address some basic human emotions. It demonstrates that love must be expressed verbally as well as physically. It suggests lovers should enjoy praising one another as a prelude to sexual fulfillment. It also shows the wonder and beauty of love without discussing rules and warnings. Such rules exist in enough other places. Love is kept simple and sensual. Lovers who imitate the book's lovers gain spontaneity and joy. They discover that their own beloved's charms may be greater than they knew. In short, they learn how to grow old in love, without the love growing old.[1]

Questions for Reflection

1. What is the best way to interpret Song of Songs?
2. How would the author of the Song of Songs define love?

Note

1. Further study is available in G. Lloyd Carr, *The Song of Solomon,* vol. 17 in *Tyndale Old Testament Commentaries* (Downers Grove, Ill.: Inter-Varsity Press, 1984); Marvin Pope, *Song of Songs,* vol. 7 in *The Anchor Bible* (Garden City, N.Y.: Doubleday, 1977); R. E. Murphy, *The Song of Songs,* Hermeneia (Philadelphia: Fortress, 1990).

17
Ecclesiastes: *How to Search for Meaning in Life*

Major Themes: The search for meaning, life's vanity, the value of wisdom, and the fear of Yahweh
Character: Qoheleth
Plot: Qoheleth searches for life's meaning. He finds all of life's activities empty, yet he does discover the value of fearing God.

Introduction

Proverbs, Ruth, and the Song of Songs are basically positive books. They show that life's problems can be overcome. Therefore, readers may misunderstand their message. Readers may think these books present life as a simple sequence of causes and effects. When rules are kept, when people are righteous, and when love exists, all will be well. Job should have ended such fantasies, but desires for an easy life die hard.

Ecclesiastes helps Job balance Proverbs in the Old Testament Wisdom Literature. Like Job, it poses relevant and realistic questions about the meaning of life. Unlike Job, it does so in an almost totally negative tone. It thereby forces readers to decide what is positive about life. The book's ultimate conclusions do not conflict with Proverbs. It simply seeks to correct all who think Proverbs' path to wisdom is easy to walk.[1] By including different perspectives, the Old Testament offers a realistic view of life.

Various suggestions have been made about Ecclesiastes's authorship. First, many scholars think Solomon wrote the book.[2] The author identifies himself only as Qoheleth, which means "preacher" in Hebrew, yet adds that he is "the son of David, king in Jerusalem" (1:1, KJV). Of course, Solomon was David's son. Jewish tradition thereby linked the book to him. This individual also possesses much wealth (note 2:1-11), which also fits Solomon. Second, other scholars believe someone wrote Ecclesiastes long after Solomon's time.[3] Solomon is not mentioned by name anywhere in the book, which differs from Proverbs and Song of Songs. The author says he "was king over Israel" (1:12, NIV), which may imply he was dethroned. Finally, the Hebrew used in Ecclesiastes is very late, and therefore probably not from Solomon's time. Third, a few commentators claim Ecclesiastes is written from a "Solomonic perspective."[4] That is, the book tries to duplicate Solomon's attitude about life; or, Ecclesiastes may even honor Solomon as the author without this being factually so.

One of the first two options is probably correct. If Solomon wrote the book, it must have been late in his life or sometime slightly before 930 B.C. If a deposed king, such as Jehoiachin, authored Ecclesiastes, then the book must have been written shortly before or after 587 B.C. Neither suggestion gives Ecclesiastes a *specific* setting, though, so it must be interpreted as general statements on life's meaning.

Ecclesiastes's main theme is that everything in life is vain, empty, nothing, absurd. The author seeks meaning in many places, yet only finds it in fearing God. Two major ideas divide the book into two parts. First, chapters 1—6 claim "all is vanity" (KJV). Second, chapters 7—12 state that death is better than life.[5] These two concepts are supported by the author's own experiences. Readers can judge Qoheleth's comments for themselves. They must take very seriously, however, his cautions about finding meaning in worthless pursuits.

Ecclesiastes 1—6: "All Is Vanity"

Chapter 1 presents the book's first major idea. Using the Hebrew word *hebel* repeatedly, Qoheleth claims that everything in life is vain, or empty (1:2). In other words, he argues that life itself has no meaning. Generations come and go (1:4). The sun rises and sets (1:5). Winds blow here and there (1:6). Rivers flow ceaselessly (1:7). Nothing ever changes (1:8-9), and nothing new ever happens (1:9). People forget the past, so why did it happen at all (1:11)? Life is one boring repetition after another.

How can Qoheleth say such things? What are his credentials? Where does he get his information? He says he was once king of Jerusalem, and that he decided to "explore by wisdom . . . all that has been done under heaven" (1:12-13, NASB). Since he was the wisest man in Jerusalem, he thought himself capable of attempting this task (1:16-18). He admits, however, that his quest for meaning led to nothing (1:14-15).

Qoheleth sought meaning in many places. First, he pursued it in pleasure. He laughed, drank, worked, collected servants, and became extremely rich (2:1-8). Through all these experiences he maintained his wisdom (2:9), which taught him pleasure was nothing (2:10-11). Second, he considered wisdom and folly (2:12). Of course, wisdom is better than folly (2:13-14), but so what? Both fools and the wise die, both will be forgotten, so both's life-styles are vain (2:15-17). Third, Qoheleth worked hard. This too was emptiness because those who inherit his property may be fools (2:18-23). All people can do is try to enjoy the work God has given them and try not to think about its vanity (2:24-26).

His search leads Qoheleth to reflect on time. There is a time for everything. Life has its seasons and its aging processes (3:1-8). Joy and sorrow alike come and go, and people have no control over them. Worse still, God has allowed people to know about eternity, yet He does not allow them to understand it fully (3:11). Thus, time frustrates Qoheleth. What God does lasts forever, but what people do vanishes (3:14-15). Given these circumstances, people can only fear God, enjoy life, and wait for judgment (3:16-22). Nothing else has meaning.

Qoheleth also considered justice and religion. He found that oppression abounds. No one comforts the poor (4:1). They are better off dead (4:2-3). The wicked often prosper more than the righteous (4:4-6). An industrious man may have no son to inherit his wealth (4:7-8). People need friends, but people are often fickle (4:9-16). Clearly life is unjust. As for religion, vows must be kept (5:1-5). Otherwise, God may get angry (5:6). Dreams are worthless. Only fearing Yahweh matters (5:7).

Wealth is especially meaningless. Money never satisfies (5:10), for those who have money spend it (5:11). They worry about their holdings, fearing they will end up poor someday (5:12-14). Everyone enters life naked and will die naked (5:15). Therefore, to work only for money is to toil "for the wind" (5:16). The rich should enjoy their wealth and not seek more (5:18). Perhaps then they will not realize how empty life really is (5:19-20).

Other evils bother Qoheleth. Rich men have their wealth stolen by foreigners (6:2). A father of many children does not get a decent burial (6:3). Appetites for food and knowledge are never satisfied (6:7-9). Talk does not always produce wisdom (6:11). Life is like a shadow that dies in the sun (6:12). Given all these wrongs, how *can* life have meaning?

Ecclesiastes 7—12: "Death Is Better"

In Qoheleth's mind, life consists of preparing to die. People should, then, learn to mourn, to prefer sorrow over laughter, and to forget the past (7:1-10). Most of all, they should gain wisdom that will balance their lives (7:11-17). Wisdom will eliminate excessive wickedness and excessive righteousness, both of which ruin life (7:16-17). It will enable individuals to ignore slander and avoid adulterous women (7:18-29). In short, wisdom helps people prepare for judgment.

Who is wise? The person who obeys the king (8:1-5) yet realizes that those in authority are often unjust (8:6-9). Wise people fear God and enjoy life, recognizing the limits of their knowledge (8:10-17). They know that everyone dies (9:1-6). Thus, they eat well, dress well, love well, and work well (9:7-10). After all, such opportunities cease in the grave (9:10). The wise know they will usually prevail, but they also understand that fools can overcome them (9:13—10:7). Life is uncertain (10:8-20). Therefore, the wise seek wealth in many ways (11:1-6). Wisdom, then, balances the harsh realities of life with its fleeting joys.

Qoheleth concludes with some final observations on life's significance. First, he again says to enjoy life. While enjoying life, though, remember that life is futile and God will judge everyone (11:7-10). Second, remember God before it is too late (12:1). Old age will come soon. Eyes will dim, hands will grow too feeble to work, and ears will grow deaf (12:2-5). The body will die and return to dust (12:6-7). All opportunities to serve God will end then. Third, he advises everyone to fear God and keep the commandments (12:13-14). These things matter to Yahweh. All else is vanity. The person who accepts this advice will live carefully and thoughtfully. That person's death will be better than his or her life.

Conclusion

Without question, Ecclesiastes offers a dark and sometimes depressing worldview. Futility and emptiness seem to overwhelm joy and success in Qoheleth's mind. This perspective is necessary, however, for readers of the whole Old Testament to grasp how to find meaning in life. It forces us back to basics and eliminates false notions about life.

Proverbs begins with the fear of God. It then shows the blessings of fearing God. The danger of this approach is that readers may seek the blessings and forget respect for Yahweh. Ecclesiastes works in the opposite way. It argues that blessings, in and of themselves, are meaningless. Only fearing God and preparing for judgment matter. Of course, the danger of this approach is that readers will become too discouraged to serve the Lord. Both viewpoints can lead to God, though, and thus to wisdom.

Ecclesiastes teaches us to search for meaning in the proper places. Pleasure, riches, and power are meaningless. They cannot satisfy the wise. Only God can give life lasting meaning, and then only after death. Seekers of meaning must be sharp, critical, and honest. Fools will be happy to settle for temporary "answers." The wise, though, struggle through vain solutions to more lasting convictions. They thereby prepare well for their death, which will certainly come.[6]

Questions for Reflection

1. Explain how Ecclesiastes and Lamentations contribute to a Christian worldview.
2. How does a view of vanity and death contribute to a positive view of joyous life for Ecclesiastes?

Notes

1. Brevard Childs, *Introduction to the Old Testament as Scripture* (Philadelphia: Fortress, 1988), 588.

2. For example, Walter Kaiser, *Ecclesiastes: Total Life* (Chicago: Moody Press, 1979), 25-29.

3. Note R. K. Harrison, *Introduction to the Old Testament* (Grand Rapids: Wm. B. Eerdmans, 1969), 1072-1078.

4. G. A. Barton, *A Critical and Exegetical Commentary on the Book of Ecclesiastes* (New York: Scribner's, 1908), 58.

5. James L. Crenshaw, *Old Testament Wisdom: An Introduction* (Atlanta: John Knox Press, 1981), 145.

6. For further study see Michael Eaton, *Ecclesiastes,* vol. 16 in *Tyndale Old Testament Commentaries* (Downers Grove, Ill.: Inter-Varsity Press, 1983); Robert Gardis, *Koheleth: The Man and His World* (New York: Schocken, 1979).

18
Lamentations: *How to Mourn National Tragedies*

Characters: Jerusalem, Yahweh, and the exiles
Plot: Jerusalem and her exiles lament the destruction of Judah. They admit God's punishment was just; yet, they long for restoration and trust God to rebuild the nation.
Themes: Israel's sin, God's just judgment, and God's faithfulness

---

Introduction

Ecclesiastes forces readers to consider serious issues. Lamentations follows with statements about Jerusalem's destruction. No more serious, more horrible event ever occurs in Israel's history. Jerusalem's fall leaves the Israelites homeless. It revokes God's promise of land, at least for a time. Further, it leaves the people without a temple. In their minds, no temple meant God would forsake them. Obviously, they felt hopeless and utterly discouraged. How should these hurting people respond to this disaster?

Lamentations is an anonymous book. Tradition has linked it to Jeremiah, partly because of 2 Chronicles 35:25, which says he wrote a lamentation for Josiah. This possibility cannot be confirmed, however, so it is best to treat the book as an anonymous work. Lamentations was almost certainly written shortly after 587 B.C. Jerusalem's destruction provides the text's background. In the canon, Lamentations begins a series of books about the exile. It announces the exile. Esther and Daniel describe life as an exile in Persia and Babylon, respectively. Ezra-Nehemiah discusses the rebuilding of the nation's capital and spiritual life. Chronicles follows with an upbeat theological history meant to encourage those who help restore the land.

Like Psalm 119, Lamentations uses acrostic poetry. In chapters 1, 2, and 4, each succeeding verse begins with the next letter of the

Hebrew alphabet. Chapter 3 has three such poems, but it has a unified theme. Chapter 5 has 22 verses (the number of letters in the Hebrew alphabet), but it is not an acrostic. Thus, five distinct poems appear. As its name indicates, this book consists of a series of national laments similar to Psalm 137. The speaker in each poem mourns the past, yet eventually asks God to heal the situation.

National disasters force us to face reality. Sins can no longer be hidden. Pride becomes foolish. Most importantly, we must check our relationship to God. Israel has a choice. They can blame God for their defeat, or they can admit their sin. The choice they make could well determine their nation's future.

Lamentations 1: Jerusalem's Sorrow

Poets often give human characteristics to nonliving things. In Lamentations's opening poem, Jerusalem comes to life. She appears as a lonely woman, perhaps a widow, who has lost her children. She is like a lovely princess who has become a poor slave woman (1:1). All night she weeps and has no one to comfort her (1:2). Why is she so broken?

Jerusalem's pain comes from Babylon's victory (1:3). Her children are exiles in many nations (1:3). Her roads are empty, "her virgins are afflicted" (KJV), and her worship services have ceased (1:4). Jerusalem serves foreign masters (1:5). All glory she once knew has departed (1:6). In one tightly packed verse after another, the poet describes the city's pain. The mother of all Israel has become as barren as Sarah and as helpless as Naomi.

To her credit, Jerusalem admits her sins brought her downfall (1:8-9). Her uncleanness has caused Babylon's oppression (1:10-12). Yahweh was correct to punish (1:13-19). Still, Jerusalem hopes for renewal. She asks that God end the exile by defeating her enemies (1:20-22). Then the nation can prosper again.

Lamentations 2: Yahweh's Justifiable Wrath I

God has poured out tremendous destruction on Israel. This punishment reverses past blessings. For instance, once Yahweh led Israel with a "pillar of cloud by day" (Ex. 13:21, NASB). Now they are covered "with a cloud in his anger" (2:1, KJV). Once God fought for Israel, but He has now become their enemy (2:2-5). Yahweh appointed the tabernacle and altar as special places once, but now the Lord has rejected them both (2:6-7). Zion was a favored city, but no more (2:8-10).

Israel brought this wrath on themselves. They listened to false prophets (2:14). They loved idols. All the people can do now is ask God to save them (2:20-22). Perhaps Yahweh will have pity on Jerusalem and her children (2:22).

Lamentations 3: The Exile's Prayer

A new character, a "man who has seen affliction" (3:1, NIV), enters the poem. This individual has suffered through hunger (3:4), homelessness (3:6), and imprisonment (3:7). This description fits Israel's exiles. They have no security (3:10), and their strength has faded (3:18). All hope seems to be gone (3:18).

Even in his desperate circumstances, though, the exile finds hope in the Lord (3:19-21). He remembers that God's kindness never ceases (3:22). Indeed, Yahweh's compassions are "new every morning" (3:23). He exclaims to the Lord, "Great is your faithfulness" (3:23, NIV). This faithful God is the exile's hope, so he will wait on Yahweh's certain deliverance (3:24-26).

The exile decides that no one can really complain about God's punishment since everyone sins (3:39). It is far better to examine behavior, repent, and turn to God (3:40). God will punish Israel's enemies (3:46-66). If not, there is certainly nothing Israel can do to Babylon. Clearly, the exile shares Jerusalem's opinion that God has acted correctly. He also moves beyond her pleas for help to a confident statement of faith in Yahweh.

Lamentations 4: Yahweh's Justifiable Wrath II

This fourth poem largely agrees with the second, yet it offers more definite reasons for Jerusalem's downfall. God has devastated the land (4:1-12) because of wicked prophets and sinful priests (4:13). These worthless leaders teach the people to shed blood (4:13-14). They have, therefore, been scattered with the other exiles (4:15-17). Israel also fell because old enemies like Edom helped Babylon. Again, the nation can only turn such foes over to the Lord (4:20-22).

Lamentations 5: Israel's Final Plea

One last time the people ask God for help. The whole nation speaks here since "us," "we," and "our" are used often. Israel begs God to "remember" them, to "see" their shame (5:1). Yes, they have sinned (5:7,16), and they have suffered for what they have done (5:2-18). Perhaps now the eternal God will forsake them no more (5:19-20). They hope they can be restored to their former glory (5:21).

Conclusion

Lamentations instructs the nation how to receive forgiveness. First, honesty is important. Sins must be confessed, especially since they are so obvious. Second, God must be sought. No one else can deliver them from exile. Third, God must be trusted. Yahweh's faithfulness never ends. Since this is true, all repentant sinners can count on God's mercy and forgiveness. God's compassion is new every day (3:23), even for nations and individuals who rebel repeatedly.[1]

Questions for Reflection

1. How does it help you to interpret Lamentations to know that the author used an acrostic form of poetry?
2. According to Lamentations, where is God while His people suffer?

Note

1. For further information see R. K. Harrison, *Jeremiah and Lamentations,* vol. 19 in *Tyndale Old Testament Commentaries* (Downers Grove, Ill.: Inter-Varisty Press, 1973); Robert B. Laurin, "Lamentations" in *The Broadman Bible Commentary,* vol. 6 (Nashville: Broadman Press, 1971); Delbert R. Hillers, *Lamentations,* vol. 7A in *The Anchor Bible* (Garden City, N.Y.: Doubleday, 1972).

19
Esther: *How to Survive in Exile*

Major Characters: Esther, Mordecai, King Ahasuerus (Xerxes), and Haman
Minor Characters: Queen Vashti, Haman's wife and friends, and a eunuch named Harbonah
Plot: While in exile, an Israelite woman named Esther becomes queen of Persia. When vicious enemies attempt to exterminate the Israelites, Esther and her cousin Mordecai save the people.
Themes: The survival of Israel in exile and the defeat of the wicked

Introduction

Lamentations states that Israel's enemies oppress them in exile. Esther describes one such incident. This book has all the elements of a good story: interesting characters, strange twists of fate, humor, and irony. Its plot presents a terrible problem that must be solved. Israel's very existence is threatened. Will they survive? If so, how? All the worst perils of being an exiled people emerge in Esther. No wonder Lamentations paints such a dark picture of Israel's defeat.

Esther is an anonymous book. Though its author is unknown, it is possible to fix its general historical setting. The decree of Cyrus in 538 B.C. allowed the Israelites to return to Judah. Many stayed in exile, however, due to financial and other considerations. During 487-465 B.C., King Ahasuerus, better known as Xerxes I, ruled "127 provinces" in Persia (1:1). Ancient history portrays him as one who loved battles, women, and parties.[1] Esther seems to confirm this description.

Esther possibly was the last book accepted into the Old Testament canon. All the other books are mentioned or quoted in the Dead Sea Scrolls. Jewish tradition indicates that the rabbis questioned Esther's worth. Why? Because, like the Song of Songs, God is not mentioned in the book. Also, the story seems rather violent and vindictive. Thus, Esther seems more secular than sacred.

Major Post-Exilic Events	
Persia conquers Babylon	539 B.C.
Cyrus's decree	538 B.C.
First exiles return to Jerusalem	538-535 B.C.
Temple rebuilt	520-516 B.C.
Esther's era	487-465 B.C.
Ezra's and Nehemiah's ministries	about 450 B.C.

Why, then, was it finally considered Scripture? No one knows for sure, but two reasons seem logical. First, Esther describes how Purim, a permanent Israelite festival, was instituted. Purim celebrates Israel's victory over their enemies. Second, Esther demonstrates the terrors of exile. It shows how hatred for Israel threatened to eliminate the nation. Such hatred and attempts at extermination have continued into the twentieth century. Esther reveals that no peril, however great, will finish Israel. Even exile can be overcome. Israel's survival in Esther also shows how others can survive horrible times.

Esther 1:1—2:20: Esther's Rise to the Throne

King Ahasuerus enjoys parties. Therefore, he gives a party for the nobles of his kingdom during his third year in power (1:1-3). The banquet lasts seven days and includes much drinking (1:5-8). Queen Vashti holds a banquet for women at the same time (1:9). The king gets "merry with wine" (KJV) and orders Vashti to display her beauty for his guests (1:10-11). Perhaps she was to show more than her face, though it is impossible to know for certain. At any rate, she refuses to come, which infuriates the king (1:12). Vashti has humiliated him before all his guests.

Now both drunk and angry, Ahasuerus seeks advice. What shall he do to Vashti? His advisors fear all Persian women may become as rebellious as the queen (1:17-18). Therefore, they tell him to remove her at once (1:19). Perhaps then all women will fear their husbands (1:20). The king agrees, and Vashti is eliminated (1:21-22). Maybe women will stay meek and submissive now!

Eventually, the king wakes up to the fact that he has no queen (2:1). His attendants suggest a beauty contest. Beautiful young women will be brought into the harem. The one who pleases the king will take Vashti's place (2:2-4). Surely the new queen will be more obedient than her predecessor.

Esther becomes a candidate for the position. She has been raised by her cousin Mordecai, a fourth-generation exile (2:5-7). Esther is beautiful and obedient. She listens to the advice of both her cousin and the king's harem overseer (2:8-15). Soon she wins Ahasuerus's heart and with it the contest (2:16-18). Esther is queen, but she hides her nationality from the king at Mordecai's command (2:10). Exiles must be very careful.

Esther 2:21—7:10: Mordecai's Battles with Haman

Even when they are careful, exiles may make enemies. Mordecai angers Haman, the egotistical, spiteful second-in-command to Ahasuerus (3:1). All the king's servants bow in Haman's presence, but Mordecai refuses to do so (3:2-5). Mordecai is a good man. In fact, he exposes a plot against Ahasuerus, thus saving the king's life (2:21-23). Haman either does not know, or ignores, Mordecai's service to the king. He hates Mordecai so much that he decides to kill not just Mordecai, but all Israelites with him (3:6). Haman lies about Israel and gets Ahasuerus to sign a law allowing Israel's enemies to destroy them on a set day (3:7-15). Persia's laws could not be repealed, only offset by another law.

It looks very bad indeed for Israel. Mordecai mourns what has happened (4:1-3). He sits near the palace gate, weeping and wearing sackcloth and ashes (4:4). Esther sends him some clothes, but he rejects them (4:4). He wants something more substantial. Mordecai wants Esther to speak to the king on Israel's behalf (4:8). She protests and reminds Mordecai the queen can only approach the king when called (4:9-11). Remember what happened to Vashti!

Mordecai's response is half threat, half promise. He tells her she will not survive the purge (4:13); yet, more positively, he also says, "who knows whether you have become queen for such a time as this?" (4:14). Finally, she agrees. She will go to Ahasuerus, even if he kills her (4:16). She asks Mordecai to pray for her (4:16-17).

The crucial moment arrives. Esther goes before the king without being called. Will she suffer Vashti's fate? No, for the king loves her (5:2). He promises to give her what she wishes (5:3). Slyly, she invites Ahasuerus to a banquet and asks him to bring Haman (5:5-8). What does she have in mind?

Meanwhile, Haman gradually loses his battle with Mordecai. Haman hates his foe so much that he has a 75-foot-high gallows built on which he plans to hang Mordecai (5:14). He brags to his wife and friends that he has been invited by Esther to a special banquet (5:11-13). Clearly, he thinks his career is about to reach new heights.

Unfortunately, however, his pride leads to his downfall. The king finally decides to honor Mordecai for saving his life (6:1-3). He asks Haman, "What should be done for the man the king desires to honor?" (6:6). Haman assumes Ahasuerus wants to honor *him*, so he says the honoree should be placed on the king's horse and led through town by a high official (6:7-9). The king tells *him* to honor Mordecai in this way (6:10). Naturally, Haman feels humiliated. Now he covers *his* head and mourns (6:12). His wife and friends warn him that if Mordecai is an Israelite, then Haman "will surely fall before him" (6:13, NASB). The text does not say why they reach this conclusion, but they are correct.

Without sensing his fate, Haman goes to the banquet (6:14—7:1). The king asks Esther again what she wants (7:2). This time she tells everything. She reveals her nationality and exposes Haman's plot (7:3-6). Infuriated, the king leaves the room (7:7). While begging Esther for his life, Haman falls on the queen's couch (7:7-8). Just then, the king returns and accuses Haman of trying to rape the queen (7:8). Once more he asks for advice. Harbonah, a eunuch, suggests they hang Haman on the gallows meant for Mordecai (7:9). The king agrees (7:9), so Israel's terrible enemy meets his just fate.

Esther 8—9: Israel's Deliverance

Israel's troubles are hardly over. Their enemies can still kill them on the set day. Therefore, Mordecai and Esther have the king sign a law to counteract the one allowing Israel's extermination (8:1-8). The decree lets the Israelites defend themselves and gives them revenge by killing Haman's sons (8:9—9:16). Over 75,000 people die in this great slaughter (9:16). This killing may seem excessive, but it also indicates the extent of the animosity against Israel.

Because of their great victory, Israel declares a festival. They celebrate the first Purim and decree that this day must be kept "throughout every generation" (9:28, NASB). Indeed Esther makes a law establishing this observance (9:29-32). Israelites can thereby remember that their enemies cannot destroy them. All who act like Haman will die like Haman.

Esther 10: Peace and Prosperity

Israel is safe again. All enemies are vanquished. Esther remains queen, and Mordecai takes Haman's place as second-in-command (10:2-3). Mordecai's fame spreads through the whole Persian kingdom (10:2). For now, exile is less dangerous. Still, trouble may arise at anytime. Until they are back in their own land, the Israelites will never be completely secure.

Conclusion

Esther may not be an extremely spiritual book, but it is very realistic. Life in exile allows few options. Exiles must often do the best they can in harsh conditions. How, then, does one survive in exile? Perhaps by marrying a pagan king. Certainly, by maintaining personal integrity, remaining loyal to family, and working for justice. Political shrewdness and the ability to seize opportunities are also helpful. These characteristics, plus God's earlier promises, saved people in Esther's time and still do so today.[2]

Questions for Reflection

1. Why should a book like Esther be in the Bible? How does its obvious lack of theological emphases affect your answer?
2. Is Esther a model for modern women to follow?

Notes

1. Lewis B. Paton, *A Critical and Exegetical Commentary on the Book of Esther* (New York: Scribner's, 1908), 121.

2. For further study see Joyce Baldwin, *Esther,* vol. 12 in *Tyndale Old Testament Commentaries* (Downers Grove, Ill.: Inter-Varsity Press, 1984); Carey A. Moore, *Esther,* vol. 7B in *The Anchor Bible* (Garden City, N.Y.: Doubleday, 1971).

20
Daniel: *How to Maintain Distinctive Faith in Exile*

Major Characters: Daniel, Shadrach, Meshach, Abednego, King Nebuchadnezzar, King Belshazzar, and King Darius
Minor Characters: Various court officials and God's messengers
Plot: While young men, Daniel and his friends are exiled to Babylon in 605 B.C. There they live by God's standards, but they are persecuted for doing so. They endure, and Daniel receives visions about future world events.
Themes: Faithfulness to God in exile, God's deliverance of the faithful, and God's rule over future events

Introduction

Esther emphasizes the dangers Israel faces from foreign governments during the exile. Daniel continues this theme, yet also reveals the exiles' spiritual difficulties. In Babylon, Israel is sometimes ordered to worship idols. They feel great pressure to comply. Will they renounce Yahweh? If not, will God protect them? Of course, the nation will die if they reject God. In Daniel, as in Esther, Israel seems trapped between their convictions and their oppressors.

Daniel is one of the most controversial books in Scripture. First, scholars debate its authorship. Chapters 1—6 mention no author, but chapters 7—12 contain many first-person accounts by Daniel (for example, 7:1,9; 8:1; 9:2). Thus, Daniel may have written some or all of the book, or he may have told his experiences and visions to someone else. This second person may have written the book.

Second, commentators do not agree on Daniel's date. The book's events are fairly easy to fix. Daniel goes into exile in 605 B.C. and lives there until about 536 (note 1:1,21; and 6:28). His work in the governments of Babylon and Persia leads him into some perilous circumstances. Still, other factors create some confusion. For instance, the text is written in both Hebrew and its sister language Aramaic. Daniel's visions (chapters 7—12) describe events long after his death. These and other details have led some authors to conclude that someone composed Daniel as late as 167-164 B.C., when they think the last predicted event occurred.[1]

Third, Daniel's visions are difficult to interpret. Writers have attempted to decipher the strange images in chapters 7—12 for centuries. Daniel's original audience may have understood his comments; we can only offer informed, but humble, opinions on them today. No one has an infallible interpretation of these passages.

A survey like our present study cannot solve such difficult problems. It is necessary, though, to make some observations that may aid readers. As for Daniel's authorship, it is likely that either Daniel or someone who had an accurate account of his life and visions wrote the book. Such is also the case with Jeremiah, so this possibility seems reasonable. Daniel's date may thereby fall within several years of his death. The later events are predictions that come true. Daniel's interpretation must be approached cautiously. The book is not a simple guide to the end times. Quite possibly, however, Daniel predicts the rise of the Babylonian, Persian, Greek, and Roman Empires. He also speaks of the final day of Yahweh.

Most first-time readers of the Hebrew canon are surprised to find Daniel in the Writings instead of the Prophets. Why is the book not among the Prophets? Perhaps because of its literary form. Unlike the prophetic books, Daniel does not emphasize sin, punishment, and restoration. Except for chapter 9, it does not deal directly with Israel's ethical problems, nor does it explain why Israel fell. Instead, Daniel is an apocalyptic book.[2] That is, it stresses the distant future, claims God orders history, and uses symbolic language. Many other books of this type were written during and after Daniel's time.

Therefore, Daniel seems more at home in the Writings. Like Lamentations and Esther, it reveals the pain of exile. Like Ezra-Nehemiah and Chronicles, it also points to a better future for Israel. In its own way, Daniel demonstrates how to have faith while in exile, then encourages faith in the God of the future.

Daniel 1—6: Maintaining Distinctive Faith in Exile

Israel's commitment to Yahweh was challenged even before the exile. Baal worship, in particular, tempted the people repeatedly. Such temptations multiply in exile. Young people like Daniel and his three friends Hananiah, Mishael, and Azariah are taken to Babylon (1:1—3:6). They are educated in Babylonian language and literature (1:4) and are expected to enter the king's service (1:3-4). They are even given Babylonian names: Daniel (Belteshazzar), Hananiah (Shadrach), Mishael (Meshach), and Azariah (Abednego) (1:7). Will they also accept Babylon's religion?

When told to eat Babylonian food, the young Israelites face their first test. Such meals were probably unclean by Moses' standards. Daniel decides not to "defile" himself (1:8). He and his friends gain permission to eat vegetables and water (1:12), and they become healthier than the youths who eat the king's food (1:15). The king recognizes their intelligence and chooses them for his personal staff (1:19).

Another kind of test follows. King Nebuchadnezzar has a troubling dream and demands that his magicians tell him both the dream and its interpretation (2:1-3). If they cannot, they will all die; but if they can, they will be rewarded (2:5-6). The magicians protest and claim no one can know his dream (2:10). Therefore, the king orders the wise men's death, an order that includes Daniel and his friends (2:11-13).

Daniel saves the day. He asks for time to tell the king's dream (2:14-16). His friends pray for him (2:17-18), and God reveals the dream to him (2:19-45). Does he take credit for this knowledge? No. Instead, he honors Yahweh (2:20-23). His witness leads Nebuchadnezzar to marvel at God's greatness (2:47). Daniel is both dedicated and humble.

A third test soon arises. Nebuchadnezzar erects a giant idol and orders all his officials to worship it (3:1-5). Whoever disobeys will be burned in a furnace (3:6). Shadrach, Meshach, and Abednego refuse (3:12). The king gets angry, but he offers them a second chance (3:13-15). Again they refuse and claim God "will deliver us out of your hand, O King. But if not . . . we are not going to serve your gods or worship the idol you have built" (3:17-18).

This bold stand earns them a trip to the furnace. The fire devours the men who take them down, but the Israelites do not burn (3:19-27). God delivers them (3:24-25). Again Nebuchadnezzar marvels at Yahweh (3:28). He makes it illegal to speak against the Lord and promotes Shadrach, Meshach, and Abednego (3:29-30).

Despite witnessing such miracles, Nebuchadnezzar does not fully trust Yahweh. He becomes proud and even claims to have built Babylon by himself (4:30). Because of his arrogance, Yahweh strikes him with madness, and he lives like an animal for a time (4:33). Later, though, his reason returns. Then he praises Yahweh (4:34-37).

Similarly, Belshazzar, his successor, tests God. While drinking wine, Belshazzar sends for the special gold cups Nebuchadnezzar took from Jerusalem's temple (5:1-2). He and his guests drink from them and praise their gods (5:3-4). Suddenly, a hand appears, writing unknown words on the wall (5:5). Terrified, Belshazzar sends for an interpreter (5:5-9). Daniel comes and denounces the king for not learning from Nebuchadnezzar's punishment (5:17-24). He then interprets the hand's words. Because of his pride, Belshazzar is finished (5:25-28). That very night the king is killed, and Darius takes his place (5:30-31). Yahweh again acts as universal ruler.

Exiles, especially faithful ones, are never truly safe from persecution. One final test awaits Daniel. Darius plans to "appoint him over the entire kingdom" (6:3, NASB). Jealous rivals scheme to discredit him on religious grounds (6:4-5). They get Darius to pass a law ordering everyone to pray to him or be put in a lion's den (6:6-9).

Daniel pays no attention to the law. He prays to Yahweh as before (6:10-11). To Darius's dismay, he learns he must put Daniel in the lions' den (6:11-15). With Daniel among the lions, Darius does not rest (6:16-18). He hurries to the den the next day (6:19). Once again Yahweh has delivered a faithful servant (6:20-22). Daniel's attackers are fed to the hungry lions (6:24). Darius recognizes God's greatness (6:25-27).

Every test has been passed. Daniel and his friends maintain their faith despite all that has happened. Threats, persecution, and personal advancement do not change them. God alone is their judge, so they serve only God. Exile does not have to break Israel's faith.

Daniel 7—12: Visions of the Future

The book now changes to a different type of material. Dreams and visions dominate the rest of Daniel. In his first vision, Daniel sees four beasts and sees God as well. These beasts represent four kingdoms, perhaps those of Babylon, Persia, Greece, and Rome.[3] They are boastful (7:8,11), just like Nebuchadnezzar. They do not boast for long, however, because Yahweh, "the Ancient of Days," takes His throne and judges them (7:9-10). God gives their kingdoms to "one like a son of man," who will rule the earth (7:13-14, NIV). This "son of man" is probably the messiah, the coming son of David, since "his kingdom will not pass away" (7:14).

Daniel asks for an explanation (7:15-16). He learns the four beasts are four kingdoms (7:17). They will rule for a time, but God's faithful will eventually rule the world (7:18). The last kingdom will have a series of ten kings, followed by a final, particularly blasphemous leader (7:23-25). Eventually, of course, Yahweh will rule the earth (7:26-28).

Other visions follow. First, he sees a powerful ram with two horns defeating all other rams (8:1-4). This ram "magnified himself" (8:4, NASB) until a mighty goat displaces him (8:5-8). The goat has one large horn, which gets broken. It then grows four small horns, out of which comes a small, powerful, and boastful horn (8:8-9). This last horn fights against God and God's people (8:10-14).

Gabriel, an angel, tells Daniel the vision's meaning (8:15-17). The first ram is Babylon and Persia (8:20). It gives way to Greece (8:21). Greece's first king will be its greatest, but the small horn will be Greece's most blasphemous ruler (8:22-26). Even Daniel marvels at such revelations (8:27).

Next, Daniel confesses Israel's sins to God. He says the nation has been judged correctly, but he hopes they can be forgiven (9:1-19). In response, God sends Gabriel to Daniel again (9:20-23). Gabriel promises that Jerusalem will be rebuilt and that the messiah will come (9:25-26). Afterwards, however, Jerusalem will be destroyed once more (9:27). All these predictions come true: the first in Haggai's time, the second through Jesus' ministry, and the third when Rome destroyed Jerusalem in A.D. 70.

Following this vision, Daniel learns how Greece will overwhelm Persia. God has allowed the Persians a time of power, but Greece's turn has come (10:1-21). The last king of Persia will be so rich that Greece will desire his wealth (11:1-2). A mighty Greek ruler will defeat Persia (11:3-4). When he dies, his kingdom will be divided into northern and southern portions (11:5-6). These two factions will fight for years (11:10-13). After a time, a great northern king will blaspheme Yahweh and even declare himself a god (11:36-39).

These predictions also come true in history. Alexander the Great conquers Persia and much of the rest of the ancient world in 336-323 B.C. Upon his death, his kingdom is split into northern and southern sectors. About 175 B.C. a ruler named Antiochus Epiphanes gains power. He murders thousands of Israelites, sacrifices a pig in the holy of holies, and declares himself a god.

Daniel hears some final, more encouraging, words. The end of time will bring great distress, but God will rescue the faithful (12:1) just as Daniel and his friends were rescued (12:1). He learns the dead will be resurrected (12:2). Not even death can separate the faithful from Yahweh. Daniel wonders how long it will be before these events occur (12:6). Not even he receives this information (12:7-8). He is told to go his way, enjoy his rest, and believe in his ultimate resurrection (12:9-13). This text provides one of the clearest promises of the resurrection in the Old Testament.

Conclusion

Daniel demonstrated that distinctive faith can be maintained. Why? Because God, not Babylon or any other nation, rules the world.

How can such faith be maintained? By refusing to eat unclean foods, take credit for God's miracles, or bow to idols; by believing God will deliver from harm but accepting death if necessary; and finally, by knowing that Yahweh has planned the future. The faithful will always be in those plans. Thus, they can live confidently, courageously, and righteously.[4]

Questions for Reflection

1. Explain how Daniel's date and authorship does or does not affect its value as Scripture.
2. Does the Book of Daniel aid us in establishing ethical standards?

Notes

1. James A. Montgomery, *A Critical and Exegetical Commentary on the Book of Daniel* (Edinburgh: T. and T. Clark, 1927), 96; and Norman Porteous, *Daniel: A Commentary* (Philadelphia: Westminster, 1965), 20.

2. Note Paul D. Hanson, *The Dawn of Apocalyptic*, rev. ed. (Philadelphia: Fortress, 1983); H. H. Rowley, *The Relevance of Apocalyptic* (1944; reprint, Greenwood, S.C.: Attic Press, 1980).

3. Note R. K. Harrison, *Introduction to the Old Testament* (Grand Rapids: Wm. B. Eerdmans, 1969), 1128-1132. For alternatives from a conservative viewpoint, consult E. J. Young *The Prophecy of Daniel: A Commentary* (Grand Rapids: Wm. B. Eerdmans, 1949); John F. Walvoord, *Daniel: The Key to Prophetic Revelation* (Chicago: Moody Press, 1971). For critical alternatives, note Montgomery and Porteous, who think Daniel was written about 165 B.C., and thus argue that Antiochus Epiphanes's activities are reflected throughout the book. More recently, John Goldingay, *Daniel,* vol. 30 in *Word Biblical Commentary* (Dallas: Word Books, 1989) has charted a middle way between the differing viewpoints.

4. For further study see Joyce G. Baldwin, *Daniel,* vol. 21 in *Tyndale Old Testament Commentaries* (Downers Grove, Ill.: Inter-Varsity, 1978); W. Sibley Towner, *Daniel,* Interpretation (Atlanta: John Knox, 1984); Robert A. Anderson, *Signs and Wonders,* International Theological Commentary (Grand Rapids: Wm. B. Eerdmans, 1984).

21
Ezra—Nehemiah: *How to Rebuild a Nation*

Major Characters: Ezra, Nehemiah, and King Artaxerxes of Persia
Minor Characters: Sanballat, Tobiah, and Geshem—enemies of Israel
Plot: Ezra first summarizes Israel's path to renewal from Cyrus's decree to Israel's rebuilding of the temple. Next, he explains his own journey to Jerusalem and his efforts to rebuild Israel's spiritual life. Finally, Nehemiah describes the rebuilding of Jerusalem's wall and the religious renewal that follows.
Themes: God's rule over history, Ezra and Nehemiah's effective leadership, and Israel's spiritual and physical restoration

Introduction

Israel remains in exile in Esther and Daniel. The Babylonian era has passed, and the Persians now rule. Daniel offers hope for Israel's renewal, but this long-awaited event has yet to occur. Ezra—Nehemiah begins the slow, painful process of Israel's reconstruction. Ezra, a priest, and Nehemiah, a builder, prove to be great leaders. Unfortunately, they face great obstacles. The land has been wrecked for years. The people are understandably discouraged. Many enemies oppose them. That these problems are overcome demonstrates God's power, Ezra and Nehemiah's character, and the stamina of the Israelites. It also shows readers how to overcome their own seemingly impossible difficulties.

Like Samuel, Kings, and Chronicles, Ezra and Nehemiah are basically one continuous story. The main characters' careers overlap, and their work complements each other's. Thus, the Hebrew text does not separate them. The English Bible divides them, placing them after 1 and 2 Chronicles for at least two basic reasons. First,

Ezra—Nehemiah continues the history Chronicles begins. Second, Ezra 1:1-2 is identical to the last two verses of Chronicles (2 Chron. 36:22-23).

The Hebrew text prefers to have Ezra—Nehemiah finish the exile and announce Israel's return to the land. It assumes the original readers knew the basic events in Israel's history and sought the meaning of those events. Therefore, Ezra—Nehemiah fulfills the prophets' promises of restoration of temple, worship, and capital city. Chronicles follows with an enthusiastic history that reemphasizes God's love for Israel, the eternal covenant with David, and national renewal. This survey offers great hope for the nation's future. Thus, Chronicles ends the canon with hope and glory. To conclude with Nehemiah would leave the reader with an image of Nehemiah mourning Israel's sin.

Ezra and Nehemiah minister somewhere between 450 and 425 B.C. These dates can be fixed fairly easily because of references to Persia's King Artaxerxes, who began reigning about 465 B.C. (note Ezra 7:1,8; Neh. 2:1; 13:6). Despite these references, however, it is not possible to know exactly when the two men worked *together.*[1] The text is not clear on this point.

Much of Ezra—Nehemiah is autobiographical. Thus, it is likely that Ezra and Nehemiah either wrote or dictated some of the book. Their firsthand comments make the story personal and compelling.

Without question, Ezra and Nehemiah work during an extremely crucial moment in Israel's history. The nation's restoration hangs in the balance. The prophets' promises remain unfulfilled. Depression and cynicism grip the people. If these men fail, Israel may not recover for some time. If they succeed, they can propel their people into a bright and significant future.

Ezra 1—6: Israel's Return and Temple Construction

Long before Ezra or Nehemiah was born, Israel begins its renewal. Ezra notes that Persia's defeat of Babylon starts this process. To fulfill Jeremiah's prediction of a seventy-year exile (note Jer. 29:10), God moves Cyrus to let Israel return home in 538 B.C. (1:1-2). Cyrus allows the Israelites to rebuild their temple (1:2) and even returns the items Nebuchadnezzar took from the temple in 587 B.C. (1:7-11).

At last, Israel begins the return from exile. Led by Joshua, the priest, and Zerubbabel, their governor, over 40,000 people go to Israel (2:1-64). Their leaders pledge money for rebuilding the temple (2:68-70). When they arrive, the people erect an altar on the destroyed temple's foundation (3:1-2). They renew worship (3:3). During the second year, they lay a new foundation for the temple (3:8-10). Obviously, they hope to construct a whole new place of worship. This beginning causes great joy, except among older people. They still mourn the previous temple's destruction (3:11-13).

External pressures stop the construction. Some "enemies of Judah and Benjamin" (4:1, NIV) frighten the people (4:4), thus halting the work during Cyrus's time (4:5). During Ahasuerus's reign, the enemies write damaging letters to the king that claim Israel plans to rebel against Persia (4:6-16). Ahasuerus orders the builders to cease, so the enemies prevail once more (4:17-23).

Finally, Haggai and Zechariah inspire the people to try again (5:1). Zerubbabel and Joshua lead the people to rebuild the temple in 520-516 B.C. (5:2). Their enemies appeal to the king again, but this time their strategy fails. The king allows construction to continue and also gives the Israelites building materials and animals for sacrifice (5:6—6:15). With great rejoicing, the people dedicate the new temple (6:16-18). They also observe Passover (6:19). Restoration seems well under way.

Ezra 7—10: Rebuilding Israel's Spiritual Life I

About 450 B.C., Ezra gains permission from Artaxerxes to reestablish Moses' law in Israel. A priest himself, Ezra leads several other priests, Levites, and singers to Jerusalem (7:1-10). Artaxerxes gives him money for sacrifices and "the needs for the house of . . . God" (7:20, NASB). He also empowers Ezra to appoint judges who will enforce the laws of Moses and of Persia (7:25-26). They make the long trip, safe under Yahweh's protection (8:1-36). Great things seem to be about to happen.

When Ezra arrives in Jerusalem, he receives distressing news. The Israelites, including the Levites, have intermarried with the foreign women in the land (9:1-2). These women do not follow Yahweh and could lead the Israelite men to worship idols, as did Solomon's wives. Ezra mourns (9:3). He confesses Israel's sins and waits for God's answer (9:4—10:1). What good is a restored temple if the people never change?

The men decide on a drastic measure. They will divorce their foreign wives and send them away, with their children (10:2-4). Ezra commands the people to do so in three days (10:5-8). Some extra time is granted, but the nation's elders enforce the ruling (10:9-44). Israel's purity is saved by this highly unusual decision. Apparently, Ezra believes that only the strongest possible break with the past can save the situation. At any rate, Israel seems serious about being a holy nation again.

Nehemiah 1—7: Rebuilding Jerusalem's Walls

A new character enters the story. Nehemiah, Artaxerxes's cupbearer (2:1), hears that Jerusalem lies in ruins (1:1-3). This news bothers him so much that he asks the king's permission to go rebuild the city (1:4—2:3). Artaxerxes agrees but asks him to come back when the task is done (2:4-6). He also gives Nehemiah official letters that validate his mission and some vital construction material (2:7-8). Indeed he makes Nehemiah governor of Israel (note 5:14; 8:9). Artaxerxes aids efforts to restore Israel again.

Once in Jerusalem, Nehemiah wastes no time. He knows Sanballat and Tobiah, two local enemies of Israel, are opposed to his rebuilding efforts (2:10). He surveys Jerusalem and sees what must be done (2:12-16). Then, he encourages the people to work despite Sanballat, Tobiah, and Geshem the Arab's opposition (2:17-20). He supervises construction all over Jerusalem (3:1-32). The main goal is to rebuild the city walls so Jerusalem will be safe from attack.

Four obstacles soon arise. First, Sanballat and his friends ridicule the workers. They tell them a fox could topple their wall (4:1-3). Undaunted, the laborers continue. The wall grows to half its expected height (4:6). Second, the enemies threaten violence against Jerusalem (4:7-9). In response, Nehemiah arms the workers (4:10-23). They carry swords at all times (4:22).

Third, several people want to stop building so they can harvest crops (5:1). Many of them owe money to unjust lenders (5:2-5). Nehemiah eases the situation by forcing the lenders to stop charging the people interest (5:6-19). Fourth, the enemies try to discredit or intimidate Nehemiah. He ignores them. Nehemiah states, "I am doing a great work, and I cannot come down. Why should the work stop while I . . . come down to you?" (6:3, NASB). He scorns all their threats (6:19). The wall finished, Nehemiah appoints gatekeepers and counts the people (7:1-73).

Through his courageous leadership, Nehemiah has helped Israel reach a new stage of restoration. The people have a temple. They have capable religious and civic leaders. Their city can now be defended. The nation has not made such progress since Josiah's reign.

Nehemiah 8—13: Rebuilding Israel's Spiritual Life II

Ezra and Nehemiah work together for an unspecified amount of time. Both men stress the importance of repentance and worship. Ezra has already emphasized purity in marriage. Now he and Nehemiah help the people renew their covenant with Yahweh.

Ezra and the priests read and explain the law while standing on specially built platforms (8:1-8). Nehemiah has the people celebrate, instead of mourn, when they hear the teachings (8:9-12). After several days of listening (8:13-18), the people confess their national sins and plead for forgiveness (9:1-32). They also covenant to follow God in their restored land (9:33—10:39). Some of them agree to live in Jerusalem so national defense and proper worship can continue (11:1—12:47). All seems well.

Unfortunately, human sin is quite persistent. While Nehemiah is back in Artaxerxes's court, the people sin again. The high priest allows Tobiah, of all people, to live in the temple (13:4-5). Support for the Levites and the temple wanes (13:10). The sabbath is broken (13:15), and the people marry idolaters again (13:23). Nehemiah corrects these errors when he returns, but surely he must wonder when the people will be faithful. Will Israel *ever* live like a restored people?

Conclusion

Ezra and Nehemiah demonstrate that Israel can emerge from the ashes of exile. How? By appreciating the efforts of the first exiles to return, by insisting on religious and marital purity, by following unyielding and visionary leaders, by obeying God's Word and renewing the covenant. None of these tasks are easy. They demand discipline and perseverance. Still, they were keys to overcoming great obstacles then and remain so today.

Questions for Reflection

1. Discuss Ezra and Nehemiah's leadership traits and styles. Which one do you think should be imitated?
2. What does reading Ezra and Nehemiah contribute to your spiritual life?

Note

1. For options on the dating of Ezra and Nehemiah's ministry, note F. C. Fensham, *The Books of Ezra and Nehemiah* (Grand Rapids: Wm. B. Eerdmans, 1982) and H. G. M. Williamson, *Ezra, Nehemiah,* vol. 16 in *Word Biblical Commentary* (Waco, Tex.: Word Books, 1985).

22
1 and 2 Chronicles: *How to View the Past*

Major Characters: Levi, David, Solomon, Hezekiah, and Josiah
Minor Characters: Jehoshaphat and Manasseh
Plot: Before its fall, Israel experiences its greatest era during David and Solomon's reigns. After its division, the kingdom still enjoys great kings like Hezekiah and Josiah. Even some very wicked kings turn to God before they die.
Major Themes: Israel's great heritage and bright future, God's covenant with David, and the work of the priests

Introduction

The Old Testament story of Israel ends on a positive note. Ezra—Nehemiah find the people back in the land, struggling to live like Yahweh's people. They still sin repeatedly, yet they do possess Jerusalem again. How can the people find inspiration to move forward? How can future generations be sure of Yahweh's love and support? Chronicles indicates that the needed inspiration and hope will come from Israel's heritage. It discusses the best of the nation's past and, thereby, challenges each new generation to build on this strong foundation.

Chronicles is an anonymous work. It must have been written after the exile, of course, but it is impossible to tell exactly when. The book may have been composed about the same time as Ezra—Nehemiah since the books complement one another, or, Chronicles may date from an even later period. Since it is not possible to fix any certain date, it is best to view the work as a postexilic effort to encourage the nation. Its interest in the Levites may indicate that priests compiled the book.

Many readers assume that Kings and Chronicles are virtually identical. Certainly, they tell several of the same stories, but the differences are striking. Here, most of the leaders' sins are not mentioned. Rather, their best characteristics take precedence. Thus, readers can gain new insights into Israel's story.

Given the differences between Kings and Chronicles, how should readers view Israel's history? The writer of Kings portrays Israel as a flawed nation at best. Chronicles' author claims that Israel is a good nation gone bad. This upbeat history admits the nation's faults, yet transcends these faults. It gives future generations the sense that they, too, can do great things for God.

1 Chronicles 1—9: Israel's Ancestors

This section lists the major figures in Israel's past. Beginning with Adam (1:1), the list continues through Jacob's sons (2:1) and includes David's family (3:1). Judah (4:1) and Levi (6:1) receive special attention since David comes from Judah's clan, and Levi's "sons" direct Israel's worship. The genealogy ends with a list of Levites who worked at the tabernacle (9:2-44). No other Old Testament book places such emphasis on the priests and their importance in Israel.

1 Chronicles 10—29: David's Reign

Much of this material appears in Samuel, so it is not necessary to repeat it here. Several differences are important to note, though. Each one helps explain Chronicles' view of Israel's history. First, Saul's career receives only fourteen verses (10:1-14). Saul merely serves as a prelude to David. Chronicles thereby avoids discussing Saul's rebellion against God.

Second, Chronicles offers a longer account of how David brings the ark to Jerusalem than Kings. It includes a beautiful psalm recited for the occasion (16:8-36). Clearly, Chronicles focuses on David's role as benefactor of the sanctuary here. This theme will resurface later. Third, the text says nothing about the whole Bathsheba affair (note 20:1). David's character remains unsoiled. Fourth, 1 Chronicles 21:1 says Satan moved David to take the census mentioned in 2 Samuel 24:1. In Samuel, God "incited" (NIV) David to number Israel. Of course, Satan can only do what God allows, so the two ideas are not totally irreconcilable. Still, Chronicles shifts the focus from God and David at this point.

Fifth, in Chronicles David gathers all the materials for the temple (chaps. 28—29). Solomon has only to build the structure. As in the ark narrative, this account presents David as the patron of orderly, centralized worship. He strives to honor the God who has honored him so greatly.

2 Chronicles 1—9: Solomon's Reign

Solomon's life is portrayed in a similarly positive way. He asks for, and receives, wisdom from Yahweh (1:7-13). As a result of his wisdom, Israel enjoys unprecedented prosperity (1:14-17). Most importantly, Solomon builds the temple (chaps. 2—4). God's glory fills this place of worship (5:14), and Yahweh responds favorably to Solomon's dedication prayers (chaps. 6—7). Solomon follows his father's example of caring for Israel's worship center.

Chronicles does not mention Solomon's later idolatries. Rather, it stresses his days of faithful service to Yahweh (8:13-14). It reports how his wisdom thrills the queen of Sheba (9:1-12). Chronicles allows Solomon to die with dignity, honor, and esteem.

2 Chronicles 10—36: Division, Fall, and Restoration

This portion of the book deals almost exclusively with Judah's kings. Samaria's rulers are only mentioned when they are important in Judah's history. Therefore, Jeroboam appears as Rehoboam's and Abijah's opponent (note chaps. 10—13). Ahab is mentioned as Jehoshaphat's wicked ally (chap. 18). Elijah and Elisha do not appear at all.

Hezekiah (chaps. 29—32) and Josiah (chaps. 34—35) are great figures in Chronicles, just as they are in Kings. Other, less righteous, kings, however, are treated more positively in Chronicles. Most notably, Manasseh repents after exile in Babylon (33:10-17). He still commits horrible sins before then (33:1-9), yet he does change his ways in his old age.

Certainly Chronicles does not gloss over all the kings' faults. Rehoboam acts unwisely (10:1-19). Ahaz remains rebellious until his death (28:22-25). Jeroboam (13:1-12) and Ahab (18:1-34) are still wicked men. These negative assessments demonstrate Chronicles' basic honesty. Where good things can be reported, the author does so. When nothing positive occurs, the book does not invent a happy story.

Chronicles deals with Jerusalem's destruction very briefly (36:11-21). It does not want readers to dwell on this catastrophe. Instead, the book closes with Cyrus's decree that Israel can return home and rebuild the temple (36:22-23). It ends with the challenge, "Whoever there is among you of all His people, may the Lord his God be with him, and let him go up!" (36:23, NASB). In other words, the book encourages all who can to rebuild the land and to recapture the glory of the past. The same God who helped David and Solomon build the first temple will lead them to build another.

Conclusion

The past can be viewed in many ways. It can be looked upon with regret over missed opportunities, lost causes, and broken dreams. On the other hand, it can be viewed as a picture of glory. Neither perspective is totally mistaken. Chronicles believes that exiles must embrace the goodness of their heritage. They can be grateful for brilliant leaders, a beautiful temple, and an eternal covenant. They can find hope for themselves by seeing it in others.

In a very real sense, all who read the Old Testament need to adopt Chronicles' attitude. We know of Israel's (and our own) sin, and how it led to punishment. Yes, we have learned that David, Solomon, Abraham, and Moses were not perfect men. Still, as Chronicles stresses, we must look beyond punishment to renewal. God always works towards restoration and hope. When we begin to embrace this concept, we begin to grasp Chronicles' purpose. We also begin to understand the whole Old Testament as well.[1]

Questions for Reflection

1. Describe Chronicles' view of history. How valid is it?
2. How are Chronicles and Kings similar? How are they different? How does your answer contribute to the understanding of the nature of the Bible?

Note

1. For further study see H. G. M. Williamson, *1 and 2 Chronicles,* The New Century Bible Commentary (Grand Rapids: Wm. B. Eerdmans, 1982); Simon J. DeVries, *1 and 2 Chronicles,* The Forms of the Old Testament Literature XI (Grand Rapids: Wm. B. Eerdmans, 1989); Roddy Braun, *1 Chronicles,* vol. 14 in *Word Biblical Commentary* (Waco, Tex.: Word Books, 1986); Raymond B. Dillard, *2 Chronicles,* vol. 15 in *Word Biblical Commentary* (Waco, Tex.: Word Books, 1987).